SRA
Reading
Mastery®
Transformations

Reading
Textbook B

Siegfried Engelmann

Steve Osborn

Jean Osborn

Leslie Zoref

McGraw Hill

Acknowledgments

Many thanks to Lynda Gansel and Crystal Weber for their help in preparing the manuscript.

CREDITS

The Circuit
Copyright by Francisco Jiminez; reprinted by author's permission.

The No-Guitar Blues
"The No-Guitar Blues" from BASEBALL IN APRIL AND OTHER STORIES by Gary Soto. Copyright © 1990 by Gary Soto. Reprinted by permission of Houghton Mifflin Harcourt Publishing Company. All rights reserved.

In Time of Silver Rain
"Additional rights by permission of Harold Ober Associates Incorporated."

"In Time of Silver Rain" from THE COLLECTED POEMS OF LANGSTON HUGHES. Copyright 1994 by the Estate of Langston Hughes.

Trees
From THE LITTLE HILL by Harry Behn. Copyright 1949 Harry Behn. C Renewed 1977 by Alice L. Behn. Used by permission of Marian Reiner.

PHOTO CREDITS

2 (c)National Archives and Records Administration (NLR-PHOCO-A-8150(29); **3** (b)National Archives and Records Administration; **23** (t)urbancow/E+/Getty Images; **59** (t)BrianLasenby/iStockphoto/Getty Images, (c)Cal Vornberger/Alamy; **60** (t)Don Keith/iStock/Getty Images Plus/Getty Images; **61** (b)Tammy Fullum/iStock/Getty Images; **64** (b)stormcastle/123RF; **66** (t)Daniel Dempster Photography/Alamy; **70** (b)Jim Parkin/Getty Images, (b)Figure8Photos/E+/Getty Images; **100** (b)Photo by George E. Marsh, NOAA, Dept. of Commerce; **101** (b)Department of Commerce/NOAA; **104** (br)Library of Congress Prints & Photographs Division [LC-USF34-018895-E]; **105** (br)Library of Congress Prints and Photographs Division [LC-DIG-fsa-8b29516]; **109** (b)Library of Congress Prints and Photographs Division [LC-DIG-ppmsca-17962]; **119** Chris Willig, (tr)Sallyrango/Getty Images, (bl)NOAA, (bc)jukree/iStock/Getty Images, (br)Frank Leung/Getty Images; **123** (b)anek_s/iStockphoto/Getty Images; **124** (br)Westend61/Westend61/Getty Images; **125** (br)catshiles/Getty Images; **126** (br)Chris Hill/Shutterstock.com; **135** (b)Bettmann/Contributor/Getty Images; **140** Bettmann/Contributor/Getty Images; **145** (tc)Sporting News/Contributor/Getty Images; **146** (b)©Everett Collection Historical/Alamy; **149** (t)Archive Photos/Getty Images; **156** (t)©Bettmann/Corbis; **159** (cl)Olivier Blaise/Moment Open/Getty Images, (b)H Lansdown/Alamy, (bl)Gerald Nowak/Westend61/Getty Images, (br)iStockphoto/Getty Images, (br)©Image Source/PunchStock; **160** (t)©Sergey YAkovlev/Alamy, (tr)Wibofoto/Getty Images; **227** (t)Patrick Herrera/Getty Images; **228** (t)SasPartout/age fotostock; **230** (t)©Arco Images GmbH/Alamy, (t)Glen Allison/Getty Images; **69** (b)Figure8Photos/E+/Getty Images, (b)Jocelyn Augustino/FEMA; **L063 EX1** PBNJ Productions/Getty Images.

mheducation.com/prek-12

Send all inquiries to:
McGraw-Hill Education
8787 Orion Place
Columbus, OH 43240

ISBN: 978-0-07-905424-1
MHID: 0-07-905424-2

Printed in the United States of America.

1 2 3 4 5 6 7 8 9 LWI 24 23 22 21 20

Table of Contents

Table of Contents

A WORD LISTS

1 | Hard Words

1. develop
2. receive

2 | Word Practice

1. alligator
2. couple
3. eyesight
4. jerky
5. return

3 | Word Family

1. domestic
2. domesticate
3. domesticated
4. domestication

4 | Place Names

1. Africa
2. Asia
3. Egypt
4. India

5 | Vocabulary Words

1. advantages
2. generation
3. keen
4. prey
5. relatives

B VOCABULARY DEFINITIONS

1. **advantages**—The *advantages* of a plan are the ways the plan is better than another plan.

2. **generation**—A *generation* is a group of people who grow up at the same time. Your grandparents are one generation. Your parents are another generation.

3. **keen**—If you have *keen* hearing, your hearing is very good.
• What kind of eyesight do you have if your eyesight is very good?

4. **prey**—An animal that is hunted by another animal is called *prey*.

5. **relatives**—Your *relatives* are the people who are part of your family, such as your aunts, uncles, cousins, and grandparents. Animals have relatives, too. Those relatives are animals from the same family of animals. Cats, tigers, lions, and leopards are relatives. They are all members of the cat family.
• What do we call members of the same family?

The Domestication of Animals
Part 1

All animals can be divided into two groups: wild animals and domestic animals.

Wild animals do not live with people. Instead, they live in forests, jungles, rivers, oceans, and other wild places. Bears, tigers, snakes, eagles, alligators, and sharks are wild animals.

Domestic animals live with people. They live in people's houses or on people's farms. Dogs, horses, cows, chickens, and goats are domestic animals.

More than twenty thousand years ago, all animals were wild. But some of those animals were relatives of animals that are now domesticated. There were wild dogs that looked like wolves. There were wild goats that climbed mountains, wild horses that ran across the prairies, even wild chickens and wild sheep.

Domestication of Dogs

The first animal to become domesticated was probably the dog. The dog became domesticated thousands of years ago, when many people still lived in caves. The cave people had to hunt to stay alive, but they were not very good hunters. They could not run as fast as the wild animals, and they were not as strong as many of these animals.

We don't know exactly how the cave people domesticated dogs. Possibly, the wild dogs came near the cave during the cold winter months. They might have smelled the food cooking inside. They might have felt the warmth of the fire. They might have been hungry.

The people inside the cave might have tried to get rid of the wild dogs by throwing heavy bones at them. The dogs might have fought over the bones and then returned to the mouth of the cave, howling and waiting for more bones.

Puppies may have been the first wild dogs to come inside the caves and live with people. The puppies were wild, but a young wild animal is easier to tame than an older one. If a puppy receives food and warmth from people, the puppy will learn to love people, just as a wild puppy learns to love the dogs that it lives with in a pack. ◆

Dogs and Hunting

Cave people may have learned to hunt with their dogs by accident. A couple of puppies may have followed the cave people as they went hunting. When the puppies became full-grown dogs, the cave people may have discovered that dogs could do things that people couldn't do. Dogs could track other animals by following the scent of those animals. Dogs could warn the cave people of danger before the people could see or hear the danger. If a dangerous animal was near, a dog's fur would stand up, and the dog would growl.

When the tame dogs grew up, they had puppies. These tame puppies lived with the cave people. The tame puppies responded to the cave people in the same way that wild puppies respond to the leaders of a pack of wild dogs. Wild puppies learn to obey the leader dogs; tame puppies learn to obey people.

When the dogs were fully tamed by the cave people, they became domestic animals.

Domestication of Other Animals

For thousands of years, cave people hunted with their dogs. This plan worked well, but hunting had problems. The main problem was that people had to follow the wild animals they hunted. When deer and other wild animals moved from one place to another, people had to follow them or starve. Wild animals moved around a lot, which meant that people were on the move all the time, going from one place to another. ✦

Then people started to work out better plans. Some of them domesticated animals other than dogs, such as wild goats and wild sheep. The people took these animals with them as they hunted. If hunting was not good, they would kill one of these animals and eat it.

Domestication and Farming

Other people developed a different plan. Instead of following wild animals from place to place, they stayed in one place and raised domestic animals and plants. These people were the first farmers.

Farming had a big advantage over hunting. When a hunter kills a wild goat or sheep, the only food the hunter gets is the meat of the goat or sheep. But when a farmer raises goats or sheep, the farmer gets milk for many years. When the goats or sheep get old, the farmer can still kill them for meat.

When people became farmers, they no longer had to move from place to place to find food. Instead, they used domesticated plants and animals to get most of the food they needed.

D   MAIN IDEA

Write the main idea for each passage.

1. Maria looked through a lens.
   Then Maria said, "Smile."
   Then Maria pushed a button on her camera.

2. The dog dug a hole.
   The dog put a bone in the hole.
   The dog filled the hole with dirt.

3. Tina put the pencil into the sharpener.
   Then Tina turned the handle.
   Then Tina pulled the pencil out of the sharpener.

4. Some hammers are made of steel.
   Some saws are made of steel.
   _s are made of steel.
   _ers.
   _hers.
   _thers.

E   COMPREHENSION

Write the answers.

1. Use details from the article to explain the main differences between wild animals and domestic animals.

2. How does a puppy learn to love people?

3. Why did the cave people have to keep moving from place to place?

4. Why didn't the farmers have to move from place to place?

5. What are some uses that people today get from domestic goats?

F WRITING

Write a passage that compares hunting and farming thousands of years ago.

Use details from the article to answer these questions in your passage:

1. Why did people hunt thousands of years ago?

2. What domestic animals helped them hunt?

3. What was the main problem with hunting?

4. What advantages did farming have over hunting?

5. What are two domestic animals that early farmers used?

Write at least six sentences.

END OF LESSON 47

A WORD LISTS

1 | Hard Words
1. popular
2. talons

2 | Word Endings
1. domestication
2. Egyptian
3. generation

3 | Animal Names
1. camel
2. cheetah
3. cobra
4. falcon

4 | Animal Names
1. ferret
2. hawk
3. llama
4. mongoose

5 | Vocabulary Review
1. advantages
2. generation
3. prey
4. relatives

B READING INFORMATIONAL TEXT: Science

The Domestication of Animals
Part 2

When people started to farm, they continued to use dogs for hunting. They also began domesticating other animals for different uses. Over time, people developed three main uses for domestic animals:
- Helping people hunt.
- Giving people food and other products.
- Carrying things.

Animals That Hunt

The house cat was first domesticated as a hunting animal. The domestication of the cat took place in Egypt more than three thousand years ago. By that time, people had been using dogs as hunting animals for many years. But the Egyptians had a hunting problem that dogs could not solve.

The Egyptians raised grain, which they stored in large buildings. Mice and rats would get into the storage buildings and feast on the grain. Dogs couldn't help the Egyptians because dogs are not very good at catching mice and rats. Instead, cats solved the problem because they can easily catch mice and rats.

By placing cats in their storage buildings, the Egyptians protected their grain. They were so grateful to cats that they made large statues of the animals, and they treated them with great respect. Over time, cats began living in people's houses, just as they do today.

Other people trained larger members of the cat family, such as cheetahs. These cats are as big as large dogs, and they can run fast—up to sixty miles per hour. Because of their speed, they became popular with hunters in India.

People also trained many other hunting animals, including ferrets and mongooses. A ferret is half the size of a cat, but it can catch rats and rabbits. A ferret can move some parts of its body so quickly that people can't see the movement. If a ferret turns its head from side to side, you don't see the movement. You simply see the head looking one way, and then, an instant later, you see the head looking the other way.

In India, the mongoose was domesticated to kill cobras, which are poisonous snakes that can kill people with just one bite. The mongoose is smaller than a cat, but it is extremely powerful. Its fast, jerky movements permit it to kill cobras with ease. When a mongoose fights a cobra, the cobra rears up and leans back. Then the mongoose bites the cobra's head, cracking the snake's skull with its powerful bite.

People all over the world have domesticated falcons and other types of hunting birds. These birds of prey have strong claws, called talons. They also have keen eyesight and good speed. They can catch other birds in the air or small animals on the ground.

Animals That Give Food

Animals such as sheep, cattle, and chickens are important to people because they give meat and other food. Sheep and cattle give milk, chickens give eggs, and they all give meat.

But people use food-giving animals for many things besides meat, milk, and eggs. The thick skin from cows and pigs is used to make leather. Sheep fur is used to make wool. Goose feathers are used to fill jackets and blankets. ♦

Animals That Carry Things

Animals that carry things are called carrier animals. The camel was one of the first carrier animals to be domesticated. People all over Asia and North Africa loved the camel because it could be trained to carry large loads for long distances.

Donkeys and horses were also trained to carry loads. In South America, the llama was widely used for carrying. The llama is good at climbing mountains and walking in places without roads. In Africa and India, people were able to domesticate elephants. These huge animals can carry tremendous loads and can easily lift an entire tree.

Since the invention of cars, trucks, trains, and planes, people don't depend as much on carrier animals as they did in the old days.

Animal Breeding

After they learned how to domesticate animals, people discovered a process for changing animals to make them more useful. This process is called animal breeding.

Let's say a person who hunts has several male and female dogs. One of the male dogs is much better at hunting than any other male because it has a keen sense of smell. One of the female dogs is also better at hunting than the other females. ✦

If these two good hunting dogs have puppies, some of their puppies will be better hunters than any of the other dogs in the pack. If the person keeps breeding only the best hunting dogs, some of their puppies will be even better hunters. After several generations of breeding, the last-bred dogs will be much better at hunting than the dogs the person used to start the breeding process.

Chickens, horses, and goats changed in the same way dogs changed. When farmers kept only the chickens that laid the biggest eggs, the chickens' eggs grew larger and larger from generation to generation. At first, the eggs were no bigger than ping-pong balls. But after many years, the eggs were much bigger than ping-pong balls.

The same thing happened with horses. Farmers kept only the biggest and most powerful horses, so the horses changed from generation to generation. After hundreds of years, the newest horses were much bigger than the horses the earlier farmers had.

Before people discovered how to breed domestic animals, there were only a few types of each animal. Now there are many types. Along with hunting dogs, for example, there are herding dogs, sled dogs, and guard dogs. People developed all these different types of dogs through breeding.

C MAIN IDEA

Write the main idea for each passage.

1. The bear in the cave slept.
   The wolf in the cave slept.
   The lion in the cave slept.

2. Rowboats go into the water.
   Sailboats go into the water.
   Tugboats go into the water.

3. John swung a bat.
   Later John threw a ball to first base.
   Later John caught a line drive.

4. The horses heard a gun go off.
   The horses jumped over barriers.
   At last the horses crossed the finish line.

D COMPREHENSION

Write the answers.

1. Why were Egyptians so grateful to cats?

2. Use details from the article to explain what happens when a mongoose fights a cobra.

3. Why don't people today depend on animals that carry things as much as people did in the past?

4. Use details from the article to explain how people could breed sheep with thicker fur.

5. If you were a goat, would you rather be a wild goat or a domesticated goat? Explain your answer.

Write a passage that explains the process of animal breeding.

Use details from the article to answer these questions in your passage:

1. Why did people want to change animals?

2. What type of animals did people select for breeding?

3. How did people make sure the animals kept changing?

4. What are some examples of animals that have been changed through generations of breeding?

Write at least six sentences.

END OF LESSON 48

A WORD LISTS

1 Hard Words	2 Word Practice	3 Word Endings	4 Vocabulary Words
1. factual	1. comb	1. domestication	1. bargain
2. fantasy	2. combed	2. fiction	2. gnaw
3. realistic	3. flavor	3. imagination	3. pounce
4. Rudyard	4. flavored	4. nation	4. shall
		5. selection	

B VOCABULARY DEFINITIONS

1. **bargain**—When you *bargain* with someone, you try to make a deal with that person.
- What's another way of saying *Edna tried to make a deal with Jamal?*

2. **gnaw**—When you bite or chew something hard, you *gnaw* it.
- What's another way of saying *The dog chewed on the bone?*

3. **pounce**—When you quickly attack something, you *pounce on* that thing.
- What's another way of saying *The tiger quickly attacked the rabbit?*

4. **shall**—*Shall* is another word for *will.*
- What's another way of saying *I will give it to you?*

STORY BACKGROUND

Fact and Fiction

Some of the material you read presents facts. The article in the last two lessons, for example, presented facts about the domestication of animals. Because the main purpose of the article is to present facts, it is called a **factual article.**

Another type of reading material is **fiction,** such as short stories and novels.

Fiction is a story that somebody makes up. *The Wonderful Wizard of Oz* is fiction. "A Horse to Remember" is fiction.

Not all fiction is the same. "A Horse to Remember" is fiction, but the things that happen in the story actually could happen.

Farm horses like Nellie can win steeplechases. The Grand National does take place near Liverpool. The problems that Tara had when she was learning to jump are real problems that anybody could have when learning to jump. So although "A Horse to Remember" is fiction, it is close to fact. Fiction that is close to fact is called **realistic fiction.**

Some fiction, such as *The Wonderful Wizard of Oz*, is far from fact. The Land of Oz doesn't really exist, and scarecrows can't talk or think. Fiction that is far from fact is called **fantasy.**

READING LITERATURE: Fantasy

The Cat That Walked by Himself
Rudyard Kipling
Chapter 1

Once upon a time, all animals were wild. The dog was wild, and the cow was wild, and the horse was wild, and the sheep was wild—as wild as wild could be—and they walked in the wild woods. But the wildest of all the wild animals was the cat. He walked by himself, no matter where he went.

Of course, the man was wild, too. He was very wild. He didn't even begin to be tame until he married the woman. She told him that she did not like his wild ways.

She picked out a nice dry cave to live in, and she lit a nice fire at the back of the cave, and she spread clean sand on the floor, and she said, "Wipe your feet when you come in, dear, so we can keep our house neat and clean."

That night, the man and the woman ate wild sheep that had been roasted on the fire and flavored with wild onion and wild pepper. The man was very happy, and he went to sleep in front of the fire; but the woman sat up and looked at the fire.

Out in the wild woods all the wild animals gathered together where they could

_____

[Adapted for young readers.]

see the light of the fire a long way off, and they wondered what it meant.

Then the wild horse stamped with his wild foot and said, "Oh, my friends and enemies, why have the man and the woman made that great light in that great cave, and what harm will it do us?"

The wild dog lifted up his wild nose and smelled the smell of roast sheep and said, "I will go to the cave and see, for I think something smells good. Cat, come with me."

"No," said the cat. "I am the cat who walks by himself, no matter where I go. So I will not go with you."

"Then we can never be friends," said the wild dog, and he trotted off to the cave. But when the wild dog had gone a little way, the cat said to himself, "It doesn't matter where I go, so I will go and see what happens." The cat followed the wild dog softly, very softly, and hid himself where he could hear everything.

When the wild dog reached the mouth of the cave, he lifted his nose and sniffed the beautiful smell of the roast sheep. The woman heard him and said, "Wild Dog, what do you want?"

The dog said, "What smells so good?"

Then the woman picked up a roasted sheep bone, threw it to the wild dog, and said, "Wild Dog, taste and try."

The wild dog gnawed the bone, and it was more delicious than anything he had ever tasted. When he was finished, he said, "Give me another."

The woman said, "Wild Dog, if you help my man to hunt during the day and guard this cave at night, I will give you as many roasted bones as you need." ♦

"Ah," said the cat, listening. "This is a very wise woman, but she is not as wise as I am."

The wild dog crawled into the cave and laid his head on the woman's lap and said, "Good friend, I will help your man to hunt during the day, and at night I will guard your cave."

"Ah," said the cat, listening. "That is a very foolish dog." And the cat went back through the wild woods, walking by himself and waving his wild tail. But he never told anybody what he had seen and heard.

When the man woke up, he said, "What is Wild Dog doing here?" And the woman said, "His name is not Wild Dog anymore. His new name is First Friend because he will be our friend forever. Take him with you when you go hunting."

That day, the woman cut great green armfuls of fresh grass from a meadow in the wild woods. She dried the grass by the fire.

Out in the wild woods, all the wild animals wondered what had happened to the wild dog, and at last the wild cow stamped her foot and said, "I will go and see why Wild Dog has not returned. Cat, come with me."

"No!" said the cat. "I am the cat who walks by himself, no matter where I go. So I will not go with you." But secretly, he followed the wild cow, very softly, and hid himself where he could hear everything.

When the wild cow reached the mouth of the cave, she lifted her nose and sniffed the beautiful smell of the dried grass. The woman heard the cow and said, "Wild Cow, what do you want?"

The wild cow said, "Where is Wild Dog?" But the cow kept staring at the dried grass.

The woman laughed and said, "Wild Cow, I think you are more interested in grass than you are in Wild Dog."

The wild cow said, "That is true. Give me the grass to eat."

The woman said, "Wild Cow, if you will give me your milk, I will let you eat the wonderful grass three times a day."

"Ah," said the cat as he listened from his hiding place. "This is a clever woman, but she is not as clever as I am."

The wild cow said, "I will give you my milk if you give me the wonderful grass."

"Ah," said the cat. "That is a very foolish cow." And the cat went back through the wild woods, walking by himself and waving his wild tail. But he never told anybody about what he had seen and heard. ✦

When the man and the dog came back from hunting, the man said, "What is Wild Cow doing here?"

And the woman said, "Her name is not Wild Cow anymore, but Giver of Good Food. She will give us warm white milk forever, and I will take care of her while you and First Friend go hunting."

On the next day, the woman gathered grass again. Then she sat in front of the cave and made a collar from animal skins.

That night, the wild animals got together again to talk about the wild dog and the wild cow. At last, the wild horse said, "I will go and see why they have not returned. Cat, come with me."

"No," said the cat, "I will not come." But he secretly followed the wild horse, very softly, and hid himself where he could hear everything.

When the wild horse reached the cave, he smelled the dried grass. The woman heard him and said, "Wild Horse, what do you want?"

The wild horse said, "Where are Wild Dog and Wild Cow?" But the horse kept staring at the grass.

The woman laughed and said, "I think you are more interested in grass than in Wild Dog or Wild Cow."

The wild horse said, "That is true. Give me the grass to eat."

The woman said, "If you will wear this collar and be our servant, I will let you eat the grass three times a day."

"Ah," said the cat, as he listened from his hiding place. "This is a very clever woman, but she is not as clever as I am."

The wild horse said, "I will wear the collar and be your servant if you give me the wonderful grass."

"Ah," said the cat, listening. "That is a very foolish horse." And he went back through the wild woods, walking by himself and waving his wild tail. But he never told anybody what he had seen and heard.

When the man and the dog came back from hunting, the man said, "What is Wild Horse doing here?"

And the woman explained, "His name is no longer Wild Horse, but First Servant. He will carry us from place to place forever. You can ride on his back when you go hunting, and he will pull the animals you kill."

That night, the wild animals had another meeting. The wild sheep said, "I'm not going to that cave. No animal that has gone to that place has come back."

The wild chicken, the wild goose, and all the other animals agreed. So no animal went to the cave that night. Instead, they all went back to their homes.

E MAIN IDEA

Write the main idea for each passage.

1. The Atlantic Ocean contains salt water.
   The Pacific Ocean contains salt water.
   The Indian Ocean contains salt water.

2. Los Angeles is in California.
   San Diego is in California.
   San Francisco is in California.

3. Willie put his letter into an envelope.
   Willie put a stamp on the envelope.
   Willie put the envelope into a mailbox.

4. Frank picked up his cell phone.
   Frank pressed seven numbers.
   Frank said, "Hello."

F COMPREHENSION

Write the answers.

1. What are the main differences between fantasy and realistic fiction?

2. How do you know that "The Cat That Walked by Himself" is fantasy?

3. Why was the wild dog attracted to the cave?

4. Why were the wild cow and the wild horse attracted to the cave?

5. Do you think those animals made good bargains with the woman? Explain your answer.

G WRITING

- "The Cat that Walked by Himself" has two chapters.

Write what you think will happen during chapter 2.

Use evidence from chapter 1 to answer these questions in your passage:

1. What happens to the cat?

2. What happens to the other animals?

3. What happens to the man?

4. What happens to the woman?

Write at least six sentences.

END OF LESSON 49

A WORD LISTS

1 | Hard Words

1. avoid
2. digest
3. variety

2 | Word Practice

1. accept
2. bargain
3. entertain
4. fantasy
5. flavored

3 | Vocabulary Words

1. abnormal
2. access
3. environment
4. facilities

B VOCABULARY FROM CONTEXT

1. It is normal to sleep eight hours a night. It is **abnormal** to sleep sixteen hours a night.
 • What does abnormal mean?

2. Horses living in the wild **have access to** food at all times. Tame horses only eat when they are fed by people.
 • What does have access to mean?

3. The **environment** in forests is peaceful and quiet. The environment in cities is loud and busy.
 • What does environment mean?

4. Factories are **facilities** for making things. Kitchens are facilities for cooking. Dentists' offices are facilities for fixing teeth.
 • What are facilities?

C READING LITERATURE: Fantasy

The Cat That Walked by Himself

Chapter 2

The man and the woman were now living with three animals. On the day after the wild animals decided not to send any more animals to the cave, the cat waited to see what the wild animals would do. No animal moved from the wild woods, so the cat walked to the cave by himself. He saw the woman milking the cow, and he saw the light of the fire in the cave, and he smelled the warm white milk.

The cat went up to the woman and said, "Where are Wild Dog, Wild Cow, and Wild Horse?" ⚙

The woman laughed and said, "Wild Cat, go back to the wild woods again, for we have all the friends and servants we need."

The cat said, "I am neither a friend nor a servant. I am the cat who walks by himself, and I want to go into your cave."

The woman said, "I saw you hiding near the cave when First Friend came here. If you wanted to come inside, why didn't you come in with First Friend on that first night?"

The cat grew very angry and said, "I want to go inside."

The woman laughed and said, "You are the cat who walks by himself, no matter where you go. You are neither a friend nor a servant. You have said it yourself. So go away and walk by yourself."

Then the cat pretended to be sorry and said, "Can't I ever come into the cave? Can't I ever sit by the warm fire? Can't I ever drink the warm white milk? You are very wise and very beautiful. You should not be cruel, even to a cat."

The woman smiled and said, "I knew I was wise, but I did not know I was beautiful." She gazed at the cat for a few moments. Then she said, "I think you are very cunning, and you are trying to trick me. But I will make a bargain with you. If I ever praise you, you may sit near the mouth of the cave forever."

"And if you praise me twice?" said the cat.

"I never shall," said the woman, "but if I praise you twice, you may sit in the back of the cave by the fire."

"And if you praise me three times?" said the cat.

"I never shall," said the woman, "but if I praise you three times, you may drink the warm white milk anytime you wish."

Then the cat arched his back and said, "I accept your bargain." And he went away through the wild woods, walking by himself and waving his wild tail. ♦

That night when the man and the horse and the dog came home from hunting, the woman did not tell them about the bargain she had made with the cat, because she was afraid they might not like it.

The cat went far away and hid himself in the wild woods. After many days passed, the woman forgot all about him and the bargain she had made. A bat that hung inside the cave knew where the cat was hiding, and every evening the bat would fly to the cat with news of what was happening in the cave.

One evening the bat said, "There is a baby in the cave. He is new and fat, and the woman is very fond of him."

"Ah," said the cat, listening. "And what is the baby fond of?"

"Let's see," the bat said thoughtfully. "He is fond of things that are soft, and he is fond of warm things he can hold in his arms when he goes to sleep. And he is very fond of being played with."

"Ah," said the cat, with a cunning smile. "The time has come for me to move into the cave."

The next morning, the cat walked through the wild woods and hid near the cave until the man and the dog and the horse went hunting. The woman was busy trying to cook that morning, and the baby's crying bothered her. So she carried the baby outside the cave and gave him pebbles to play with. But still the baby cried.

The cat approached the baby, put out his paw, and patted the baby softly on the cheek. The baby cooed and smiled. The cat rubbed against the baby's knees and tickled the baby under his fat chin with his tail. The baby laughed, and the woman heard the baby laugh.

The bat said, "Woman, that baby is happy because a wild animal is entertaining him."

Without going outside of the cave, the woman said, "That wonderful animal is a marvel. That animal has done a great service for me."

Suddenly, the woman noticed the cat sitting quite comfortably inside, near the mouth of the cave. "Woman," said the cat, "you have praised me, and now I can sit in the cave forever. But remember, I am the cat who walks by himself, no matter where I go."

The woman was very angry. She shut her lips tightly, picked up a ball of thread, and began to sew.

Suddenly, the baby cried because the cat was no longer entertaining him. The woman went outside, but she could not hush the baby. The baby struggled and kicked and cried. ✶

"Woman," said the cat, "give me a ball of thread, and I will show you how to make your baby laugh as loudly as he is now crying."

"I will do so," said the woman, "but I will not praise you if you do it."

She gave the cat a ball of thread, and the cat ran after it. He patted it with his paws and rolled head over heels and tossed the thread backward over his shoulder and chased it between his legs and pretended to lose it and pounced down upon it again. The baby started to laugh loudly and to scramble after the cat all around the cave. Then the baby grew tired. He put his arms around the soft cat and held it.

"Now," said the cat, "I will sing the baby a song that will put him to sleep for an hour." The cat began to purr, loud and low, until the baby fell fast asleep. The woman smiled as she looked down upon the two of them and said, "That was wonderful. You are a very clever cat."

Suddenly, the cat was sitting quite comfortably at the back of the cave, close to the fire.

"Woman," said the cat, "you have praised me twice, and now I can sit by the warm fire at the back of the cave forever. But remember, I am the cat who walks by himself, no matter where I go."

Now the woman was very, very angry. She resolved not to praise the cat again.

Hours later, the cave grew so still that a little mouse crept out of a corner and ran across the floor.

"Woman," said the cat, smiling, "I see that a little mouse lives in your cave."

"Oh, no," said the woman.

"Ah," said the cat. "Then you should do something to get rid of it."

The woman said, "Oh, please get rid of it, and I will always be grateful to you."

The cat made one jump and caught the mouse. The woman said, "A hundred thanks. Even First Friend is not quick enough to catch little mice. You are a very skillful animal."

The cat walked over to a bowl and began lapping up the warm white milk. Then he paused and licked his chops. "Woman," he said, "you have praised me three times, and now I can drink the warm white milk any time I wish. But remember—I am still the cat who walks by himself, no matter where I go."

Then the woman laughed and said, "Cat, you are as clever as I am, and I will be glad to keep my bargain with you."

That evening, when the man and the dog came into the cave, the woman told them the story of the bargain.

And the cat just sat by the fire and smiled.

D NEITHER-NOR SENTENCES

Rewrite the sentences using *neither* and *nor*.

1. The man was not happy and was not sad.

2. She would not play and would not study.

3. The boy would not smile and would not talk.

4. The dog could not fight and could not hunt.

E MAIN IDEA

Write the main idea for each passage.

1. The desk in his house was dusty.
   The table in his house was dusty.
   The chair in his house was dusty.

2. Men have emotions.
   Women have emotions.
   Children have emotions.

3. Nellie jumped over the highest barriers.
   Nellie jumped over the middle-sized barriers.
   Nellie jumped over the lowest barriers.

F COMPREHENSION

Write the answers.

1. Why didn't the woman want to let the cat into the cave?

2. Why did the cat tell the woman that she was wise and beautiful?

3. The woman was afraid the man and the dog might not like the bargain she had made with the cat. Why wouldn't they like the bargain?

4. At the end of the story, what did the cat mean when he said, "I am still the cat that walks by himself"?

5. Which animal do you think made the best bargain with the woman? Explain your answer.

G WRITING

Write a passage that answers this main question:

- How does "The Cat That Walked by Himself" compare with the facts that you know about the domestication of animals?

Use details from the story and "The Domestication of Animals" to answer these questions in your passage:

1. Which parts of the dog domestication are based on fact?

2. Which parts of the cow and horse domestication are based on fact?

3. Which parts of the cat domestication are based on fact?

4. Which parts of the story are fantasy?

Write at least six sentences.

END OF LESSON 50

51

A WORD LISTS

1 | Words About Teeth

1. baby teeth
2. permanent teeth
3. incisor
4. molar
5. speculum

2 | Vocabulary Words

1. grit
2. infected
3. instinct
4. oval
5. sedative

B VOCABULARY DEFINITIONS

1. **grit**—Loose bits of stone and sand are called *grit*. Foods that have grit are called gritty foods.
• What might make your food gritty when you eat on a beach?

2. **infected**—A cut that is *infected* becomes swollen and painful.
• What's another way of saying *A swollen and painful wound?*

3. **instinct**—An *instinct* is a behavior that people and other animals are born with.

4. **oval**—Something that is *oval* is shaped like an egg.
• What is an oval shaped like?

5. **sedative**—A *sedative* is a medicine that makes you sleep or feel relaxed.
• What's a medicine that makes you feel relaxed?

C READING INFORMATIONAL TEXT: Science

What Big Teeth

Like humans, horses need dental care. But horses need it much earlier in their lives. A horse that is only two weeks old already has sixteen teeth!

A horse dentist checks to see whether a young horse's teeth line up properly. If they do not, the horse could develop serious problems.

A wild horse's diet is much different from that of its tame relatives. Horses living in the wild eat a variety of foods. These include grasses, grains, leafy plants, twigs, and bark. A horse's teeth are designed for eating these natural foods. The front teeth are for tearing heavy grasses. These teeth are called **incisors.** The back teeth, called **molars,** are for grinding the food.

The food in a natural environment keeps a horse's teeth in balance. All the teeth are used the same amount, so they wear down the same amount. Tame horses, on the other hand, eat food that is much less rough. Also, they do not get to eat as often. Horses living in the wild have access to natural food at all times. Tame horses eat what and when they are fed.

Tame horses do not usually eat the gritty foods that would wear down their teeth naturally and evenly. That is why they need dentists. Horse dentists use tools to wear down and smooth the horses' teeth.

Tooth Problems

It is normal for a horse's teeth to wear away. The baby teeth will be replaced, but even the permanent teeth are designed to wear away. This is because a horse's teeth keep growing.

A horse's permanent teeth are about four inches long. Only a part of the tooth shows in the horse's mouth. The rest of the tooth is deep in the horse's gums and jaws. The part of the tooth that can be seen wears down. At the same time, more tooth grows out from the gums.

Most of a horse's tooth problems are caused by its chewing pattern. As a horse grinds its food, the lower jaw moves in an oval motion. It slides to one side, drops, moves to the other side, and lifts back again.

Tame horses do not need to work as hard to grind their food. Therefore, sharp edges and points form on the parts of the teeth that are not being used much. These sharp edges and points can be very painful for a horse. They can cut a horse's tongue, cheeks, and gums. Deep cuts might become infected and result in serious diseases.

Sharp edges also keep the molars from lining up correctly. Good contact between the molars is needed for a horse to grind its food properly. If the food is not chewed well, the horse could develop other problems, such as choking. Also, the horse could have trouble digesting its food, which can lead to stomach pain and weight loss. ♦

Dentist examining horse's teeth

Dental Exams

Most horse dentists recommend dental exams or checkups one or two times per year. These exams should be provided in all stages of a horse's life.

Sometimes a horse will need extra care. One sign that a horse needs to see a dentist is that a lot of food drops from the horse's mouth while the horse is eating. Another warning sign is that a horse turns its head sideways to chew. The most obvious sign occurs when a horse stops eating. That horse needs to see a dentist at once.

Special facilities are not needed for a dental exam. A clean horse stall works just fine. The most important thing is keeping the horse's head still during the exam.

Some dentists keep the horse's head still by putting it into a cradle. The cradle holds up the horse's head so the dentist has a good view of the mouth. A cradle also helps keep the horse comfortable during the exam.

After the horse's head is in position, the dentist rinses its mouth with water, which removes bits of food from between the teeth. Then the dentist gives the horse a sedative to keep it calm. Next, the dentist uses a metal device called a **speculum** to hold the horse's mouth open. The speculum must be positioned with care.

It is not possible to do a thorough exam without a speculum and a sedative. These tools do not hurt the horse if they are used correctly. Only a trained expert should perform these steps of the process. ✦

The dentist works on the molars first by leveling and rounding off "hooks," "ramps," "waves," and "points." These are some of the abnormal tooth conditions that horses develop. Each of these terms describes the shape of the problem tooth.

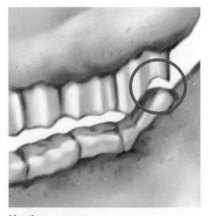

Hooks

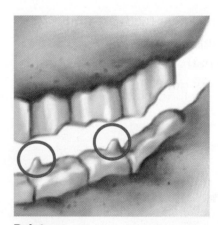

Points

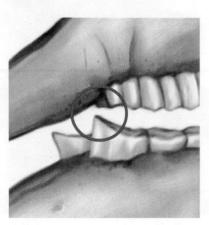

Ramps

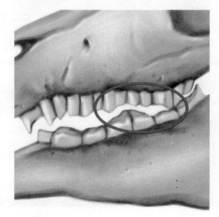

Waves

A dentist has many tools for grinding a horse's teeth. The most commonly used tool is a hand file. This is a long, narrow piece of metal with ridges. The ridges of the file work like sandpaper, shaping and smoothing the teeth.

Sometimes the problem is too severe for a hand file. For these cases a dentist uses power tools. Small saws, drills, and sanders help to cut into the teeth and smooth them.

After the molars are corrected, the dentist works on the incisors. These teeth must also be trimmed and shaped with care. A horse cannot bite and chew properly if its incisors are uneven or too long. When the horse bites, the back teeth and the front teeth should close at the same time.

Regular Checkups

Horses are like eating machines. Their instinct to eat is so strong that it can cause them to ignore pain. That is why many horse owners do not know when their horse is having trouble with its teeth.

This situation can be avoided with regular dental checkups. The earlier a problem is noticed, the easier it is to correct. Skilled horse dentists have the training and tools needed to help horses live longer, healthier lives.

D COMPREHENSION

1. Use details from the article to explain why a tame horse's teeth don't wear down evenly.

2. How are a horse's permanent teeth different from a person's permanent teeth?

3. What problems do tame horses have with their teeth?

4. What are some warning signs that a horse needs to see a dentist?

5. What is the main thing dentists do to a horse's teeth with a hand file?

E WRITING

Write a passage that answers this main question:

- How do the problems people have with their teeth compare to the problems that tame horses have with their teeth?

Use details from the article and your own knowledge to answer these questions in your passage:

1. What are some problems people and tame horses have with their teeth?

2. What causes those problems?

3. How can those problems be prevented?

Write at least six sentences.

END OF LESSON 51

A | WORD LISTS

1 | Hard Words

1. flood
2. summary
3. necessary
4. unnecessary

2 | Related Words

1. devastate / devastation
2. erode / erosion
3. erupt / eruption
4. volcano / volcanic

3 | Vocabulary Words

1. absorb
2. landslide
3. restore
4. sediment

4 | Vocabulary Words

1. hazard
2. seawall
3. volcanic eruption

B | VOCABULARY DEFINITIONS

1. **absorb**—When something *absorbs* water, it soaks up the water.
- What's another way of saying *A sponge soaks up water?*

2. **landslide**—A *landslide* occurs when large amounts of mud and rock slide down from a hill or a mountain.
- What happens when a landslide occurs?

3. **restore**—When you repair something to make it look like new, you *restore* it.

- What's another way of saying *Workers repaired the old house to make it look like new?*

4. **sediment**—Small pieces of rock and sand that settle at the bottom of a river, lake, or ocean are called *sediment.*
- What do we call small pieces of rock and sand that settle at the bottom of a river, lake, or ocean?

C | VOCABULARY FROM CONTEXT

1. Heavy rains can be a **hazard** because they can trigger landslides.

2. The giant waves destroyed the **seawall** at the entrance to the harbor.

3. The land was covered with lava after the **volcanic eruption.**

Changing Landscapes

Two types of forces change how the world looks. Some forces make slow changes and other forces make sudden changes.

Slow Changes

The main forces that make slow changes are wind and water. As rivers and streams run downhill, they carry mud, stones, and rocks from higher places to lower places. When the water in the river slows, the water drops the material it is carrying. So the mountains wear away and the lowlands fill up with material.

In the ocean, big waves also carry stones. These stones rub against rocks as the waves roll through shallow water near the land. The force of the waves grinds the rocks into smaller and smaller pieces. After millions of years pass, the rocks have been worn down to the tiny grains of sand you see on beaches.

Snow, rain, and wind also change the shape of mountains and valleys. Ice makes tiny cracks in rocks. Over many years, the cracks become larger until parts of the rocks break off. In time, mountains are worn down to hills as ice, snow, water, and wind slowly wear the mountains away.

Fast Changes

Some forces make fast changes in how the world looks.

During some **volcanic eruptions,** rivers of hot melted rock called lava bubble up from inside the earth and flow onto the surface of the land. When these rivers of lava cool down, they make a large mountain that is shaped like a cone.

Some **earthquakes** cause the earth to split. The split may create huge cliffs in places that were flat.

Landslides change the landscape by moving lots of rocks and soil all at once. Heavy rains can be a hazard because they can trigger landslides in hilly areas. The ground becomes soaked and can't hold any more water. Rocks and soil begin to slide downhill, usually moving faster and faster. If enough rocks and soil tumble down, the whole hillside can collapse.

Landslides are sometimes caused by earthquakes or volcanic eruptions. These forces loosen and move rocks and soil down hillsides. Landslides can move with the speed and power of an express train. This force makes landslides very dangerous. They can cause millions of dollars in damage.

Landslides often happen in hilly areas that have no trees and few plants. When there are no trees and few plants, there is nothing to stop the land from sliding downhill.

In hilly areas that do have trees and plants, the roots of the trees and plants help keep the soil in place. The roots also absorb water in the soil. These types of hilly areas are less likely to have landslides.

Hurricanes also change the landscape. Hurricanes are powerful storms that form over the ocean. As a hurricane nears land, the wind may create waves more than 40 feet high. The waves cause a lot of devastation when they reach land, smashing through storm barriers and seawalls. The waves wash away sand from beaches. After a hurricane, a shore that had a large sandy beach may now have no beach and only large jagged rocks.

HOW A WETLAND WORKS

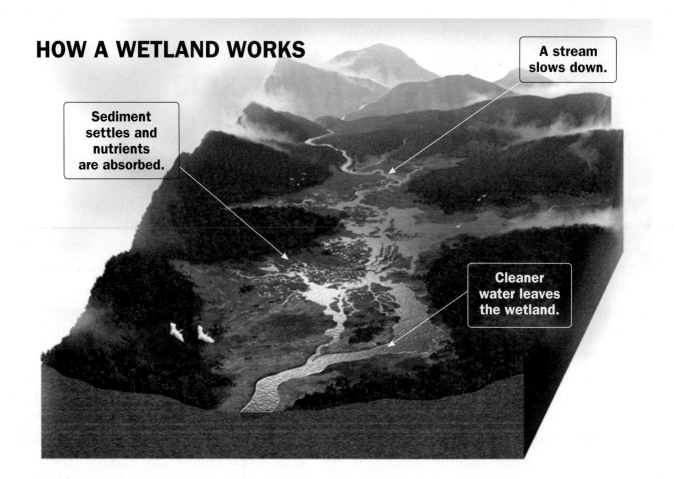

Sediment settles and nutrients are absorbed.

A stream slows down.

Cleaner water leaves the wetland.

The rain from a hurricane can cause **floods.** During a flood, shallow rivers overflow their banks. The sand and sediment from the river are carried into flooded areas and dropped there.

Wetlands that are next to the ocean help protect inland areas from hurricanes. When a hurricane hits the shore, it pushes a wall of water in front of it. Wetlands absorb and slow down the wall of water. As the wall of water slows, it becomes smaller and less dangerous.

Fixing the Damage

When people remove natural features such as sand dunes and wetlands, more **erosion** can occur. In places where people cut down trees and remove plants to build roads or houses, landslides are more likely. Roots of trees and other plants are no longer there to hold the earth in place, so soil is carried away, and landslides may occur.

To help slow down erosion and prevent landslides, we can plant trees and plants that have long, deep roots. Another way to slow down erosion is by restoring wetlands and dunes. People who live near the coast are realizing that they need to restore wetlands and sand dunes to reduce erosion farther inland.

It is possible for us to fix a damaged area. First we need to know what is causing the damage. Then we need a good plan to change what is happening.

Summary

Wind, water, ice, and snow cause slow changes in our landscapes. Natural disasters such as volcanic eruptions, hurricanes, and landslides can change the landscape quickly. We can't prevent natural disasters, but we can restore the landscape to reduce unnecessary erosion.

E COMPREHENSION

Use details from "Changing Landscapes" to answer the questions.

1. What are the two types of forces that change the landscape? Give at least two examples of each type.

2. How do streams and rivers wear down mountains?

3. How do waves make sand?

4. How can heavy rains trigger landslides?

5. Explain the two ways that trees and plants can help prevent landslides.

6. How do wetlands protect inland areas from hurricanes?

F WRITING

- Pretend you live in a place that has snowy winters and warm springs. You visit the same park near your house during winter and spring. The park landscape has lots of trees, flowers, and birds.

Write a passage that answers this main question:

- How does the park landscape change from winter to spring?

Your passage should also answer these questions:

1. What do the trees look like during the winter?

2. What happens to the flowers during the winter?

3. Where are the birds during the winter?

4. What do the trees look like during the spring?

5. What happens to the flowers during the spring?

6. Where are the birds during the spring?

Write at least six sentences.

A WORD LISTS

1	Word Endings
1.	bitterly
2.	doubtfully
3.	exactly
4.	hardly
5.	quietly
6.	ugly

2	Place Names
1.	Alaska
2.	Canada
3.	Dawson
4.	Klondike
5.	Skagway
6.	Yukon

3	Vocabulary Words
1.	lean
2.	slosh
3.	treacherous

4	Vocabulary Words
1.	coil
2.	exchange
3.	flicker
4.	hurl

B VOCABULARY DEFINITIONS

1. **lean**—People who are *lean* have very little fat on their bodies.
- What's the word that describes somebody with very little fat?

2. **slosh**—When liquid *sloshes*, it splashes around.
- When liquid splashes around, what is it doing?

3. **treacherous**—Something that is very dangerous is *treacherous*.
- What's another way of saying *The trail was very dangerous?*

C VOCABULARY FROM CONTEXT

1. He wound the rope around his hand until the rope was in a neat **coil.**

2. The butcher **exchanged** his dull knife for a sharper knife.

3. The fire burned brightly at first, but then the flame began to **flicker.** After a while, the fire burned out.

4. Kareem **hurled** the rock into the lake as far as he could.

Journey to Dawson

In the next lesson, you will begin reading an exciting story that takes place during the Klondike Gold Rush. Gold was discovered in 1896 along the Klondike River in northern Canada, near a tiny town named Dawson. During the next few years, more than 100,000 people set out for Dawson to find gold, but only 30,000 reached the town, and only 4,000 found gold.

Pretend you are living during the 1890s. You hear about the Klondike Gold Rush, and you decide to go to Dawson to find your fortune in gold.

The map shows the route you will take to reach Dawson. Your route is more than 400 miles long and is marked with a dotted line that begins in Skagway, Alaska. From Skagway, you climb steep mountains to Bennett Lake in Canada, where the Yukon River begins. You will take a boat several hundred miles on the Yukon River until you reach Dawson. Then you will look for gold along the Klondike River.

In Skagway, you make arrangements to travel to Dawson. Other people seeking gold will go with you, and each person will have to pay a small fortune for the guide who takes you on the treacherous journey.

The guide leads you and the others as you tramp overland from Skagway through

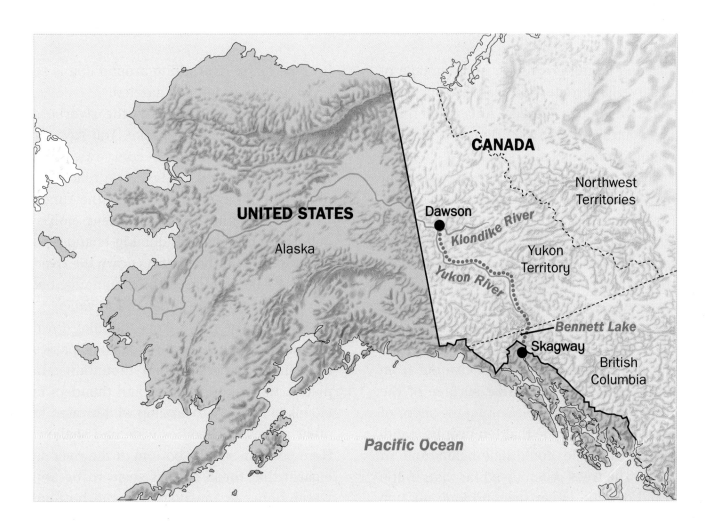

amazing mountain passes. In the middle of this overland route, you cross the border of Alaska and enter Canada. At last you reach the south end of Lake Bennett. You are ready to start on your boat trip.

It is early morning, and you can see your breath, although it is still summertime. The lake, which is more than 30 miles long, is surrounded by mountains with their peaks hidden in the clouds. The only sounds are those of occasional fish splashing in the lake and early morning birds. Some chirp, some cry, and some seem to scream.

As you and the others seat yourselves in the small riverboat, ripples move out from the boat across the mirror surface of the water. Some of the trees along the shore of the lake are so huge that ten people, standing side by side, could hide behind one of them. The trees reach up so far that, if you stand directly under one and look up, you

become dizzy. Everything around you is so grand that your mind is dazzled.

You and the others row the riverboat north across the glassy lake. You row for hours, and your hands become raw from pulling on the oars. At last, you reach the north end of Lake Bennett. Here the Yukon River starts, and for the moment, you're delighted. Your delight quickly changes to fright when your boat starts down the river. Bennett Lake is high in the mountains, but Dawson is far below in the Yukon Valley.

As the river flows from the lake down into the valley, it roars through steep passes that snake between great mountains. In places, the Yukon tumbles and thunders in clouds of spray and dazzling white water. In other places, it becomes wide and shallow. Here you can see the bottom of the river so clearly that there doesn't seem to be any water between the boat and the bottom.

Even in places where the water is ten feet deep, the water is so invisible that if you peer over the edge of the boat and look down, you feel as if you are floating ten feet in the air. ◆

When you come to these still places in the river, you observe the things around you. You see fish—thousands of them—in the river. Some are three or four feet long, and they move in great schools. You also look at the trees and the jagged rocks that line the banks of the river.

When you come to places where the river roars down through a narrow pass, you don't think of anything except scrambling through the pass. Above the roaring water you hear the guide shouting directions, "Pull right! Pull right!" His voice is nearly drowned in the thunderous sound of the great river as it hammers and bounces the tiny boat through the snarling, icy water. When the river again slows down, your hands are numb from the cold, and your feet ache from being in the freezing water that sloshes around in the bottom of the boat.

At last the river reaches the Yukon Valley. Now the water moves more steadily, north and west. You still must travel hundreds of miles to reach Dawson. ★

The days move by slowly. You see wild animals—wolves, deer, moose, and millions of birds. On all sides are fantastic mountains, topped with a dazzling white mantle that reaches down to the broad, green valley on either side of the river. The valley is dotted with wildflowers and birds and with an occasional bear standing on its hind legs looking at the strange sight of a boat on the river.

When you reach Dawson, your hands are lean and hard. You feel as if you've left everything you know far, far behind. Even your memories of cities and people are dull. As you stand inside this strange little town, you seem to be a part of the northern country. At the same time, you feel like a lonely stranger who doesn't belong here.

The cold air, the crystal waters, and the green meadows do not belong to people, but to the wild things that grow here. The great mountains stand like gigantic guards, keeping people out. But you are here because hidden in those mountains are great riches.

E MAIN IDEA

Write a complete main-idea sentence for each paragraph.

- Name the main character.

- Tell the main thing that character did.

- Tell when and where the character did that main thing.

1. In August, Clara went to the department store. She looked at clothing. She looked at sporting equipment. Then she recalled that she needed to fix her bike. So, she found a bike-repair kit and paid for it. Then she left the store.

2. At noon, Sidney followed the other students into the lunchroom. But Sidney was not hungry, so he sat at one of the tables. He took a paper and pencil from his backpack and began to write. Soon, Sidney was finished. Here is what he wrote:

The lunchroom has a lot to eat:
Milk and bread and cheese and meat.
But on this day I would rather think
Than get some things to eat and drink.

F NEITHER-NOR SENTENCES

Rewrite the sentences using *neither* and *nor*.

1. He could not swim, and he could not dive.

2. She was not happy, and she was not sad.

3. They could not walk, and they could not run.

G COMPREHENSION

Write the answers.

1. The story says that you decide to "find your fortune in gold." What does that mean?

2. Why does your delight change to fright when you move from Bennett Lake to the Yukon River?

3. Why do you feel as if you're floating on air when you travel on the calm parts of the Yukon River?

4. Using details from the story, name at least five animals you see in the Yukon Valley.

5. According to the article, who do the cold air, the crystal waters, and the green meadows in the Yukon Valley belong to?

H WRITING

- "Journey to Dawson" describes what you see, hear, and feel on your journey, such as mountains, lakes, rivers, trees, and animals.

Reread the descriptions in "Journey to Dawson." Then write a passage that describes where you are sitting right now.

Your passage should answer these questions:

1. What people and objects do you see?

2. What sounds do you hear?

3. What things do you smell?

Write at least six sentences.

END OF LESSON 53

A WORD LISTS

1	Word Practice
1.	baggage
2.	cricket
3.	exchange
4.	mine
5.	miner
6.	Thornton

2	Compound Words
1.	downstream
2.	hillside
3.	overhead
4.	waterfall

3	Vocabulary Words
1.	bud
2.	gee
3.	linger
4.	murmur

4	Vocabulary Words
1.	runners
2.	sap
3.	stagger
4.	whittle

B VOCABULARY DEFINITIONS

1. **runners**—The long, thin strips of metal under a sled are called *runners*. The runners are the only part of the sled that comes in contact with the snow.
• What do we call the strips of metal under a sled?

2. **sap**—The liquid underneath the bark of a tree is called *sap*. The sap carries water from the tree's roots to its branches and leaves.
• What do we call the liquid underneath the bark of a tree?

C VOCABULARY FROM CONTEXT

1. The tree branches were covered with young **buds** that would soon become full-grown leaves.
• What does *buds* mean in that sentence?

2. The wagon driver said, **"Gee!"** and the horses turned right.
• What does *Gee* mean in that sentence?

3. In Alaska, it was dawn by three o'clock in the morning, and twilight **lingered on** till nine o'clock at night.
• What does *lingered on* mean in that sentence?

4. In the forest, you could hear the **murmur** of insects and other living things.
• What does *murmur* mean in that sentence?

5. The man was so tired and cold that when he tried to walk, he **staggered** and almost fell.
• What does *staggered* mean in that sentence?

6. John Thornton **whittled** a branch with his knife and shaped the branch into an axe handle.
• What does *whittled* mean in that sentence?

Dog Sleds

The story that you will read today takes place near Dawson, in the Yukon Valley. The story begins in early spring, just as the ice is melting. Because the Yukon River is frozen during the winter, miners who are looking for gold can use dog sleds to ride on top of the solid ice.

A dog sled is built to carry heavy loads. It has runners along the bottom that slide over snow and ice. Its sides are high enough to hold baggage.

The sled is pulled by a team of dogs. Sled dogs are big and strong. The best dog, called the "lead dog," is at the front of the team. Some sleds have two lead dogs at the front of the team.

The dogs learn to work together, and they learn the commands the driver gives. When the driver says, "Mush on!" the dogs start running. When the driver says "Gee!" the dogs turn right. When the driver says "Haw!" the dogs turn left.

For the Love of a Man

Jack London

Chapter 1

It was beautiful spring weather along the Yukon River. Each day, the sun rose earlier and set later. It was dawn by three in the morning, and twilight lingered on till nine at night. The whole long day was a blaze of sunshine. The ghostly winter silence had given way to the great spring murmur of awakening life.

This murmur arose from all the land and filled it with the joy of living. The murmur came from the things that lived and moved again, things that had been almost dead and had not moved during the long months of winter. The sap was rising in the pines. The trees were bursting out in young buds, and shrubs and vines were putting on fresh green leaves. Crickets sang in the nights, and in the days all kinds of creeping, crawling things came out into the sun. Squirrels were chattering, and birds were singing. Overhead, the wild geese flew up from the south in V's that split the air.

From every hillside came the trickle of running water, the music of unseen waterfalls. Everything was thawing, bending, snapping. The Yukon was straining to break loose from the ice that held it motionless. The river flowed under sheets of ice and ate away at the ice from below; the sun ate from above. Cracks formed in the ice on the river's surface, and thin sheets of ice fell into the river.

Adapted for young readers.

John Thornton stepped out of his small tent and looked down the Yukon. He could hear the ice cracking, and he wondered how long it would be before the water flowed freely again. Thornton looked to the north and saw the spot where the White River joined the Yukon. He looked to the south and saw a dog sled coming slowly up the frozen river. He looked at the dog sled for a long time, and he did not like what he saw.

A full hour went by before the dogs and their two drivers staggered into Thornton's camp. When they arrived, the dogs dropped down as though they had all been struck dead. One of the drivers sat down on a log to rest. He sat down very slowly and carefully. He looked very stiff. The other man stood next to the sled and did the talking.

Thornton was whittling the last touches on an axe handle he had made from a stout branch. He whittled and listened, gave brief replies and good advice. He knew the kind of driver he was talking to, and as he gave advice, he was certain the man would not follow it. ♦

The man sneered and said, "They told us down at Skagway that the trail on the frozen river wasn't safe and we shouldn't try to take the sled to Dawson. They told us we couldn't make it this far, but here we are."

"And they told you true," Thornton answered. "The bottom's likely to drop out of the trail at any moment. Only fools, with the blind luck of fools, could have made it.

I tell you straight, I wouldn't risk my body on that ice for all the gold in Dawson."

"That's because you're not a fool, I suppose," said the man. "All the same, we'll go on to Dawson." He uncoiled his whip and yelled to the lead dog, "Get up there, Buck! Get up there! Mush on!"

Thornton went on whittling. It was a bad idea to get between a fool and his foolish ideas; the world would not change with the loss of these two fools.

But the dog team did not get up at the command. The team had passed into the stage where whipping was required to get it moving. The whip flashed out. Thornton bit his lip.

An old husky was the first to crawl to its feet. A brown dog followed. A white mutt came next, yelping with pain. A fourth dog made painful efforts. Twice he fell over, but on the third attempt he was able to rise.

The lead dog, Buck, made no effort to get up. He lay quietly where he had fallen. He neither whined nor struggled. Several times Thornton started to speak, but he changed his mind. Tears came into his eyes. At last he stood up and walked away.

This was the first time Buck had failed, and his failure drove the foolish man into a rage. He exchanged the whip for a club. Buck still refused to move. Like his mates, he was barely able to get up, but unlike them, he had made up his mind not to get up. He had a feeling of disaster because he had felt the thin ice under his feet all day. He sensed death, out there ahead on the ice where his master was trying to drive him. He refused to stir. ★

Buck had suffered so greatly that the spark of life within him flickered and went down. It was nearly out. He felt strangely numb. Then, the last feeling of pain left him. He no longer felt anything.

Suddenly, Thornton uttered a cry that was like the cry of an animal. He sprang upon the man who held the club and hurled him backward. The man fell as if struck by a falling tree. The other man looked on, but he was too stiff and cold to get up.

Thornton stood over Buck, struggling to control himself. He was too angry to speak.

"If you strike that dog again, I'll lay into you," he at last managed to say in a choking voice.

"It's my dog," the man replied. "Get out of my way, or I'll fix you. I'm going to Dawson."

Thornton stood between the man and Buck. The man pulled out a hunting knife. But Thornton quickly rapped the man's knuckles with the ax handle, knocking the knife to the ground. He rapped the knuckles again as the man tried to pick up the knife. Then Thornton stooped, picked up the knife himself, and cut Buck's harness with two strokes.

The man had no fight left in him. Besides, Buck was too near death to be of further use in hauling the sled. A few minutes later, the two men started the sled down the river. Buck heard them go and raised his head to watch. The dogs were limping and staggering. One man guided the sled from the side, and the other stumbled along in the rear.

As Buck watched them, Thornton knelt beside him and with rough, kindly hands searched for broken bones. He found nothing more than many bruises and a state of terrible hunger. Dog and man watched the sled crawling along over the ice. Suddenly, they saw its back end drop down. A scream came to their ears as one man fell through the ice. They saw the other man turn and make one step to run back.

Just then, a whole section of ice gave way, and the dogs and the second man disappeared. A yawning hole was all that was to be seen. The bottom had dropped out of the trail.

Thornton and Buck looked at each other.

"You poor beast," said Thornton, and Buck licked his hand.

F MAIN IDEA

Write a complete main-idea sentence for each paragraph.

- Name the main character.
- Tell the main thing that character did.
- Tell when and where the character did that main thing.

1. Rochelle went to her closet on the first day 'of April and took out her kite. Then she tied some string to the kite and went to the park. She held the string in her hand and started to run. The kite went into the air. Rochelle stopped running and let out more string. She watched the kite dart back and forth in the sky. After several hours, she pulled the kite back in and walked home.

2. Veronica wanted birds to live in her yard. Last weekend, she went to the lumber yard and bought several pieces of wood. She went back to her yard and nailed some of the pieces together to make a box. Then she put a roof on the box and cut a hole in one side to make a door. Finally, she filled the box with birdseed and hung it in a tree.

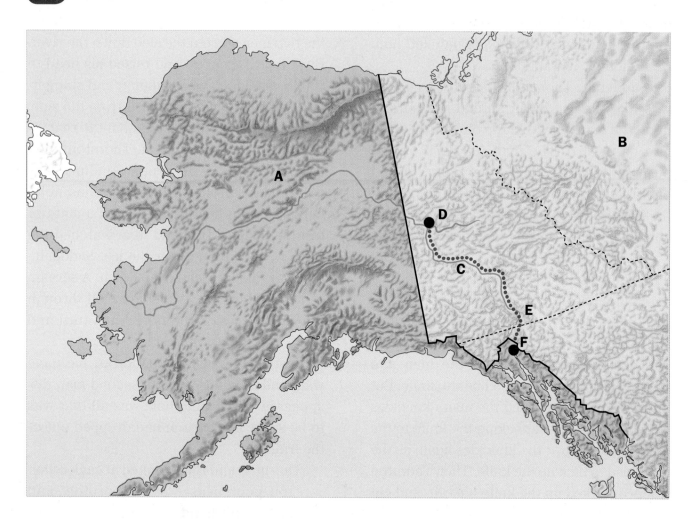

Write the name of each place.

1. State **A**

2. Country **B**

3. River **C**

4. Town **D**

5. Lake **E**

6. Town **F**

Write the answers.

1. The story says, "The Yukon was straining to break loose from the ice that held it motionless." Explain what that sentence means.

2. Why do you think the driver ignored Thornton's advice about the river?

3. At first, why did Thornton walk away when the driver was whipping Buck?

4. Why did Buck refuse to get up?

5. Why did Thornton change his mind about helping Buck?

Reread the description of springtime along the Yukon River at the beginning of "For the Love of a Man." Then write a passage that answers this main question:

- What happens when winter changes to spring where you live?

Your passage should also answer these questions:

1. How do the weather and the days change?

2. How do the plants and animals change?

3. How do people change?

Write at least six sentences.

55

A WORD LISTS

1 | Hard Words

1. affection
2. afterward
3. Hans

2 | Word Endings

1. comfortable
2. grumble
3. muscle
4. scramble
5. tumble

3 | Vocabulary Words

1. embrace
2. grapple
3. haunted
4. ideal
5. naked
6. recover
7. tolerate

B VOCABULARY FROM CONTEXT

1. He threw his arms around his mother and gave her a warm **embrace.**
- What does *embrace* mean in that sentence?

2. The two fighters didn't have any weapons, so they began to **grapple** with their bare hands.
- What does *grapple* mean in that sentence?

3. The bad dream **haunted** Isra every night for months, but then it went away.
- What does *haunted Isra every night* mean in that sentence?

4. Rance was so good in all his schoolwork that he was an **ideal** student.
- What does *ideal* mean in that sentence?

5. Some rocks were covered with moss, but other rocks were **naked.**
- What does *naked* mean in that sentence?

6. He was sick for two weeks, but then he began to **recover.**
- What does *recover* mean in that sentence?

7. Loretta didn't like green beans, but she could **tolerate** them if there was nothing else to eat.
- What does *tolerate* mean in that sentence?

For the Love of a Man
Chapter 2

John Thornton had been staying in the tent for two months. He had come down the Yukon with two other men, Pete and Hans. But Thornton had frozen his feet, and his partners had left him there to recover while they went up the river to get logs for a raft. They planned to take the raft to Dawson later that spring. Thornton was still limping slightly at the time he rescued Buck, but with the continued warm weather, the limp went away.

Buck slowly got his strength back. He would lie by the riverbank during the long spring days, watch the running water, and listen to the songs of birds and the hum of nature. Buck's wounds healed, his muscles swelled out, and the flesh came back to cover his bones.

Thornton was an ideal master. Other men took care of their dogs in a business-like way. But Thornton treated Buck as if he were his own child. He always had a kindly greeting and a cheering word. He would sit down for long talks with Buck. At these times, he would take Buck's head between his hands and rest his own head on

Buck's. Then he would shake Buck back and forth and talk softly to him. Buck knew no greater joy than Thornton's embrace and the sound of his voice.

Buck had a strange way of showing his love for Thornton. He would often seize Thornton's hand in his mouth and hold it so tightly that teeth marks would show for some time afterward. For the most part, however, Buck kept his love to himself. He went wild with happiness when Thornton touched him or spoke to him, but he did not beg for the man's affection.

Buck would lie for hours at Thornton's feet and look up into his face. He would follow each expression with keen interest. Sometimes, he would lie farther away and watch the outlines of the man and the movements of his body. The strength of Buck's gaze would often make Thornton turn his head. The man would return the gaze without speaking. Thornton's love shone out of his eyes, just as Buck's did.

For a long time after his rescue, Buck never let Thornton out of his sight. From the moment Thornton left the tent to the moment he entered it again, Buck would follow at his heels. The dog remembered that all of his former masters had left him. He was afraid that Thornton would pass out of his life, just as they had. ♦

Even in Buck's dreams, he was haunted by the fear of Thornton leaving. At such times, he would shake off sleep and creep through the chill to the flap of the tent, where he would stand and listen to the sound of his master's breathing.

Buck responded with joy to only one person—Thornton. Other gold rushers might praise or pet Buck, but he was cold toward them, and he would often get up and walk away. When Hans and Pete finally arrived on the raft, Buck refused to notice them until he learned that they were Thornton's friends. After that he tolerated them. They were very much like Thornton, living close to the earth, thinking simply and seeing clearly. They soon understood Buck and his ways.

Buck's love for Thornton seemed to grow and grow. Nothing was too great for Buck to do when Thornton commanded. One day, the men and Buck were sitting on the edge of a cliff that fell away, straight down, to naked rock three hundred feet below. Thornton was sitting near the edge, with Buck at his shoulder. Hans and Pete were nearby.

"Get ready to grab Buck," Thornton said to Hans and Pete. Then Thornton commanded, "Jump, Buck!" and pointed over the cliff. Buck sprang forward. An instant later, the three men grappled with Buck on the edge of the cliff; then they dragged him back to safety. ★

"I don't want to be the man that lays hands on you while that dog is around," Pete said, nodding his head toward Buck.

The very next day, Buck and the men got on the raft and headed down the Yukon to Dawson. Several days later, all four of them were walking around the muddy streets of the town, when they came upon two men having a fight. Thornton stepped between the men to try to stop them from fighting. Buck lay down in the street, put his head on his paws, and watched his master's every move.

Suddenly, one man struck out, straight from the shoulder. He hit Thornton and sent him spinning. Thornton fell down.

Those who were looking on heard what was neither bark nor yelp, but something more like a roar. They saw Buck's body rise up in the air as he left the ground. The man threw out his arm and was hurled backward to the street, with Buck on top of him.

The crowd quickly descended on Buck and pulled him off the man. Buck growled furiously and attempted to rush back in. Hans and Pete had to struggle to hold him back. A "miners' meeting" was called on the spot. The miners who saw what had happened decided that the dog was only protecting his master, so Buck was set free. But he was now famous, and from that day, his name spread through every mining camp along the Yukon.

D MAIN IDEA

Write a complete main-idea sentence for each paragraph.

- Name the main characters.

- Tell the main thing those characters did.

- Tell when and where the characters did that main thing.

1. It was the Fourth of July. Mr. and Mrs. Dunbar woke up early and began to prepare for the day's big event. Mr. Dunbar made chicken sandwiches and a big potato salad. He put the sandwiches and salad in a large basket, then he woke up the children. Meanwhile, Mrs. Dunbar put gas in the car and checked the oil and tires. Then she picked up the family and the food and drove to Red Rock State Park. When they got to the park, the Dunbars got out of the car and put some blankets on the ground. Then they ate all the food.

2. The Comets were one of the best softball teams in Springfield. In September, they played in the City Championship game. At the end of three innings, they had a five-run lead. But the other team started to come back. In the last inning, the Comets were one run behind, and they failed to score. The Comets were brokenhearted, but they went over to congratulate the other team.

E COMPREHENSION

Write the answers.

1. Why did Thornton have to stay in the tent while Hans and Pete were gone?

2. Why do you think Buck showed his love for Thornton by biting his hand?

3. Why did Buck follow Thornton everywhere?

4. Why did Thornton order Buck to jump off a cliff?

5. Copy the sentence in the story that explains why the miners decided to set Buck free.

F WRITING

Write a passage that answers this main question:

- Do you think Thornton did the right thing when he ordered Buck to jump off a cliff?

Use details from the story to answer these other questions in your passage:

1. Why did Thornton order Buck to jump?

2. Why did Buck obey Thornton?

3. What could have gone wrong?

4. In what other ways could Thornton have proved his point about Buck?

Write at least six sentences.

END OF LESSON 55

A WORD LISTS

1 Hard Words	2 Word Endings	3 Vocabulary Review	4 Vocabulary Words
1. ashore	1. apparently	1. embrace	1. clutch
2. Eldorado	2. desperately	2. grapple	2. flush
3. lunge	3. instantly	3. haunt	3. guilty
	4. particularly	4. ideal	4. jut out
		5. recover	5. rear up
		6. tolerate	6. stretch

B VOCABULARY DEFINITIONS

1. **flush**—When your face turns red and hot, it *flushes*.
- What happens to your face when it flushes?

2. **guilty**—Somebody who makes a mistake is *guilty* of the mistake.
- A person who makes a mistake is …

C VOCABULARY FROM CONTEXT

1. He reached out and **clutched** the slippery rocks with both hands.
- What does *clutched* mean in that sentence?

2. The rocks **jutted out** so far into the river that the boat could hardly get around them.
- What does *jutted out* mean in that sentence?

3. When the horse **reared up,** the rider fell off and landed behind the horse.
- What does *reared up* mean in that sentence?

4. They paddled through a bad **stretch** of rapids.
- What does *stretch* mean in that sentence?

For the Love of a Man
Chapter 3

In the fall of that year, Buck saved John Thornton's life. The three partners were moving a long and narrow boat down a bad stretch of rapids on the Forty Mile Creek. Hans and Pete moved along the bank and guided the boat with a rope. Thornton remained in the boat and pushed it along with a pole. From time to time, Thornton shouted directions to his partners on the bank. Buck ran along the bank beside the men. He was worried and anxious, and he never took his eyes off his master.

They came to a particularly bad spot where a ledge of rocks jutted out into the river. The boat started to fly downstream in a swift current. Hans and Pete tried to stop the boat by yanking on the rope. But the boat hit the rocks and flipped over. Thornton was flung out. He floated downstream toward the worst part of the rapids—a stretch of wild water in which no swimmer could live.

Buck sprang into the water instantly. At the end of three hundred yards, in the middle of a mad swirl of water, he caught up to Thornton. When he felt the man grasp his tail, Buck headed for the bank. He swam with all his splendid strength. But the progress to the bank was slow, while the man and the dog traveled downstream with amazing speed. ♦

Thornton and Buck could hear the loud roaring of rapids below them. They could see the rocks that thrust through the water like the teeth of an enormous comb. They could feel the current becoming swifter. Thornton

knew it would be impossible to reach the shore. Suddenly, he was hurled into a rock with crushing force. He let go of Buck and clutched the rock's slippery top with both hands. Then he shouted, "Go, Buck!"

Buck could not hold his own, and he was swept farther downstream, struggling desperately, but unable to swim back to Thornton. When he heard Thornton's command repeated, he reared up in the water, threw his head high, then turned toward the shore. He swam powerfully and was dragged ashore by Pete and Hans.

They knew that Thornton could cling to the slippery rock for only a few minutes. They ran as fast as they could up the bank to a point far above where Thornton was hanging on. They attached the rope to Buck's neck and shoulders and threw him into the stream. He struck out boldly, but not far enough into the stream. He came within six feet of Thornton, but then the current carried him past the struggling man.

Hans promptly pulled with the rope, as if Buck were a boat. The dog was jerked under the surface, and he remained under the surface until his body struck against the shore and he was hauled out. He was half drowned, and Hans and Pete threw themselves upon him, pounding the breath into him and the water out of him. He staggered to his feet and fell down.

Just then, the faint sound of Thornton's voice came to them, and although they could not make out the words, they knew that he could not hold on any longer.

His master's voice acted on Buck as if it were an electric shock. He sprang to his feet and ran up the bank ahead of the men to the point he had jumped from before.

Again the rope was attached, and again Buck was thrown into the raging stream. But this time he swam far out into the stream. He had made a mistake once, but he would not be guilty of it a second time. Buck swam on until he was directly upstream from Thornton. Then he turned, and with the speed of an express train, he headed down toward his master. Thornton saw him coming. ★

Buck struck him with the whole force of the current behind him. Thornton reached up and grabbed Buck's shaggy neck with both hands. Hans tied the rope around a tree, and Buck and Thornton were jerked under the water. The man and the dog were dragged over the jagged bottom, sometimes one on top and sometimes the other. At last, they came toward the bank.

As soon as they reached the shore, both man and dog passed out. When Thornton came to, he looked for Buck. Hans and Pete were standing over Buck's limp and apparently lifeless body. Thornton was bruised and battered, yet he got up and went carefully over to Buck. He found that the dog was alive, but he had broken ribs.

"That settles it," he announced. "We camp right here." They camped until Buck's ribs mended and he was able to travel again.

• • •

That winter at Dawson, Buck did something that made him even more famous than he already was. The incident started with a conversation in the Eldorado Hotel.

Some men were bragging about their favorite dogs. These men were claiming that Buck was not the best dog. Thornton spoke loudly in Buck's favor. One man stated that his dog could start a sled with five hundred pounds on it and walk off with it. A second man bragged six hundred, and a third seven hundred.

"That's nothing," said Thornton. "Buck can start a sled with a thousand pounds on it."

A rich miner named Matthewson demanded, "Are you saying he can walk off with it for a hundred yards?"

"Yes, walk off with it for a hundred yards," Thornton said coolly.

"Well," Matthewson said slowly so that all could hear, "I would offer a prize of one thousand dollars to any dog who could pull such a load. But I don't believe that any dog alive could do it." So saying, he slammed down a sack of gold dust the size of a rolling pin.

Nobody spoke. Thornton could feel a flush of warm blood creeping up his face. His tongue had tricked him. He did not know whether Buck could start a sled with a thousand pounds on it. Half a ton! He had great faith in Buck's strength and often thought he was capable of starting such a load. But he had never tested the idea. The eyes of a dozen men fixed upon him, silent and waiting.

E COMPREHENSION

Write the answers.

1. When Buck first tried to rescue Thornton, why did Buck move so slowly toward the bank? Use details from the story to explain your answer.

2. Explain how Buck, Hans, and Pete rescued Thornton from the creek. Use details from the story.

3. After the rescue, why did the men decide to camp by the river?

4. In the hotel, Thornton made a claim about Buck that he wasn't sure of. Why do you think he made that claim?

5. The story says that Thornton's "tongue had tricked him" in the hotel. What does that mean?

F WRITING

Write a passage that answers this main question:

• Do you think Thornton is a good master for Buck?

Use details from the story to answer these other questions in your passage:

1. In what ways is Thornton a good master?

2. In what ways is Thornton a bad master?

3. What details from the story support your opinion?

Write at least six sentences.

END OF LESSON 56

A WORD LISTS

1	Word Family		2	Vocabulary Words
1.	admiration		1.	grate
2.	affection		2.	lunge
3.	condition		3.	quiver
4.	conversation		4.	witness

B VOCABULARY DEFINITIONS

1. **grate**—When something rubs against a hard surface and makes a harsh sound, it *grates*.
- What's another way of saying *The shovel grinds against the rocks?*

2. **lunge**—When you charge forward suddenly, you *lunge*.
- What are you doing when you charge forward suddenly?

3. **quiver**—*Quiver* is another word for *tremble* or *shake*.
- What's another way of saying *The tree branches shook in the wind?*

4. **witness**—When you see an event happening, you *witness* that event.
- What are you doing when you see an event happening?

C READING LITERATURE: Realistic Short Story

For the Love of a Man
Chapter 4

Matthewson looked at Thornton coldly and said, "I've got a sled standing outside now with twenty fifty-pound sacks of flour on it. That's a thousand pounds."

Thornton did not reply. He did not know what to say. He glanced from face to face like a man who has lost the power of thought. The face of Jim O'Brien, an old-time comrade, caught his eyes.

O'Brien shook his head solemnly and said, "I don't have much faith that the beast can pull such a load."

The men poured out of the Eldorado into the street to see the test. The tables were deserted. Soon, several hundred men in heavy fur coats stood around the sled.

The sled, loaded with a thousand pounds of flour, had been standing for a couple of

hours in the intense cold. The temperature was sixty below zero, and the runners had frozen fast to the hard-packed snow.

O'Brien and Matthewson argued about starting the sled. O'Brien suggested that Thornton could knock the runners loose from the ice before Buck began pulling. Matthewson insisted that Buck would have to pull the sled with the runners as they were—in the frozen grip of the snow. Most of the men who had witnessed the argument decided in Matthewson's favor.

Not one man besides Thornton thought that Buck would succeed. As Thornton looked at the sled, he was heavy with doubt.

"Three thousand," Matthewson suddenly shouted. "Thornton, I'll pay you three thousand dollars if your dog can pull that load!"

Thornton's face showed his doubt, but his fighting spirit was up. That spirit failed to recognize the impossible. The regular team of ten dogs was curled up in the snow in front of the sled. The team was unhitched, and Buck, with his own harness, was put in front of the sled. He sensed the excitement, and he felt that in some way he must do a great thing for John Thornton. ♦

The crowd began to murmur with admiration at Buck's splendid appearance. He was in perfect condition, without an ounce of extra flesh. His furry coat shone like silk. His muscles showed in tight rolls underneath his skin. The men felt these muscles and said they were as hard as iron.

Suddenly, a tall man said, "Gad, sir! Gad, sir! I offer you eight hundred dollars for him, sir, before the test, sir; eight hundred for that dog just as he stands."

Thornton shook his head no and stepped to Buck's side.

The crowd fell silent. Everybody knew that Buck was a magnificent animal; but the thousand pounds of flour was more than any dog could pull.

Thornton knelt by Buck's side. He took the dog's head in his two hands and rested his cheek on Buck's cheek. He did not playfully shake him or murmur softly. But he whispered something in the dog's ear. Buck whined eagerly.

The crowd was watching curiously. The affair was growing mysterious. It seemed like a magic trick. As Thornton got to his feet, Buck seized Thornton's hand between his jaws, pressing in with his teeth and releasing slowly. It was Buck's answer.

Thornton stepped back. "Now, Buck," he said.

Buck pulled his harness tight, then let it slacken a bit.

"Gee!" Thornton's voice rang out, sharp in the tense silence.

Buck followed the command. He swung to the right, ending the movement in a lunge that jerked the harness. The load quivered, and a crisp crackling rose from under the runners.

"Haw!" Thornton commanded.

Buck made the same move, this time to the left. The crackling turned into a snapping. The sled turned slightly, and the runners began to grate against the ice. The sled was broken out. Men were holding their breath. ✦

"Now, MUSH ON!"

Thornton's command cracked out like a shot. Buck threw himself forward, tightening the harness with a jarring lunge.

His whole body was gathered together in the tremendous effort. His muscles knotted under his silky fur. His great chest was low to the ground, his head forward and down. His feet flew, and his claws scarred the hard-packed snow. The sled swayed, trembled, and started forward. One of Buck's feet slipped, and one man groaned aloud. Then the sled slowly moved ahead.

Men gasped and began to breathe again, unaware that for a moment they had stopped breathing. Thornton was running behind, encouraging Buck with short, cheery words. The distance had been measured off, and as the dog neared the pile of firewood that marked the end of the hundred yards, the men began to cheer loudly.

The cheer burst into a roar as Buck passed the firewood and halted at command. Every man was clapping wildly, even Matthewson. Hats and mittens were flying in the air. Men were shaking hands, and they did not care whose hand they shook.

Thornton fell on his knees beside Buck, head against head. Thornton was shaking him back and forth. Those who gathered close heard him talking to Buck. He talked softly and lovingly.

"Gad, sir! Gad, sir!" sputtered the tall man. "I'll give you a thousand for him, sir, a thousand, sir—twelve hundred, sir."

Thornton rose to his feet. His eyes were wet. The tears were streaming down his cheeks. "No, sir," he said to the tall man. "No, sir. You can't buy this dog for any amount of money."

Buck seized Thornton's hand in his teeth. Thornton shook him back and forth.

The men drew back a ways, and none dared to disturb the man and his dog.

D COMPREHENSION

Write the answers.

1. At the beginning of the chapter, why were the runners of the sled stuck to the ground?

2. Why do you think Matthewson said Buck had to break the runners free?

3. How did the tall man's offer for Buck change during the story? Why did it change?

4. Why did Buck bite Thornton's hand?

5. Why do you think the men didn't dare to disturb Thornton and Buck?

E WRITING

Write a passage that answers this main question:

- How did Buck change during the story?

Use details from the story to answer these questions in your passage:

1. What did Buck look like at the beginning of the story?

2. What did Buck look like at the end of the story?

3. How did Buck's feelings and attitude change during the story?

Write at least six sentences.

END OF LESSON 57

58

A WORD LISTS

1 | Compound Words

1. birthplace
2. groundhog
3. homeowner
4. housekeeper
5. woodchuck

2 | Vocabulary Words

1. beam
2. bough
3. drowsy
4. lullaby
5. rhyming couplet
6. stanza

B VOCABULARY DEFINITIONS

1. **beam**—A ray of light is sometimes called a *beam* of light.
- What's another way of saying *a ray of morning sun?*

2. **bough**—A main branch of a tree is called a *bough.*
- What's another way of saying *They hung the swing from a main branch of the oak tree?*

3. **drowsy**—*Drowsy* is another word for *sleepy.*
- What's another way of saying *People get sleepy in the spring?*

4. **lullaby**—A song that is used to put children to sleep is called a *lullaby.*
- What do we call a song that is used to put children to sleep?

5. **stanza**—A group of lines in a poem is called a *stanza.*
- What's another way of saying *The poem had three groups of lines?*

6. **rhyming couplet**—A pair of lines that rhyme in a poem is called a *rhyming couplet.*
- What's another way of saying *The poem had four pairs of lines that rhymed?*

Trees

Harry Behn

Trees are the kindest things I know,
They do no harm, they simply grow
And spread a shade for sleepy cows,
And gather birds among their boughs.

They give us fruit in leaves above,
And wood to make our houses of,
And leaves to burn on Hallowe'en,
And in the spring new buds of green.

They are the first when day's begun
To touch the beams of morning sun,
They are the last to hold the light
When evening changes into night.

And when a moon floats on the sky,
They hum a drowsy lullaby
Of sleepy children long ago ...
Trees are the kindest things I know.

In Time of Silver Rain
Langston Hughes

In time of silver rain
The earth puts forth new life again,
Green grasses grow
And flowers lift their heads,
And over all the plain
The wonder spreads
    Of life,
    Of life,
    Of life!

In time of silver rain
The butterflies lift silken wings
To catch a rainbow cry,
And trees put forth new leaves to sing
In joy beneath the sky
As down the roadway
Passing boys and girls
Go singing, too,
In time of silver rain
    When spring
    And life
    Are new.

E COMPREHENSION

Write the answers.

1. The poem "Trees" gives several reasons to explain why trees are so kind. Use details from the poem to name at least three of those reasons.

2. How could trees "hum a drowsy lullaby"?

3. In the poem "In Time of Silver Rain," what could the narrator mean when he says, "The butterflies lift silken wings to catch a rainbow cry"?

4. What is different about the narration in "Trees" and "In Time of Silver Rain"?

5. The rhyme scheme for the first stanza of "Trees" is AABB. What does that mean?

F WRITING

- The poem "Trees" explains what the narrator likes about trees.

Write a poem that answers this main question:

- What animal do you like best and why?

Your poem should also answer these questions:

1. What does the animal look like?

2. What sounds does the animal make?

3. What does the animal do during the day?

Write at least six lines. Your poem does not have to rhyme.

A WORD LISTS

1 Hard Words	2 Poetry Words	3 Country Names	4 Vocabulary Words
1. chinook	1. beat	1. Brazil	1. identify
2. molt	2. couplet	2. Colombia	2. migrate
3. salmon	3. meter	3. Ecuador	3. plentiful
4. scarce	4. rhythm	4. Peru	4. spawn
5. scientist	5. stanza		5. volunteer
6. tanager	6. verse		

B VOCABULARY DEFINITIONS

1. **identify**—When you tell what something is, you *identify* that thing. When you tell the name of a kind of fish, you identify the fish.
- What are you doing when you tell the name of a kind of fish?

2. **migrate**—When you move from one area to another area, you *migrate* to the other area.
- What's another way of saying *The geese moved from the north to the south?*

3. **plentiful**—When something is *plentiful,* it's in good supply.
- What's another way of saying *Wild food is in good supply in the spring?*

4. **spawn**—Fish eggs are called *spawn,* so a place where fish lay eggs is called a *spawning ground.*
- What is a spawning ground?

5. **volunteer**—When you offer to help, you *volunteer.*
- What's another way of saying *The students offered to help clean up the classroom?*

C READING INFORMATIONAL TEXT: Science

Amazing Animal Journeys

During the next two lessons, you will read four short articles about four different animals. One of the animals is a brightly colored bird, another is a magnificent fish, *the third is a shy mammal, and the last is a small butterfly. These animals are different in almost every way except one: they all take amazing journeys.*

The All-American Flyer

Every year, thousands of beautiful scarlet tanagers migrate back and forth between North and South America. These small birds spend summers in the United States and Canada and winters in Colombia, Ecuador, Peru, and Brazil.

To make the long journey between North and South America, scarlet tanagers fly across the Gulf of Mexico and Central America. No tanagers get lost—not even the young ones. Yet the trip is almost four thousand miles!

Feathers for All Weathers

When tanagers arrive in May to spend the late spring and summer in North America, they are in what scientists call summer dress. The wing and tail feathers of the male birds are jet black, and the rest of their feathers are bright red. The female birds' feathers are greenish-yellow.

As the summer passes, tanagers begin shedding their old feathers and growing new ones for the long flight back to South America. This process is called **molting.**

By August, the birds look ragged. Males lose their scarlet-red feathers and grow green ones in their place. Females don't appear to change as much, because their new feathers are almost the same color as the old ones.

By September, both sexes are in green winter dress. Not a single tanager is scarlet now.

Flying for Food

During September, the days grow shorter. The weather gets colder, and the insects that tanagers eat become scarce. So the birds begin moving southward.

Male tanagers leave first. After a few days, the female tanagers follow them.

Male tanager in summer dress

Female tanager in summer dress

Male tanager molting from summer to winter dress

Flocks from the East head toward Florida, taking a route called the Atlantic Flyway. Midwestern birds head for Texas, using a different route—the Mississippi Flyway.

Tanagers fly during the night. Each morning, the birds land and eat as many insects, fruits, and seeds as they can. Then they rest and eat some more. At dusk, their long journey continues.

The birds reach South America during the rainy season. Forest trees have new leaves, and food is plentiful.

The rainy season lasts for several months, but then the dry season begins, and food gets scarce. Before that happens, the tanagers molt and leave. Traveling in summer dress, they fly back to North America on the same route they used on their way south. Some even return to the places where they started their trip.

Bands Tell the Tale

How do we know about the tanager's migration between North and South America? The United States Fish and Wildlife Service has been studying bird migrations for years. Volunteers in North and South America catch the birds in nets, put bands on their legs, and release them. Each band has its own number. When other volunteers catch the birds months later, they report the numbers on the bands.

Thousands of reports about scarlet tanagers are now on file. The reports show that tanagers travel about eight thousand miles a year, avoiding winter in North America and the dry season in South America. Their journey is amazing. But then, tanagers are amazing birds. ♦

When the Salmon Come Home

People who fish have always told great stories, but none as strange as the one about salmon. More than a hundred years ago, people who fished for a living said that salmon spent a few years in the deep ocean and then returned to the rivers where they were born.

Was the story true? How could anyone prove it? How could anyone tell one fish from another? Long ago, Izaak Walton, an English writer, tied ribbons on the tails of fish to find out where they went. But either he never saw the fish again, or the fish lost their ribbons.

Clipping and Tagging

Eventually scientists discovered a way to identify salmon. The scientists caught young salmon soon after the salmon were born in spawning grounds, which are places along the bottom of a river where salmon lay their spawn, or eggs. The scientists made a mark in each young salmon by clipping off part of the salmon's fins. The location of the clip changed from river to river. If some of the clipped salmon were later caught out in the ocean, the location of the clip would show which river they came from.

Meanwhile, scientists on fishing boats out in the ocean used little plastic or metal tags to mark salmon. When these scientists caught salmon with clipped fins, they tagged the fish and recorded where they were caught. Then they released the salmon back into the ocean.

Back in the rivers, the chance of finding any salmon that were both clipped and tagged was slight. But in time, many clipped and tagged salmon were picked up near their spawning grounds.

Here was solid proof that salmon do return to their birthplace. Their spawning ground may be located in a distant upper branch of a big river, yet somehow the salmon find their way home.

A Long Way Home

How far do salmon travel to get home? A large chinook salmon was tagged in the Pacific Ocean fifteen hundred miles from the coast and was later found a thousand miles upstream in the Columbia River. Its homeward journey was twenty-five hundred miles! *

Most salmon do not take such a long trip, but those that are born in long rivers like the Columbia or the Yukon in North America may travel hundreds of miles to reach their spawning grounds. Others, like the pink salmon, go only a few miles.

How long do the salmon stay in the sea? The pink, which is small, stays two years. The chinook, the largest of the salmon, stays two to five years. Food is plentiful in the ocean, and the salmon grow big and fat before they start for home. As soon as the salmon reach their home rivers, they stop eating. While swimming upstream, they live off the fat they stored in their bodies while at sea.

Swimming Upstream

Some salmon come home in the spring, and others come home in the fall. Before they start swimming up a river, thousands of the same kind of salmon gather at the place where the river flows into the sea. As the salmon begin rushing up the river, the water seems to boil. The fish swim so fast that their upstream journey is called a run.

Salmon climbing a fish ladder next to a dam

Swimming against the current, the salmon often cover fifty miles a day.

The run slows down in places where dams have been built. Since salmon can't scale the high walls of a dam, they are provided with a kind of stairway called a fish ladder. Water flows down the steps of the ladder, and the salmon leap from step to step until they are above the dam. Then they continue rushing upstream to their spawning grounds.

By the time salmon reach their spawning grounds, they are thin and exhausted. Yet they dig nests in the riverbed, mate, and lay eggs. When the salmon have done what they set out to do, they die. Soon afterward, baby salmon hatch from the eggs. Like their parents, they will take an amazing journey to the ocean and then come back home.

D | MAIN IDEA AND SUPPORTING DETAILS

Write the main idea and supporting details of this paragraph.

Wild horses live in a natural environment, and they eat many kinds of food, such as grasses, grains, leafy plants, twigs, and bark. These foods contain little bits of stone and sand called grit. When wild horses eat, the grit wears down their teeth smoothly and evenly.

E | COMPREHENSION

Write the answers.

1. Use details from the article to describe what happens when tanagers molt.

2. Use details from the article to name two reasons tanagers fly south in September.

3. In what body of water were the fins of young salmon clipped? In what body of water were they tagged?

4. What did scientists prove when they found clipped and tagged salmon in a river?

5. Use details from the article to describe the four actions that salmon take after they return to their spawning grounds.

F | WRITING

- Pretend you are either a male or a female scarlet tanager.

Write a passage that describes a year in your life, beginning with your arrival in North America during the spring.

Use details from the article to answer these questions in your passage:

1. How do you change while you are in North America?

2. Why do you fly to South America?

3. What do you do in South America?

4. When and why do you leave South America?

Write at least six sentences.

END OF LESSON 59

A   WORD LISTS

1 | Hard Words

1. autumn
2. cocoon
3. hibernate
4. nectar

2 | Animal Names

1. caterpillar
2. marmot
3. monarch butterfly
4. squirrel

3 | Names

1. Minnesota
2. Sierra Madres
3. Urquhart

4 | Vocabulary Words

1. commotion
2. deflate
3. enlarge
4. mysterious

B   VOCABULARY FROM CONTEXT

1. The students made such a **commotion** that the teacher told them to be quiet.
- What does *commotion* mean in that sentence?

2. The basketball had too much air inside, so the coach **deflated** it a little bit.
- What does *deflated* mean in that sentence?

3. They decided to **enlarge** their house by adding a room.
- What does *enlarge* mean in that sentence?

4. The old castle was strange and **mysterious.**
- What does *mysterious* mean in that sentence?

Amazing Animal Journeys

In the last lesson, you read about two animals that take amazing journeys: the scarlet tanager and the salmon. In this lesson, you will read about two more. One is a woodchuck and the other is a butterfly. Their journeys are just as remarkable as the tanager's and the salmon's.

Journey to Death's Door

Call it a woodchuck, a groundhog, or a marmot. It doesn't matter which name you use. The woodchuck is really just a big squirrel—one that lives on and under the ground.

Here's a question about woodchucks: How much wood could a woodchuck chuck if a woodchuck could chuck wood? The answer is none, because woodchucks don't "chuck" (eat) wood.

Like its squirrel relatives, the woodchuck gnaws with its front teeth. You might think a woodchuck gnaws wood, but it really eats softer foods, such as clover, grass, and garden vegetables. Woodchucks eat so many of these plants that some farmers think of them as pests. ✿

Woodchuck with mouthful of food

Home, Sweet Den

The woodchuck's home is an underground den with a front entrance and a back entrance and another hole that's used for a quick escape. Like little office workers, woodchucks leave home in the morning, spend the day at work, and then come back to sleep at night.

The woodchuck's den is about three feet underground and has runways connecting separate rooms. Like many homeowners, woodchucks keep improving their dens. Every spring they add new rooms or enlarge some of the old ones.

Woodchucks are good housekeepers except for one messy thing. In the fall, they store plants and other food in their dens, just like their squirrel relatives. Some of the food gets moldy and rots because woodchucks don't eat everything they have "squirreled away."

Winter Slowdown

Woodchucks hibernate in their dens when cold weather comes. When animals **hibernate,** they sleep through the winter. To hibernate, the woodchuck travels just three feet under ground; but those three feet are a journey to the door of death.

To get ready for hibernating, the woodchuck plugs the entrances to its den with dirt and grass. When the woodchuck is snugly holed up, its breathing slows down. Then its body temperature starts to fall to just a few degrees above freezing. Its heart beats only four times a minute. The woodchuck scarcely moves. It seems to be dead.

In the spring, many hours of warmth are needed to bring the woodchuck out of its winter sleep. When warm weather gets underway, the woodchuck wakes up and comes out of its den. Again, it travels only three feet, but this time it takes a journey back to life. ♦

The Mystery of the Butterfly Trees

What has six legs and flies south for the winter? The answer is a monarch butterfly. About fifty years ago, thousands of people helped discover this fact by working together. Scientists had observed that monarchs from east of the Rocky Mountains fly south in the fall. But no one had the faintest idea where they went.

From Caterpillar to Monarch

Most of the monarch's life was well-known. In spring, it lays its eggs on milkweed. The caterpillar that hatches from these eggs eats and grows. Then it covers itself with a case called a **cocoon.** Over the next two weeks, the caterpillar inside the cocoon changes completely.

When the caterpillar comes out of its cocoon, it has changed into a lovely monarch butterfly with four orange and black wings. All summer long, the monarch flies from flower to flower in search of nectar. This sweet liquid is the monarch's food.

This group of seven pictures shows the life cycle of a monarch butterfly. The butterfly begins as an egg on a milkweed plant. A caterpillar hatches out of the egg and begins eating. Then the caterpillar forms a cocoon and turns into a butterfly.

On the Wing

In early autumn, monarchs start flying south during the day. When night comes, they gather on the bark of certain trees, where they rest. They take off again the next morning.

But where do they go? The only way to track them is to tag them. A couple named

Life cycle of a monarch butterfly

Fred and Norah Urquhart discovered a label that would stick to a butterfly's wings. They had thousands of these labels printed with numbers and instructions. Then they called for volunteers to help tag monarchs. ✦

News of the tagging program spread, and people from Maine to Mexico became butterfly watchers. They caught monarchs in nets and tagged them. After hundreds of thousands of monarchs were tagged, it became clear that monarchs fly all the way to the Sierra Madres, which are mountains in Mexico.

Mountain Hideout

Just where in the Sierra Madres did themonarchs go? Some Mexicans offered aclue. They told of mysterious trees covered with butterflies, high in the mountains. But they were not sure where the trees were.

Years passed before the Urquharts found the trees. Led by guides, the couple climbed ten thousand feet to a stretch of forest where all the trees looked orange. Every tree was covered with monarchs—millions of them! Staring in wonder, the Urquharts noticed a tagged butterfly that had come from Minnesota. It had traveled two thousand miles.

Butterflies on Parade

The story of the monarchs that live west of the Rocky Mountains is different. Instead of going from north to south, western monarchs go from cool mountains to warm valleys. In the town of Pacific Grove, California, a place where monarchs spend the winter, school children welcome them with a parade. Tourists come to see the trees on which they settle.

East or west, monarchs are always welcome. Of all the animals that migrate, they are the smallest. Their journey is amazing. But then, the tanager, the salmon, and the woodchuck also make amazing journeys!

D MAIN IDEA AND SUPPORTING DETAILS

Write the main idea and supporting details of this paragraph.

Sometimes a horse will need extra dental care. One sign that a horse needs to see a dentist is if a lot of food drops from the horse's mouth while the horse is eating. Another warning sign is if a horse turns its head sideways to chew. If a horse stops eating, it needs to see a dentist at once.

E COMPREHENSION

Write the answers.

1. Why is the article about woodchucks titled "Journey to Death's Door"?

2. Describe what a woodchuck's den looks like and where it's located. Use details from the article.

3. Describe how a woodchuck's body changes when the woodchuck hibernates. Use details from the article.

4. Describe how a caterpillar turns into butterfly. Use details from the article.

5. Why did the Urquharts put tags on butterflies?

F WRITING

Write a passage that answers this main question:

- How does a scarlet tanager's migration compare with a woodchuck's hibernation?

Use details from the article to answer these other questions in your passage.

1. When and why do scarlet tanagers migrate to South America?

2. When and why do woodchucks hibernate?

3. How do the scarlet tanager's reasons for migrating compare to the woodchuck's reasons for hibernating?

Write at least six sentences.

END OF LESSON 60

A WORD LISTS

1 | Hard Words

1. agency
2. coyote
3. federal
4. surface

2 | Related Words

1. agile / agility
2. flexible / flexibility
3. govern / government
4. manage / management

3 | Vocabulary Words

1. avalanche
2. obedient
3. relationship
4. unstable

B VOCABULARY DEFINITIONS

1. **agility**—Someone who moves quickly and easily has *agility*.
   Here's another way of saying *The cat moved quickly and easily: The cat had agility.*
   * What's another way of saying *The basketball player moved quickly and easily?*

2. **avalanche**—A landslide of snow, ice, and rock is called an *avalanche*.
   * What's another way of saying *The landslide of snow, ice, and rock raced down the mountain?*

3. **obedient**—When you obey orders, you're *obedient*. Someone who is obedient has obedience.

Here are two ways of saying *The soldier obeyed orders:*
The soldier was obedient.
The soldier had obedience.
   * What are two ways of saying *The dog obeyed orders?*

4. **relationship**—When two things are connected in some way, they have a *relationship*.
   * What's another way of saying *Thornton had a good connection with Buck?*

5. **unstable**—Things that **aren't** likely to change are *stable*. Things that **are** likely to change are *unstable*.
   * What's the opposite of a ladder that is stable?

Search and Rescue Dogs

A town is hit hard by a storm. High winds knock down buildings and homes, and people who are trapped need help. Rescuers do their best to save them, but the rescuers often need help themselves. A person may be trapped somewhere inside a building that collapsed, but how do rescuers locate the person? They call their search and rescue dogs! These dogs are smart and light, and they can move quickly.

A dog's best search tool, however, is its nose. A dog's sense of smell can be one thousand to ten thousand times stronger than a human's sense of smell.

A search and rescue dog named Coyote once found a missing woman in less than ten minutes. This was after a team of people had searched for the woman for eighteen hours. Coyote's handler first let the dog sniff something that belonged to the missing woman. As soon as Coyote knew the woman's scent, he quickly found her, lying behind some bushes where people could not see her.

Early Training Exercises

Search and rescue dogs begin their training when they are three months to ten months old. The first step is to build a close relationship between a dog and its handler. A search and rescue dog must follow all commands the handler gives. These commands go far beyond "sit," "stay," and "shake hands."

The dog might be told to ride a chairlift to the top of a ski slope, or it might be told to step into a harness and be lifted into a flying helicopter. For the dog to obey these commands, it must practice routines that will be needed when the dog and handler are actually searching for a person. ◆

The relationship between dog and handler goes both ways. Handlers learn to trust their dog's instincts. A handler watches the dog closely as it searches. Search and rescue dogs may give different signals when they find something. One dog might stop moving and stand with its tail still, but another might jump into the air. Many dogs signal by barking a certain way. A handler has to know the dog's signals.

Early training exercises are like games of hide-and-seek. At first the game is simple. A search and rescue dog may watch its handler go into a nearby area and hide. The handler then gives a command for the dog to find the handler. Gradually the game gets harder. In later training exercises, several people hide in different places. The dog is given an item belonging to one of those people. The dog sniffs the item and tries to find that particular person. These games are repeated often to build a dog's skills.

Advanced Training

After a search and rescue dog learns to trail a scent on the ground, it may be taught to pick up scents in the air. Shifting winds can be troublesome, sometimes sending a dog off track. But a search and rescue dog's keen sense of smell is not easily fooled. The dog may seem to be confused when it runs in circles or zigzags, but it's really running back and forth across a search area to measure the strength of the scent it is following. Once the dog finds where the scent is strongest, the dog follows the scent trail to the person or thing that gives off the scent.

Some search and rescue dogs are trained to search for avalanche victims.

In practice sessions, human volunteers lie in tunnels carved out beneath the snow. The dog starts searching when it hears the words "Go find!" Experienced dogs are able to quickly find the spots where trainers lie buried deep in the snow. The dog digs at the snow to show it has found them.

Search and rescue dogs are trained in obedience. Following commands is only one part of obedience. The dog must also learn not to be distracted by other animals, people, or noise. ✸ There is often a lot of commotion at a rescue site, and the search and rescue dog must ignore the racket and focus on its work. The only signals the dog attends to are voice signals and hand signals from the handler.

Search and rescue dogs must also have agility, which is a combination of quickness, balance, and flexibility. The dogs may have to climb ladders or squeeze through tunnels and windows that are partly open. Sometimes they are told to walk across unstable piles of slippery metal. This skill can be hard for dogs to learn because they don't like to walk on wobbly surfaces. However, top search and rescue dogs are able to complete these exercises, which help the dogs learn to move safely through treacherous areas.

The FEMA Test

The Federal Emergency Management Agency (FEMA) is part of the United States government. FEMA helps with many kinds of disasters in which people are hurt, trapped, or lost. These disasters include hurricanes, tornadoes, and earthquakes.

Some handlers think this work is too dangerous for their dogs, but others eagerly take on the challenge. Passing FEMA's test for search and rescue dogs requires hundreds of hours of training for handlers and their dogs.

FEMA holds training and testing sessions at mock disaster sites that look like real disaster sites. Trainers hide in piles of rubble that represent collapsed buildings or wrecked trains. Search and rescue dogs have to make their way through piles of concrete, splintered wood, and bent steel to find the trainer. Or the dogs might simply lead a trainer to safety. In advanced tests, a search and rescue dog is expected to find as many as six people. Dogs that can pass these tests will be ready when they receive a real call for help.

Search and rescue dogs and their handlers do not earn much for their efforts. Usually they are unpaid volunteers. Most handlers say the greatest reward is finding a person alive. The greatest reward for the dogs is praise. Another special treat for hardworking search and rescue dogs is playing with a favorite toy. Tattered squeaky toys and deflated balls might seem like junk to us, but to rescue dogs they are prizes for a job well done.

D MAIN IDEA AND SUPPORTING DETAILS

Write the main idea and supporting details of this paragraph.

Farming had a big advantage over hunting. When a hunter kills a wild goat, the only food the hunter gets is the meat of the goat. But when a farmer raises goats, the farmer gets goat milk for many years. When the goat is old, the farmer can still kill the goat for its meat.

E COMPREHENSION

Write the answers.

1. Use evidence from the article to explain at least three features that make dogs excellent helpers for rescue workers.

2. Use evidence from the article to explain why a rescue dog needs to build a close relationship with its handler.

3. Why does a rescue dog sniff an item belonging to a person before it searches for that person?

4. How do dogs know they are getting closer to a person, even if they can't see or hear the person?

5. What are the only signals that dogs attend to when they are searching?

F WRITING

Write a passage that describes how a handler trains a search and rescue dog.

Use details from the article to answer these questions in your passage:

1. What kind of relationship does the handler build with the dog? Why?

2. When does the handler teach the dog commands?

3. What different training exercises does the dog have to perform?

4. What test does the dog have to pass before it can help with real disasters?

Write at least six sentences.

A WORD LISTS

1 | Hard Words

1. aching
2. coax
3. wrestling
4. North Carolina

2 | Word Endings

1. incredible
2. snuggle
3. tickle
4. tumble

3 | Vocabulary Words

1. limp
2. litter
3. reluctant
4. sensitive

4 | Vocabulary Words

1. intense
2. misery
3. tussle

B VOCABULARY DEFINITIONS

1. **limp**—When you *limp,* you have trouble walking.
• What's another way of saying *Elena had trouble walking because of the cast on her foot?*

2. **litter**—A *litter* is a group of animals that are born to the same mother at the same time.

3. **reluctant**—When you are *reluctant* to do something, you really don't want to do it.

Here's another way of saying *Erik really didn't want to go to the party: Erik was reluctant to go to the party.*
• What's another way of saying *Hama really didn't want to wear a coat?*

4. **sensitive**—Something that can detect things that are very faint is *sensitive.* Someone with a sensitive nose can detect very faint smells.
• What do we call ears that can detect very faint sounds?

C VOCABULARY FROM CONTEXT

1. They wore sunglasses to block the **intense** light.

2. The student felt great **misery** when he failed the test, so he started to cry.

3. The puppies began to **tussle** and fight, and they rolled all over the floor.

Adventure on the Rocky Ridge

Donna Clearwater

Chapter 1

Little Martha never knew she was almost given away when she was still a tiny puppy. She didn't know she was a runt, the smallest puppy in a litter of twelve hounds. And she didn't know that her mother was a prize hunting dog owned by people who raised the best hunting dogs in North Carolina. Little Martha didn't understand that the owners kept only the best puppies from each litter. Those were the biggest and the strongest. The rest were given away.

Little Martha's first memories were of great happiness and terrible sadness. Her eyes were still closed when she was born, and they remained closed for two weeks. While her eyes were closed, Martha experienced great joy when she snuggled next to her warm mother. She also felt great despair when one of the large puppies in the litter pushed her away, leaving her shivering and cold.

Martha would squeal little sounds of misery as she lay there, but her mother couldn't do much to help her. There were just too many puppies in the litter, and her mother could not take care of all of them. So during her first days of life, Martha spent a lot of time aching from hunger and shivering from cold.

Julie Owl saved Martha. Julie was the twelve-year-old daughter of the people who owned Martha. She pleaded with her father not to give away the little runt. "I'll take care of her, Dad," she said. "Really, I will. I'll feed her and you'll see. She'll be a fine dog."

Mr. Owl was reluctant to keep the runt. "Julie," he explained, "why don't you take one of the other puppies? I'll give you any other puppy in the litter. But that runt won't be as healthy as the others. It will always be …"

Mr. Owl stopped short as he looked at Julie's pleading eyes. He suddenly realized why she wanted the puppy. It was because she saw herself in the puppy. Like the puppy, Julie wasn't as healthy as other children, and she walked with a leg brace.

After a moment, Mr. Owl smiled and said, "Maybe you're right. Maybe that puppy will grow up to be a fine dog."

Julie's face brightened, and she threw her arms around her father's neck. "Oh, thank you, Dad!" she exclaimed. "I'll take good care of her. And I'll name her Martha."

That was a very strange name for a hound dog. Outside in the kennel were dogs named Boomer, Flash, Duke, and Queenie. There were Prince and Princess, Dodger, and Digger. But no dog had a name like Martha.

Julie mothered Martha. She got a little bottle and fed Martha six times a day. She made a warm bed for Martha next to her own bed. She held Martha and petted her and talked to her and kissed her. She loved Martha the way a mother loves her baby. ♦

All the dogs that Mr. Owl raised had a powerful sense of smell. Although Mr. Owl didn't know it at the time, Martha's nose was more sensitive than the nose of any other dog he had ever raised. In fact, it was better than the nose of any other dog in North Carolina.

Even when Martha's eyes were still closed, she recognized Julie's smell. At first, however,

Martha wasn't wild about this smell. Whenever Julie's smell came near, it meant that Martha would be removed from the wonderful smells of her mother and the smells of her brothers and sisters. But after a while, Martha began to love Julie's smell. She learned that the smell meant warm milk and soft petting and a nice blanket to keep her warm.

Shortly after the puppies' eyes opened, Mr. Owl tested the puppies to see which ones would be the best hunting dogs. The test was simple. He placed all the puppies in a shallow box. He put a screen over the top of the box so that if a puppy tried to climb or jump out of the box, the puppy would bang its head on the screen. Then he put the mother dog just outside the box and waited.

Some of the puppies kept banging and banging and banging their heads. Those were the puppies that would probably make the best hunting dogs. When they grew up, they would probably hunt and hunt, no matter how rough the country was or how tired they were.

Julie put Martha in the box with the other puppies. The other puppies whined and cried, and they kept jumping up to bang their heads against the screen. Martha whined and cried, too, but she didn't jump up, not once.

Julie knew that her father would think Martha was no good, so she tried to coax Martha to jump. But still Martha sat there without jumping as the other puppies pushed her around. At last, Julie removed her from the box. She held Martha and said, "It's all right. You're still going to be the best dog in the world."

• • •

After the puppies learned to run and jump, they began to play. Sometimes Martha's brothers and sisters would get too rough for her, but she still loved playing. She was happy just to be with them, even when they were rough. ★

One of them would usually start playing by grabbing another's droopy ear and taking a nip. Then the tussling would begin. The two puppies would tumble over each other and growl. Soon the others would join in. When the wrestling became too rough, one of them would run from the group, waiting for the others to follow. Then there would be more growling and tumbling.

The only experience that is more exciting to a young hound than playing is catching the scent of a wild animal, such as a rabbit or a deer. When a hound catches the scent of another animal, the hound feels delighted. The hound is so delighted that it wants more and more and more. It wants to keep following that scent forever. For the hound dog, following a scent is the greatest experience in the world.

Martha first discovered this marvelous experience when she was watching her brothers and sisters tussle in the meadow behind Julie's house. The puppies were now three months old. Martha had been wrestling with the others, but they were too rough for her. One of her brothers had knocked her down so hard that she had lost all interest in playing.

As Martha watched the puppies tussling, she suddenly smelled something that was more interesting than anything else she had ever smelled. The wind carried the scent. Martha held her nose high in the air and tried to catch more of it. Then she let out a little howl and tried to get closer to the smell.

Martha left the others and put her nose near the ground. She began sniffing very

quickly. "Yes, yes," her nose told her. "Get closer. Follow it." So she did, even though she could hardly run. Her ears were so long that when she tried to run with her nose to the ground, she kept stepping on her ears with her front paws.

Just as the smell was becoming so intense that Martha could hardly stand it, she caught another scent—Julie's. Julie picked her up and said, "You can't go hunting yet. You have to stay with the others."

Martha cried and squirmed and tried to get away. But Julie held on to her and limped slowly back to the place where the other puppies were playing.

E MAIN IDEA AND SUPPORTING DETAILS

Write the main idea and supporting details of this passage.

Water makes slow changes to the landscape. As rivers and streams run downhill, they carry mud, stones, and rocks from higher places to lower places. When the water in the river slows, the water drops the material it is carrying.

Big waves also carry stones. These stones rub against other stones as the waves roll through shallow water. The force of the waves grinds the stones into smaller and smaller pieces that turn into sand.

Water that freezes into ice also changes the shape of mountains. Ice makes tiny cracks in rocks. Over many years, the cracks become larger until parts of the rocks break off and are carried away by rivers and streams.

F COMPREHENSION

Write the answers.

1. At first, why did Mr. Owl want to give Martha away?

2. Mr. Owl believed that Julie saw herself in Martha. Explain why Julie might feel that way.

3. Use details from the story to show how Julie treated Martha like a human baby.

4. Why would the dogs that kept banging their heads during the test probably be the best hunting dogs?

5. Do you think Martha will be a good hunting dog? Why or why not?

G WRITING

Write a passage that compares Martha with the other puppies.

Use details from the story to answer these questions in your passage:

1. How was Martha's size different from the other puppies?

2. How was Martha's sense of smell different from the other puppies?

3. How was Martha's physical ability different from the other puppies?

Write at least six sentences.

END OF LESSON 62

A | WORD LISTS

1	Word Practice
1.	chill
2.	chilly
3.	moist
4.	moisture
5.	Yodeler

2	Vocabulary Words
1.	dwarf
2.	kennel
3.	ledge
4.	quail
5.	ridge

B | VOCABULARY DEFINITIONS

1. **dwarf**—*Dwarf* is another way of saying *very short*. Grass that doesn't grow very high is sometimes called dwarf grass.
   - What do we call trees that don't grow very high?

2. **kennel**—A *kennel* is a place where dogs or cats are kept. Often a kennel has a fenced-in place where the animals can run and an indoor place where they can sleep.
   - What do we call a place where dogs or cats are kept?

3. **ledge**—A flat shelf on the side of a cliff or a wall is called a *ledge*.
   - What do we call a flat shelf on the side of a cliff or a wall?

4. **quail**—A *quail* is a bird that's about the same size as a pigeon.

5. **ridge**—A long, narrow hilltop is called a *ridge*.
   - What do we call a long, narrow hilltop?

C | READING LITERATURE: Realistic Short Story

Adventure on the Rocky Ridge
Chapter 2

When Martha and the other puppies were six months old, they were all interested in hunting, but they weren't allowed to run free. Julie still kept Martha in her room, but Martha's brothers and sisters lived in a kennel with the other hounds. The hounds in the kennel howled and ran back and forth, trying to get out of the kennel, but the only time Mr. Owl let them out was when he trained them.

Even though a hound has a magnificent nose, training a young hound to hunt properly takes a long time. The problem is that a young hound wants to hunt everything. The hound may start out following the scent of a deer. But if it comes across the scent of a rabbit or a quail, the hound will quickly forget about the deer and follow the new scent. Young hounds must work hour after hour learning how to stay with one scent and ignore the others.

Martha didn't go hunting with her brothers and sisters because Martha was a pet. She was Julie's constant companion. She slept under Julie's bed and stayed inside during the day while Julie was in school. When Julie returned from school, Martha wagged and wiggled and whined. But when Julie left, Martha felt lonely and sad. The hours seemed to drag until she caught Julie's scent or heard the sound of her voice.

One day after school, Julie had just finished cleaning the kennel when she saw her father on the rocky ridge of a distant hill. The path up to the ridge was steep and dangerous. Julie's father did not allow her to go up there because of her leg. As Julie watched her father, she knew he was returning from a training session with Martha's brothers and sisters. He had taken Leader with him. Leader was the best hound in the kennel. Mr. Owl took Leader along so that the other dogs could imitate him and learn from him.

Julie could tell by the way her father was walking that he was disappointed. When he was disappointed, his shoulders drooped

and he plodded along slowly. As she watched him climb down from the ridge, she knew why he was disturbed. Ever since she could remember, he had talked about raising a dog that could track an animal over the rocky ridge. No dog in the county had ever done it because the ridge did not hold the scent of animals. It had no long grass or moisture to hold the scent. Instead, the ridge was nothing but hard, polished rock, with tiny patches of dwarf grass here and there.

A constant wind blew over the rocky ridge, and that wind blew away what little scent any animal left on the rocks. Julie had often watched hounds try to track animals over the ridge. They would easily follow the scent through the long grass below the ridge. Then they would move upward, to places where there were more rocks and less grass. Here, they would become confused. They would whine and run in circles, trying to pick up the scent. Sometimes, the best hounds—like Leader—would run farther, almost to the edge of the ridge. But even Leader would lose the scent on the ridge and run aimlessly this way and that. ♦

As the dogs came off the ridge, they saw Julie and Martha. They ran ahead, jumped all over Julie, and began wrestling with Martha. They quickly stopped playing, however, because they were tired from their long outing.

A few minutes later, Julie's father sat down on the grass next to her. The half-grown hounds climbed on him and licked his face. He laughed and pushed them aside. Then he explained to Julie, "Around noon, I saw a large deer climbing the rocky ridge. I was hoping that one of the young hounds would be able to track it over the ledge. But …" His voice trailed off.

"Maybe one of them will be better than Leader," he continued, pointing to one of the half-grown hounds. "Yodeler over there did as well as Leader. But when the dogs reached the top of the ridge, they lost the scent."

• • •

Three months later, when Martha and the other dogs from the litter were nine months old, a terrible thing happened. It was late fall, and the nights were very cold, with raw winds and the smell of winter.

Julie came home from school, greeted her mother, and limped into the living room. She sat down to read a book as her mother worked in her home office. Then Martha jumped into Julie's lap.

"Get out of here," Julie said, laughing. "You're not a little puppy anymore. You have to stay on the floor."

Julie pushed Martha down and returned to her reading. But Martha wanted to play, so she grabbed Julie's shoe and started to wrestle with it.

"Cut it out," Julie said. "I'm busy." Martha sat down with her tail wagging and looked up at Julie.

"All right," said Julie. She stood up and walked over to a box in the corner of the room. Then she took a rubber ball from the box and rolled it across the floor. Martha took off after the ball. She caught it and began to wrestle with it. Then she began to chew on it as Julie sat down and started reading again. After a couple of minutes had passed, Martha brought the ball over to Julie and dropped it by her feet. She let out a little bark. Julie picked up the ball and rolled it across the floor again.

The game went on for a while. Then Julie played another game with Martha. Julie took one of her old mittens. She let Martha smell it for a few seconds. Then she hid it behind the couch. "Go find the mitten," she told Martha.

Martha held her head high and sniffed the air. She trotted in a circle and suddenly stopped. She turned and went directly to the mitten. Julie had hoped the game would keep Martha busy for a while, but Martha's nose was so good that it took her only a few seconds to find anything inside the house. In fact, when Julie had played the same game outside, Martha would always find the mitten in a few minutes, even when it was hidden far out in the middle of the meadow. ✦

Suddenly, Julie noticed that her mother was standing by the living room door, looking outside into the darkness. "I wonder what happened to your father," she said thoughtfully, still peering into the darkness. "He should have been back hours ago."

"Where did he go?" Julie asked as she put the book aside.

"I think he went out with Yodeler and the others," her mother replied. "But I don't think he intended to stay out after dark."

Julie suddenly felt anxious. She limped over to the door and opened it. A raw wind sent a chilly blast into the room and almost pushed the door out of her grip.

"Close the door, honey," her mother said. "I'm sure your father will be home shortly."

Three hours later, the house was silent. Julie and her mother were sitting at the table, but neither had eaten very much. They sat without saying a word, trying not to think about why Julie's father hadn't yet returned.

• • •

Mr. Owl had a good reason for not returning. He couldn't walk. He had taken Leader, Boomer, and the other dogs from the litter up to the rocky ridge. Two of the young dogs had seen a deer and had chased it down the other side of the ridge.

Julie's father tried calling the dogs back, but they didn't return, so he followed them. He soon came to a treacherous place where the trail was just a narrow ledge above a cliff. He tripped on a rock in the trail and fell more than twenty feet. He landed sharply in an awkward position. The severe pain from his right leg told him that the leg was broken.

Climbing back up to the ledge was impossible. So Mr. Owl called Boomer and Leader close to him. He curled up with the dogs and tried to stay warm. Then he began to wait, trying to ignore the intense pain in his leg.

• • •

Julie looked out the window of her living room. Suddenly, she noticed some forms in the yard.

"Look, Mom," she said, pointing out the window. "There's Yodeler."

Julie's mother ran to the front door and opened it. Yodeler and three other dogs from the litter ran into the house. Usually, they weren't allowed inside, but neither Julie nor her mother scolded them. Instead, they looked outside into the darkness.

"Bill?" Julie's mother called. "Bill, are you out there?"

The only response was a howl from one of Martha's sisters. Soon, five more of the dogs were inside the house, wagging their tails and sniffing everything.

Julie's mother turned to Julie. With a worried voice, she said, "Julie, I'm afraid something has happened to your father."

D MAIN IDEA AND SUPPORTING DETAILS

Write the main idea and supporting details of this passage.

Many things can cause landslides or make them more likely. Heavy rains can be a hazard because they soak the ground until it can't hold any more water. Rocks and soil begin to slide downhill, usually moving faster and faster. If enough rocks and soil tumble down, the whole hillside can collapse.

Landslides are sometimes triggered by earthquakes or volcanic eruptions. These forces loosen and move rocks and soil down hillsides. Landslides can move with the speed and power of an express train. This makes them very dangerous. They can cause millions of dollars of damage.

Landslides are more likely in hilly areas where there are no trees and few plants. The roots of trees and plants absorb water and help to keep the soil in place. When there are no trees or plants, there is nothing to stop the land from sliding downhill.

E COMPREHENSION

Write the answers.

1. Why do young hounds have trouble learning how to hunt properly?

2. Why was it difficult for hounds to track animals over the rocky ridge?

3. Why was the mitten game easy for Martha?

4. Why did Mr. Owl curl up with Boomer and Leader?

5. How do you think Julie felt at the end of the chapter? Use details from the story to explain your answer.

F WRITING

- Julie could tell her father was disappointed because his shoulders drooped and he plodded along slowly.

Write a passage that answers this main question:

- What can you tell about people's thoughts and feelings just by looking at them?

Use your own experiences to answer these other questions in your passage:

1. How can you tell if people are happy by the way they look?

2. How can you tell if people are sad?

3. How can you tell if people don't like a particular smell?

4. How can you tell if people don't want to do something?

5. How can you tell if people are impatient?

6. What other things can you tell by the way people look?

Write at least six sentences.

A WORD LISTS

1 | Related Words

1. expected / unexpectedly
2. operate / operation
3. possible / possibilities

2 | Vocabulary Words

1. chime
2. down coat
3. old-fashioned
4. stocking cap

B VOCABULARY DEFINITIONS

1. **chime**—When clocks make a ringing sound, they *chime*.
- What's another way of saying *The clock made ringing sounds at midnight?*

2. **down coat**—Soft feathers are called *down*. A warm coat filled with soft feathers is called a *down coat*.
- What's another way of saying *He wore a coat filled with soft feathers during the winter?*

3. **old-fashioned**—Something that isn't modern is *old-fashioned*. A phone that isn't modern is an old-fashioned phone.
- What do we call a TV that isn't modern?

4. **stocking cap**—A long and floppy hat is called a *stocking cap*.
- What is a stocking cap?

C TEXT STRUCTURE

1. **Sequence of events**
   The girl woke up. Then she brushed her teeth. Then she went to school.

2. **Comparison**
   The red car had four doors. The blue car had two doors. The red car was four feet longer than the blue car.

3. **Cause and effect**
   The day was hot, so the ice cream melted.

4. **Problem and solution**
   The ice cream was melting, so Ned put the ice cream in the freezer.

- **Which text structures do items 5 and 6 use?**

5. Alma was standing in the cold, so she started shivering.

6. Alma was standing in the cold, so she went back inside.

Adventure on the Rocky Ridge
Chapter 3

Julie's mother pushed the door shut, closing off the wicked wind. She then walked briskly to the telephone. The Owls didn't have a cell phone because cell phones didn't work in the hilly area where they lived. Instead, they had an old-fashioned phone that connected to a phone line mounted on telephone poles. Sometimes the wind would blow down the line and their phone wouldn't work until the line was fixed.

"I'm going to call the Whitebirds," said Mrs. Owl as she picked up the phone. The Whitebirds were their closest neighbors, even though they lived three miles away. Julie watched her mother ignore the dogs that were trying to jump on her and lick her face.

A few seconds later, Julie's mother put down the phone and said, "The phone line is dead. The wind must have blown down a telephone pole and cut the line." She went to the closet, got her coat, and threw it over her shoulders. "I'm going for help," she explained. "You put the dogs in the kennel. Then keep an eye open for your father. I may not be back for some time."

As soon as Julie's mother opened the door, the fierce wind blew it out of her hand. The door swung all the way open, making a loud banging sound as it struck the wall. Julie's mother grabbed the door, and as she pulled it shut, she smiled and said, "Don't worry, honey. Everything is going to be all right."

Julie returned Yodeler and all the other dogs except Martha to the kennel. Then she went inside and waited. "Be patient," she told herself. She tried to figure out how long it would take before she received some word about her father. Since the Whitebirds lived three miles away, it might take a while. Possibly, her father had stopped there to get out of the cold.

No, he would never let the dogs go home by themselves. And besides, not all the dogs had come home. Eight of the dogs from the litter had returned. But Boomer and Leader were still out.

Maybe the younger dogs had run away. Maybe they had come home while Julie's father had stopped at the Whitebirds.

Then Julie began to imagine darker possibilities. Maybe a bear had attacked her father. Maybe Boomer and Leader had tried to defend her father. Maybe they were ... No, don't think of that.

If only the dogs could talk and tell Julie what had happened! ♦

An old clock in the living room chimed each hour. Julie sat near the window and listened to the clock. Each time it chimed, she became more anxious. When it chimed eleven times, Julie threw her arms around Martha's neck and held her tightly. "What are we going to do?" Julie asked.

Julie knew she couldn't sleep, so she decided to try reading—but it was no use. She read the same passage over three or four times without understanding what it said. Then she put the book aside and returned to the window.

Shortly after midnight, Julie became so anxious that she opened the front door and called for her father as loudly as she could. Martha cocked her head and became very alert, glancing first at Julie and then at the darkness. Julie's voice was drowned in the sound of the wind.

At one o'clock in the morning, Julie couldn't stand it any longer. She knelt down in front of Martha, took Martha's head, and held it firmly between her hands. She looked intently into Martha's big brown eyes and said, "You've got to help me find Daddy." Martha let out a playful groan and licked Julie's face. "Please, help me," Julie said. "Please." Martha shook free and attacked Julie's hand with another playful growl.

Julie wrote her mother a note that told where she was going. She got a flashlight and tested it to make sure the beam was strong. Then she went to her room and dressed in her warmest clothes: a heavy down coat, thick mittens, a thick stocking cap, wool knee socks, and winter boots. She got a leash from the kitchen and attached it to Martha's collar. Then she found a pair of gloves her father had worn that morning. She knelt down and held the gloves in front of Martha's nose. "Daddy," she said excitedly. "These are Daddy's gloves. Go find him."

Martha grabbed the gloves and began to wrestle with them.

"No!" Julie said sharply. She then continued in a softer tone. "Don't play. You must help me find Daddy." She held the gloves in front of Martha's nose for a few moments. Then she put the gloves in her pocket and went outside.

She didn't know which direction her father had gone, so she decided to walk around the meadow that surrounded the house. Before Julie and Martha had gone three hundred feet, Martha caught a scent.

Martha held her head up and let out a howl. The dogs in the kennel responded by howling back. They wanted to join her. Martha pulled on the leash and continued to howl.

A few minutes later, Julie realized that Martha was tracking something that was moving in a circle. "It's a rabbit," she said aloud. Rabbits always circle when a hound tracks them. She bent down in front of Martha again and removed her father's gloves from her pocket. She held the gloves in front of Martha's nose and said, "Daddy. Find Daddy. Please understand. Please."

And for some reason, the dog did understand. It's hard to say why. Martha had not been trained to track. And for Martha, the scent of a person was far less interesting than the scent of a quail or a deer. Of course, Martha had the ability to track a person. Her nose could easily tell one person from another. It could also tell her which direction the person had been moving and how long ago the person had been in a particular place.

Martha easily recognized the scent of Julie's father on the gloves. The only thing Martha didn't understand was what Julie wanted her to do. When they had first gone out into the night, Martha had thought that Julie was giving her an unusual treat. It wasn't often that Julie let her sniff the magnificent smells that were in the meadow. But now, something was different.

Possibly, the cold wind made Martha become more serious. She really didn't enjoy being in the cutting wind, but something about the way Julie behaved told her there was important business out here. Somehow, Martha knew that neither she nor Julie would go back into the comfortable house until the important business had been completed.

Suddenly, Martha sniffed the gloves and looked at Julie with a serious expression, almost as if she was saying to her mistress, "I understand that we have a job to do."

Julie put her father's gloves back into her pocket and continued circling the meadow with Martha. When they came to the side of the meadow that was closest to the rocky ridge, Martha began to sniff the grass excitedly. Then she raised her head and gave a funny little bark. It wasn't the kind of howl that she always let out when she caught the scent of animals or birds. Each of those howls was a long "ooooo" that would sometimes last four seconds. The sound that she let out now in the bitter wind was an excited little bark, as if she was trying to say, "I found it!"

Martha pulled Julie this way and that as she tried to decide where the trail went. Julie did her best to keep up, but because of her bad leg, she couldn't move very fast. At last, she made a difficult decision. She took off her mittens and unfastened Martha's leash.

Julie realized the chance she was taking. If Martha caught the magnificent scent of a deer or some other animal, she might not come back. But Martha would be able to work faster if she were free. Before releasing Martha, Julie held her by the collar and once more presented the pair of gloves. Then she let go and said, "Go find Daddy!"

E COMPREHENSION

Write the answers.

1. Why did Julie's mother think made the phone line go dead?

2. Do you think it was wise of Julie to go out looking for her father? Explain your answer.

3. How did Julie give Martha her father's scent?

4. Why did Martha move in circles in the meadow?

5. Why did Julie let Martha off the leash at the end of the chapter?

F WRITING

Write the next part of "Adventure on the Rocky Ridge."

Use what you know about Julie, Martha, and Mr. Owl to answer these questions in your story:

1. What problems does Julie have as she looks for Mr. Owl?

2. What sounds does Julie hear?

3. How does the weather affect Julie?

4. How does Martha help in the search?

5. Are Julie and Martha able to find Mr. Owl?

Write at least six sentences.

END OF LESSON 64

A WORD LISTS

1	**Hard Words**
1.	fumble
2.	Taylor
3.	windblown

2	**Vocabulary Words**
1.	cast
2.	face
3.	hoarse
4.	sprawl
5.	unexpectedly
6.	wild goose chase

B VOCABULARY DEFINITIONS

1. **cast**—When hunting dogs try to find the scent of an animal by sniffing back and forth across the ground, they *cast*.
- What are hunting dogs doing when they try to find a scent by sniffing back and forth across the ground?

2. **face**—The steep side of a mountain or cliff is called the *face*.
- What do we call the steep side of a mountain or cliff?

3. **hoarse**—A voice that sounds rough and harsh is a *hoarse* voice.

4. **sprawl**—When somebody falls down awkwardly, they *sprawl*.

- What's another way of saying *The skater fell down awkwardly on the ice?*

5. **unexpectedly**—When something happens that you don't expect, it happens *unexpectedly*.
If you don't expect to win a game, but then you do, you win unexpectedly.
- What happens when you don't expect to win, but then you do?

6. **wild goose chase**—When you go on a *wild goose chase*, you are going after something you won't find.
- If somebody goes out looking for a pot of gold, they're going on a wild goose chase.

READING LITERATURE: Realistic Short Story

Adventure on the Rocky Ridge
Chapter 4

Martha circled the place where she had first caught the smell of Julie's father. She circled it three times to find out which direction the tracks led. After completing the third circle, she knew the direction. She took off quickly, leaving Julie far behind.

From time to time, Martha raised her head and barked. Julie listened for the barks and followed them as quickly as she could, but she couldn't walk very fast. Soon she was far, far behind Martha. Julie could no longer hear Martha's barks, but she knew where Martha was heading—right up the steep face of the hill with the rocky ridge.

When Julie realized that her father had gone up to the rocky ridge, a dismal feeling came over her. Julie had seen Leader and the other dogs with keen noses track animals up to the ridge. She had seen them cast aimlessly across the ridge trying to pick up the scent on the windblown rocks.

Julie followed in the direction Martha had gone. It took Julie more than half an hour to reach the steep slope below the rocky ridge. She turned on her flashlight so she wouldn't trip over the rocks that jutted out of the grass. She was wearing mittens, but her hands were beginning to ache with cold. She tried not to pay attention to the pain. From time to time, she stopped and called, "Martha! Martha!" But she had little hope that the dog would hear her.

Julie continued up the rocks. In some places, she had to climb the rocks the way you would climb a ladder. She had trouble holding the flashlight and going up. Once,

her bad leg slipped and she crashed into a rock. She hurt her ribs, and the fall damaged the flashlight. It still worked most of the time, but the light would sometimes go out. By banging the flashlight against the palm of her hand, Julie could make the beam come on.

For nearly half an hour, Julie climbed up toward the rocky ridge. She knew she wasn't following the same path her father had taken. She knew he would have led the dogs up a trail that was easier to climb than the one she was on. But she didn't know where that trail was. She knew only that he had probably climbed up to the rocky ridge. She figured that as long as she was climbing up, she would get to the ridge as well.

At last, Julie reached the rocky ridge, which was flat and narrow. The sky was clear, and the moon shone so brightly that Julie could see her shadow. She turned off the flashlight and stuffed it into her pocket. Then she cupped her hands around her mouth and called, "Martha! Martha!" She continued to call until her voice became hoarse. ♦

Suddenly, Julie saw Martha's dark form casting along the flat surface of the ridge. "Martha!" she called again. The dog stopped, turned, and ran over to her. Julie could tell from Martha's behavior that she had lost the trail.

Julie took off her mittens and tried to fasten the leash to Martha's collar. Her fingers were becoming so numb that she could hardly feel what she was doing, but she

finally managed to hook the leash onto the metal ring of the collar.

Just then, Julie noticed two dots of light in the valley to the south. She quickly took out her flashlight, pushed the button forward, and pounded the flashlight four times against her palm until the beam came on brightly. Then she pointed the flashlight in the direction of the lights below and waved it back and forth. Soon, the other lights responded by moving back and forth.

Julie then removed her father's gloves from her pocket, held them in front of Martha's nose, and said, "Daddy. Go find Daddy."

The young hound wagged her tail, turned away, and began to pull on the leash.

She was trying to return to the place where she had lost the scent. Martha had followed Mr. Owl's trail to a place where the ridge got wider, but the scent had become so faint that she had lost it.

Martha led Julie back to the wide area. As Martha sniffed the ground, she pulled Julie along, first in one direction, then in another. At last, Martha caught a very faint scent. She raised her head and let out a little yelp. Then she pulled forward with so much power that Julie almost stumbled. "Good dog," Julie said. "Go find Daddy."

Martha followed the scent for about a hundred feet, but then she started to move in small circles. She had lost the scent again. She stuffed her nose into cracks between the rocks and sniffed so loudly that Julie could hear the sniffs above the wind. Suddenly, Martha raised her head and gave another little bark.

Julie turned around and noticed that the lights from the south were approaching quickly. She didn't want to stop searching, because she was afraid that if Martha lost the faint scent, she might not find the trail again. "Go find Daddy," Julie said, and Martha began pulling on the leash again. ✦

As Julie continued to follow Martha, she heard voices calling above the wind. "Bill?" a man's voice called. "Is that you, Bill?"

"No, it's me!" Julie shouted, still following Martha.

Within a few minutes, the lights were very close, and Julie could recognize the voices. They belonged to her mother, Mr. Whitebird, and another neighbor, Mr. Taylor. The three of them were trying to find Mr. Owl on the rocky surface.

When the party grew close, Julie's mother shouted, "Julie, what are you doing out here?"

Before Julie could answer, Mr. Whitebird asked, "Where's your father?"

"I don't know," Julie said, "but Martha's on his trail."

"She can't be," Mr. Whitebird said as he trotted up to Julie. He caught his breath and then continued, "No dog alive can track over these rocks."

"Martha can," Julie said hoarsely.

Julie's mother threw her arms around her daughter. "Julie," she said, "what on earth are you doing out here? You'll freeze to death."

"Mom," Julie said, "Martha's on Dad's trail. She's followed him all the way up here."

Julie could see the dim outline of Mr. Taylor shaking his head. "You better get yourself back home," he said flatly. "That dog is just taking you on a wild goose chase."

"No, she isn't!" Julie protested. "She's tracking."

At that moment, Martha caught the scent of a rabbit. It was a marvelous scent, the kind that hound dogs dream about. With a great pull on the leash, she lunged forward and let out a long, "Oooooooooo."

She pulled Julie so hard and unexpectedly that the girl slipped and went sprawling on the rocks. Mr. Taylor helped her up, and Mr. Whitebird grabbed Martha's leash.

"No," Julie protested. "That's not the signal she makes for Dad's trail. She must have picked up a different scent. But I'm telling you she was on Dad's trail."

Then Mr. Taylor patted Julie on the shoulder. "You know," he said slowly, "you may be right."

Mr. Whitebird added, "I don't know what that dog was just tracking, but she sure was tracking something. And I've never seen a dog that could track anything up here. Maybe we should give her a chance to show what she can do."

"She'll do it," Julie said, fumbling in her pocket for her father's gloves. "She'll do it. You'll see." She held the gloves in front of Martha's nose again and told her, "Go find Daddy."

D COMPREHENSION

Write the answers.

1. Use details from the story to describe the sounds Martha made when she was on Mr. Owl's trail and when she was on a rabbit's trail.

2. Why did Julie keep searching even after she saw the lights from the valley?

3. At first, why didn't the men believe that Martha could be on Mr. Owl's trail?

4. Why did the men change their minds?

5. Why is it so hard for Martha to follow a trail on the rocky ridge?

E WRITING

• Pretend you are Julie.

Write a speech that you give to the other people to convince them that Martha will find your father.

Use details from the story to answer these questions in your speech:

1. What special talent does Martha have?

2. What has Martha already done?

3. Why do you think she'll find Mr. Owl?

Write at least six sentences.

END OF LESSON 65

A WORD LISTS

1 | Hard Words

1. brutal
2. cautiously
3. deliver
4. nourish

2 | State Names

1. California
2. Colorado
3. Kansas
4. New Mexico
5. Oklahoma
6. Texas

3 | Vocabulary Words

1. abandon
2. acre
3. flyer
4. intently
5. operate

B VOCABULARY DEFINITIONS

1. **abandon**—When you leave a place without planning to come back, you *abandon* that place.
   - What's another way of saying *Hank left his wrecked car in the ditch without planning to come back?*

2. **acre**—An *acre* is a unit of land. The size of an acre is 4,840 square yards.
   - What is an acre?

3. **flyer**—A piece of paper with an ad on it is called a *flyer*. Some flyers come in the mail, and some are put in places where people can see them.
   - What is a flyer?

4. **intently**—When you do something *intently*, you concentrate on that thing. When you are listening intently, you concentrate on listening.
   - What are you doing when you concentrate on listening?

5. **operate**—When doctors *operate*, they cut into someone's body to make repairs. This process is called an *operation*.

Adventure on the Rocky Ridge
Chapter 5

Mr. Whitebird was holding Martha's leash. Mr. Taylor was next to him. Julie and her mother were close behind. As they walked along, Mrs. Owl explained that she and the two men had been looking for Julie's father for several hours. Mr. Whitebird had driven to the base of the hill in his big van, and they had walked up from there.

Suddenly, Martha tried to follow the rabbit's trail. Julie shouted, "No!" and again let Martha smell her father's gloves. At last, Martha started to cast about for the scent.

She went across the rocky ridge, from one side to the other. Suddenly, she let out a sharp bark. "That's it!" Julie announced. "She's got it again!"

Julie heard Mr. Taylor say, "Look there! She's on a different trail now."

Both Mr. Taylor and Mr. Whitebird raised dogs, and they understood dogs well. They knew that Martha was certain about the scent she was now following. And they knew that it was not the same scent she had howled about earlier.

Martha went for another two or three hundred feet along the rocky ridge. Then she started down the other side. She was right on the trail that Julie's father had left. And she was only about a thousand feet from where he was lying at that moment. But when she started down the other side of the rocky ridge, Mr. Taylor pulled on the leash and stopped her. "I don't know," he said above the wind. "I can't picture Bill going down there. This is a very dangerous place."

Julie and her mother caught up to them. Mr. Whitebird explained. "I don't know if we should try to go down there. Maybe the dog has Bill's scent, and maybe the dog doesn't. But there are some treacherous places down there. I can't imagine why Bill would go down there."

"Martha's on his trail," Julie said sharply.

"But why would Bill go down there?" Mr. Whitebird replied.

"I don't know," Julie said. "Maybe one of the dogs got away and he went after it."

During the moment that followed, the wind blew bitterly. Finally, Mr. Whitebird said, "You may be right. There's some grass down there. Maybe one of the dogs picked up a scent and Bill went after it."

Mr. Taylor shook the leash and said to Martha, "Go find him."

Martha turned around for a moment; then she put her nose to the ground and began trying to find the scent. She was on a narrow, rocky path, so there was only one direction for her to go. She moved forward, stopping every few feet to search the cracks of the rocks for some sign. But the scent of Julie's father was now quite old and was almost gone.

The party moved slowly down the trail, but Martha gave no sign that she was tracking Julie's father. At last, they came to a place where a large clump of grass grew out of the rocks. When Martha was about four feet from the grass, she suddenly tugged forward. "Yep, yep," she said. Then much more loudly, she announced, "Arrr, arrrr."

A moment later, a response came from somewhere in the darkness ahead of them. It was the long "Oooo" wail of a hound. ♦

Everybody stopped as Mr. Taylor pulled back on Martha's leash. "Did you hear that?" Mr. Taylor asked.

"I heard something," Julie's mother said. "It sounded like Leader."

"I think it came from ahead of us," Mr. Taylor said. Then he flicked the leash and said, "Get him, Martha."

Martha pulled forward to the next patch of grass. "Arrr, arrr," she announced.

Everybody stood silently and listened intently for some sound above the wind. "Oooooooo," came the reply.

"That's Leader," Julie's mother said. "Leader!" she called. "Here, boy. Come here."

"Ooooooo," came the reply.

"Let's go," Mr. Whitebird said, and he moved forward cautiously over the jagged rocks.

"Bill! Bill!" Julie's mother called. "Can you hear us?"

Two dogs howled in response.

"That's Boomer," Julie said. Her feet were numb from the cold, but she didn't even notice them. She was exhausted from all the climbing and walking, but she wasn't thinking about how she felt. Her mind was concentrating on only one thing—any sounds that could be heard above the wind. She searched every sound of the wind for a familiar voice.

At last the party came to the place where Mr. Owl had slipped. The scent was now very plain to Martha. She could smell

Mr. Owl below her. She could also smell Boomer and Leader. She stood at the edge of the trail, held her head high, and announced with a very loud voice, "Arrr, arrr."

"Help," a dim voice replied from down below.

Julie held onto Martha's leash as Mr. Taylor, Mr. Whitebird, and her mother scrambled along the path looking for a place where they could climb safely down to Mr. Owl.

• • •

The trip back to Mr. Whitebird's van was long and cold. The men cut some branches and fastened them to both sides of Bill's broken leg. Then, one man got on each side of Bill, and they led him back up to the flat surface of the rocky ridge. From there, the party moved slowly along the ridge until they came to the path that led down to Mr. Whitebird's van. Julie's mother ran ahead to start the engine and turn on the heat.

When everybody was in the van with the heater on full blast, Mr. Taylor asked, "How are you doing, Bill?"

Slowly, Mr. Owl said, "I don't think I would have lasted the night. It was horrible."

Julie's mother put her arms around him and held her face next to his. "It's all right now," she said. "You're going to be okay."

The van had three rows of seats. The adults sat in the first two rows, and Julie sat in the back row with the three dogs. She hugged Martha and said, "Oh, thank you so much."

Everybody turned around and looked at Julie. Mr. Taylor said, "Your dad owes a lot to you, young lady. We would never have found him without your help."

Nobody said anything for a long time. They just sat there, with the humming sound of the heater filling the van with wonderful hot air.

• • •

The story of Julie and Martha went on for many years. Martha grew up and had several litters of puppies. Once, she had a litter of fourteen. The morning after Martha delivered that litter, Julie's father picked up the smallest puppy and said, "Don't worry, little one. Nobody's going to give you away. Maybe you'll be as great as your mother."

And that puppy was great, but not as great as Martha. Many people came from far off just to see Martha track. Even Leader knew that Martha was the finest hunting dog in the pack. When Leader lost a scent, he would hold his head up and look at Martha. Then he'd follow her.

Some nice things also happened to Julie. About a year after the adventure on the rocky ridge, a doctor operated on Julie's leg. The operation helped Julie walk better, but the doctor said that she would still walk with a limp.

Julie wasn't disappointed. When the doctor announced that she would still have a limp, she looked at him and said, "I don't mind. You don't have to be born perfect to be outstanding. I learned that from my dog, Martha."

D COMPREHENSION

Write the answers.

1. At first, why did the men think Mr. Owl would never have gone down the far side of the ridge?

2. When Martha came to a large clump of grass, she picked up Mr. Owl's scent. Explain why.

3. Why did Mr. Whitebird and Mr. Taylor attach branches to Mr. Owl's broken leg?

4. What did Mr. Taylor mean when he told Julie, "Your dad owes a lot to you?"

5. At the end of the story, Julie said, "You don't have to be born perfect to be outstanding." Use details from the story to explain how that statement applies to both Martha and Julie.

E WRITING

• Pretend you are Julie's mother.

Write the story of Julie and Martha as you saw it.

Use details from "Adventure on the Rocky Ridge" to answer these questions in your story:

1. Where did you go after you left your house?

2. What were you doing while Julie and Martha were searching for Mr. Owl?

3. What did you think when you saw Julie's light flashing?

4. How did you feel about Julie doing something so dangerous?

5. What did you learn from Julie and Martha?

Write at least six sentences.

END OF LESSON 66

A WORD LISTS

1 | Word Practice
1. decade
2. overlap
3. product
4. quality
5. topsoil

2 | Vocabulary Words
1. extensive
2. laborer
3. paradise
4. produce

3 | Vocabulary Words
1. drought
2. eliminate
3. pneumonia
4. sod

B VOCABULARY DEFINITIONS

1. **extensive**—Something that is *extensive* covers or affects a large area.
- What's another way of saying *The plowing covered a large area?*

2. **laborer**—A *laborer* does work that doesn't require special skills. You need special skills to become a carpenter or a plumber, but you don't need special skills to load boxes onto a truck or wash dishes.
- What other kinds of jobs do laborers do?

3. **paradise**—An ideal place to live in or visit is called a *paradise.*
- What's another way of saying *Some people think Hawaii is an ideal place to visit?*

4. **produce**—When you make or grow something, you *produce* that thing.
- What's another way of saying *The farmer grew wheat?*

C VOCABULARY FROM CONTEXT

1. The lake dried up and the ground cracked because of the **drought.**

2. The gardener tried to **eliminate** the weeds by spraying them with poison.

3. When Carlotta had **pneumonia,** she had a fever, she coughed, and she had trouble breathing.

4. After the workers dug through the soft and grassy **sod,** their shovels started to hit rocks and harder ground.

The Dirty Thirties
Part 1

Was it day or night? The confusion of darkness and gusting wind made it hard to tell. The air had a strange quality—it was gritty.

This scene was common in the Plains states of the United States during the 1930s. In that decade, dust storms blew fast and frequently. Fine soil blew up from the ground and darkened the air. The worst of the dust storms occurred in parts of five southern Plains states—Kansas, Oklahoma, Colorado, New Mexico, and Texas. The roughly oval shape that overlaps these states came to be known as the Dust Bowl.

Farmers planted seeds only to see them blown away. All that came up from the ground was dust and more dust.

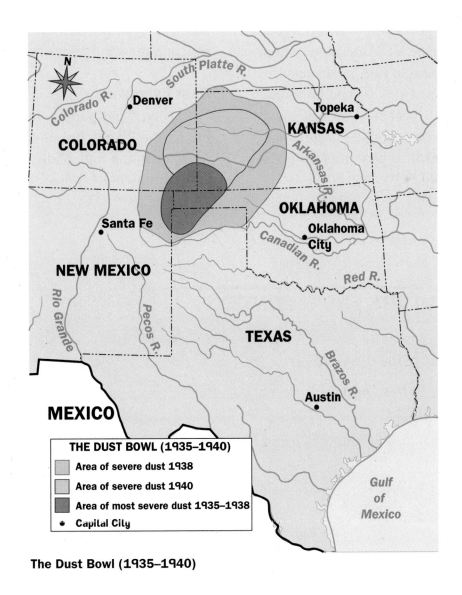

The Dust Bowl (1935–1940)

Too Much Plowing

Oklahoma was in the middle of the Dust Bowl. Farm families had begun moving to the state in the late 1800s. They had plowed millions of acres of tough sod and then planted wheat. The grain grew well in the flat, sprawling fields—as long as rain fell.

Rain fell often enough in the early 1900s for wheat crops to thrive. Farmers bought new plows and tractors. They were able to plant more acres and earn more money with less labor.

The demand for wheat increased in 1914. European countries were fighting World War One, and farmers in those countries were not able to produce as many crops. This meant more good news for farmers in America. The price of American wheat increased as supplies in Europe dropped.

After World War One, Europe no longer needed American wheat, but American farmers continued to produce large wheat crops. The supply of wheat was so great that prices dropped.

In an attempt to make a living, farmers plowed more land and planted even more wheat. But that made wheat prices drop even further. Because the price of wheat was so low, farmers now had to sell much more wheat to earn enough money to live on.

The extensive plowing ruined the land because the sturdy grasses in the sod were plowed under. Before the grasses were plowed under, they had absorbed water and held the topsoil in place with their thick roots. But now the topsoil was loosened, with only thin-rooted wheat to hold it together. To make matters worse, a brutal drought that lasted for several years began in 1931. Little or no rain came to nourish the plants, and the wheat crops failed. Now there were not even wheat roots to anchor the topsoil, and the wind started to blow it away.

Dust Everywhere

Strong wind had always been a fact of life on the Plains. But as the wind began to blow dust far and wide, all forms of life were threatened by dust storms.

Dust storm approaching a farm in the Dust Bowl during the 1930s

A tractor in the Dust Bowl half-buried in a dune of dust

The wind blasted topsoil into powdery dust, sometimes piling it into dunes. Plants were eliminated from the landscape. With nothing to graze, many animals starved. Others died from breathing or swallowing too much dust. Countless people suffered from "dust pneumonia," which caused them to cough up mud. People of all ages lost their lives to this disease.

Wind forced dust through the tiniest cracks in houses. People stuffed papers and wet rags around windows and doors to keep the dust out. Still the dust found its way in, coating clothes, furniture, and dishes. After strong storms, some families used shovels to remove dust from their homes. Even when the winds were calm, dust hung in the air. People slept with a damp cloth over their face to keep dust from settling in their nose and mouth.

People began to refer to this decade as the "Dirty Thirties." Farmers kept hoping for rain and tried their best to get by, but with no crops to sell, no money was coming in, and other jobs were nearly impossible to find. Many people living in the Dust Bowl began to look elsewhere for hope. They found that hope in flyers that began to appear in their towns.

Many of the flyers came from California, known as the Golden State. The flyers said farmers in the Golden State needed lots of laborers to harvest their plentiful crops. They also said that people from the Dust Bowl would be welcome in California.

California sounded like paradise. Food and jobs would be plentiful. Many Dust Bowlers decided to abandon their farms and move west.

E SUPPLY AND DEMAND

Work the items.

- **supply**—The amount of a product that is for sale is called the *supply*.

- **demand**—How much people want to buy a product is called the *demand*.

1. A grocery store receives 100 cartons of eggs a day, and it sells 100 cartons of eggs a day.
- Are the supply and demand for eggs *different* or *the same?*

2. If the supply increases, the demand will be **less than** the supply.
- What happens to the demand if the supply goes up?

3. The grocery store can change the demand by changing the price.
- If the store **lowers** the price of a carton of eggs, will the demand for eggs *increase* or *decrease?*

4. If the store **raises** the price of eggs, will the demand *increase* or *decrease?*

5. If the store receives 200 cartons of eggs a day but sells 100 cartons a day, how can it change the price for a carton of eggs so the demand is higher?

F COMPREHENSION

Write the answers.

1. Use details from the article to explain why the demand for American wheat increased during World War One.

2. Use details from the article to explain why the price of American wheat fell after World War One.

3. Use details from the article to explain why too much plowing helped create the Dust Bowl.

4. Name two ways that people tried to protect themselves from the dust.

5. Use details from the article to explain why many Dust Bowlers decided to move to California during the 1930s.

G WRITING

- Pretend you are a wheat farmer in the Dust Bowl during the 1930s with a large family. Your farm is ruined, and you have to decide between staying on your farm or moving to California.

Write a passage that explains what you decide to do.

Use details from the article to answer these questions in your passage.

1. Why is your farm ruined?

2. What reasons do you have for staying on your farm?

3. What did the flyers say about jobs in California?

4. Do you think the flyers are telling the truth? Why or why not?

5. What reasons do you have for moving to California?

6. What have you decided to do?

Write at least six sentences.

END OF LESSON 67

A WORD LISTS

1 Hard Words

1. carriage
2. community
3. communities
4. jalopy
5. nectarine
6. Okie

2 Related Words

1. enthusiastic / enthusiastically
2. hesitant / hesitantly
3. migrate / migrant
4. populate / population
5. translate / translation

3 Vocabulary Words

1. determined
2. misled
3. poverty
4. resent

4 Vocabulary Review

1. drought
2. eliminate
3. extensive
4. paradise
5. pneumonia

B VOCABULARY DEFINITIONS

1. **determined**—When you plan to do something no matter what, you are *determined* to do that thing.
   If you plan to go swimming no matter what, you are determined to go swimming.
   - What's another way of saying *The girl planned to climb the mountain no matter what?*

2. **misled**—When you are *misled*, somebody tricks you.
   - What's another way of saying *The ad tricked people about the used car?*

3. **poverty**—When you are very poor, you live in *poverty.*
   - What's another way of saying *The beggar was very poor?*

4. **resent**—When you *resent* a person or a thing, you are angry with that person or thing.
   - What's another way of saying *Andrea was angry with Hilary for taking her seat on the bus?*

The Dirty Thirties

Part 2

Migration to California

From 1935 to 1940, more than one million people left the Plains states for California. It was one of the largest migrations in the country's history. The migrants came from all over. But more came from the center of the Dust Bowl—Oklahoma—than from any other state, so people in other states called the migrants Okies.

Jalopy driven to California in the 1930s by migrant workers

scorching desert heat were too much for many old cars and trucks.

When the jalopies broke down, the Okies would try to find odd jobs in nearby towns. The money they earned would pay for repairs, gas, or oil. While the families were waiting for repairs, they camped in or near their car or truck. At night they lit a campfire. If they were lucky, they cooked a bit of food.

Some migrant families had beat-up old cars or trucks called jalopies. These families piled their jalopies high with supplies for their new life, including beds and mattresses, tables and chairs, pots and pans. The jalopies formed an odd parade as they moved slowly down the highway.

Some migrants did not even have a jalopy. These determined Okies set out for the West Coast on foot. They pulled wagons and pushed baby carriages. The hope for a better life urged them on.

The trip to California was long and difficult. The jalopies often gave out. Tires and engines blew under the tremendous weight. Steep mountain roads and

The Okies looked forward to working the land in California. They expected that one day they would have farms again—that they could earn a decent living and provide good homes for their children. They believed the flyers they had read and seen posted on telephone poles.

Low Wages

When Dust Bowl migrants arrived in California at last, they found they had been misled. Okies were not welcome. People in California did not want them in their towns.

Okies thought that even if they were not accepted in local communities, they could at least work in the fields. But they had been deceived here as well.

At that time, farming was the most important business in California. As technology had advanced, however, most small family farms in the Golden State had vanished. They were absorbed into large farms owned by big companies. These huge farms needed lots of workers to harvest the crops. But they kept wages low.

During planting and harvest times in California, there was a great demand for labor. That is why all the flyers about California had appeared in Dust Bowl towns. Growers in the Golden State knew the Dust Bowlers needed work. They drew the Okies west to flood the job market—not to give them jobs, but to lower labor prices.

As the supply of labor increased, the wages workers received dropped. Local residents resented the Okies who had come in and driven down their wages. When a job opened, three or four workers fought to get it. If one person refused to work for only 25 cents an hour, plenty of others would agree to such low wages. No family could live on so little income, but for many the income was better than nothing.

Growers paid workers 35 cents an hour for picking plums and nectarines. They paid only 20 cents an hour for picking lettuce and potatoes. For peaches, workers earned only two and a half cents for each box. That meant they earned only one dollar for picking one ton (2,000 pounds) of peaches.

Farm Labor Camps

Many migrants remained homeless and jobless. They made housing from scraps of tin and cardboard. They crafted tents from old blankets, and they lived in open fields, under bridges, and on the banks of ditches. They washed themselves and their clothes in rivers. They used the woods as bathrooms.

Migrant mother and children in 1936

Disease soon broke out among the migrants. Unclean conditions and poor diets caused deadly illnesses. The migrants barely survived this dismal way of life. In 1936, the federal government in Washington, DC, started assisting the migrants by building several farm labor camps in California. The camps provided better housing for the migrants.

The new camps were not fancy by any means, but the one-room cabins and tents had a floor. One building in each camp had shower and bathroom stalls. The facilities seemed like palaces to migrants who had been living outdoors.

It cost a family one dollar per week to stay at a government camp. If a family did not have the money, they could pay the rent by doing chores. ✦

One of the camps was named Arvin Federal Camp. It was located near the small towns of Arvin and Weedpatch, and it came to be known as Weedpatch Camp. About three hundred people at a time, many of them children, lived at Weedpatch.

The Weedpatch School

At the camps, migrant children received breakfast for one penny a day. The camps also gave children a chance to go to school. Many children had lived their entire lives on the move and in poverty. No one had taught them to read or write. Because the migrant children were behind in their studies, local students often made fun of them. Some teachers ignored them because they believed the migrant children were unable to learn.

One kind man, Leo Hart, knew differently. Hart understood that migrant children just needed a chance. He knew they were like any other children with hopes and dreams. Hart ran for the office of local school chief with a secret plan. He intended to help the migrant children.

Hart won the election. One of his top goals was to help migrant children fit in at the public schools they attended. But he found that it was too difficult for them to fit in. Hart decided that the only way migrant children could receive the education they deserved was for them to have their own school. He rented 10 acres of land next to Weedpatch Camp and hired really good teachers.

In September 1940, Hart, eight teachers, and 50 young people from Weedpatch Camp built their own school. Weedpatch School became much more than a building. To the students, it was a sign of their strength and self-worth. It was a place where they could be among friends, a place of pride and honor. More important, for the generation of the Dirty Thirties, the Weedpatch School offered hope in lives that were choked with dust.

People who lived in the towns of Arvin and Weedpatch began to hear stories about Weedpatch School. The school was rumored to have the best teachers and well-behaved students. These local residents changed their minds about migrant children and tried to enroll their own kids in Weedpatch School. In 1944, Weedpatch School became part of the local school district.

The success of Weedpatch School was a sign that life was slowly getting better for the Okies in California during the 1940s. Many Okies found good-paying jobs and remained in the Golden State. Others returned to Oklahoma and neighboring states, where the drought and the dust storms had ended. As the 1940s came to a close, the Dust Bowl and the Dirty Thirties were just distant memories.

D SUPPLY AND DEMAND

Work the items.

1. What happens to the price of a product if the supply is **greater than** the demand?

2. What happens to the price of a product if the supply is **less than** the demand?

3. Wages paid to workers also depend on supply and demand.

- Pretend that the **supply** of workers for a factory is the same as the **demand** for workers by the factory owners. The supply and demand are **equal,** so the workers' wages remain the same.

- Why do the workers' wages remain the same?

4. What can happen to the workers' wages when the **supply** of workers increases?

5. What could make wages go up?

E COMPREHENSION

Write the answers.

1. Use details from the article to explain why many Okies migrated to California during the 1930s.

2. The flyers made two false claims about California. For each claim, tell what the claim was and what the truth was. Your answer should use this format: *The flyers claimed A, but …*

3. Use details from the article to explain why growers in California were able to save money after the Okies arrived.

4. Name two ways the farm labor camps were better than the other places Okies lived in California.

5. What did Leo Hart do to help the children who lived in Weedpatch Camp?

F WRITING

- Pretend you are a student at Weedpatch School.

Write the story of your experiences in California.

Use details from the article to answer these questions in your story.

1. What did you hope California would be like?

2. What did you discover about your hopes when you arrived in California?

3. Where did you live at first?

4. How is where you live now better than where you lived at first?

5. Why are you proud of Weedpatch School?

Write at least six sentences.

END OF LESSON 68

A WORD LISTS

1 | Hard Words

1. foreman
2. galvanized
3. italic
4. parentheses
5. risen

2 | Spanish Words

1. listo
   [LEES-toh]
2. braceros
   [brah-SEHR-ohs]
3. carcanchita
   [car-cahn-CHEE-tah]

3 | Spanish Phrases

1. es todo
   [ess TOH-doh]
2. mi olla
   [mee OY-ya]
3. ya es hora
   [yah es OH-ra]

4 | Spanish Names

1. Fresno
   [FREZ-noh]
2. Jalisco
   [hah-LEES-koh]
3. Jiménez
   [hee-MEH-nez]
4. Panchito
   [pahn-CHEE-toh]

5 | Vocabulary Words

1. circuit
2. detect
3. kerosene
4. sharecropper

B VOCABULARY DEFINITIONS

1. **circuit**—When you travel in a circular path, you make a *circuit*.
- Here's another way of saying *The judge traveled in a circular path around the state: The judge made a circuit around the state.*
- What's another way of saying *Pedro traveled in a circular path around the town?*

2. **detect**—When you notice something, you *detect* it.
- What's another way of saying *Oprah noticed a faint noise?*

3. **kerosene**—*Kerosene* is a type of gasoline that is used in lights and heaters.
- What is kerosene?

4. **sharecropper**—A *sharecropper* is someone who rents land from a farmer.
- What's a sharecropper?

On the Move

In today's story, "The Circuit," a narrator describes his experiences as a migrant farmworker in California during the 1950s. Even though the story takes place long ago, the conditions it describes are still true today. Farmers still need migrant farmworkers to harvest their crops, and those workers still have difficult lives.

Like many farmworker families in the United States, the narrator's family is from Mexico. Farmworker families stay in one place until the crops have been harvested in that place. These crops are often fruits, such as strawberries and grapes. When the crops are harvested, the family moves to another place. Sometimes families stay in as many as six different places in one year. They live in labor camps, shacks, and sometimes garages, just like the narrator's family.

During the harvest season, farmworkers work for many hours every day. Sometimes they work seven days a week. The crops must be harvested when they are ready, so there's no time to waste. The work is hard, and usually the sun is hot. Children often work alongside their parents.

The family in the story speaks Spanish. The narrator uses some Spanish words to make his story more accurate. The first time the Spanish words appear, they are in *italics*. The narrator translates some of these words in parentheses, but he doesn't tell you how to pronounce them. For example, he writes, "*Es todo*" (that's it) and "*Mi olla*" (my pot). Other times you will see Spanish words in italics without a translation. You can figure out what these words mean by using the other words in the sentence.

Migrant worker near Fresno, California

The Circuit

Francisco Jiménez

Part 1

It was that time of year again. Ito, the strawberry sharecropper, did not smile. It was natural. The peak of the strawberry season was over and the last few days the workers, most of them *braceros*, were not picking as many boxes as they had during the months of June and July.

As the last days of August disappeared, so did the number of braceros. Sunday, only one—the best picker—came to work. I liked him. Sometimes we talked during our half-hour lunch break. That is how I found out he was from Jalisco, the same state in Mexico my family was from. That Sunday was the last time I saw him.

When the sun had tired and sunk behind the mountains, Ito signaled us that it was time to go home. "*Ya esora,*" he yelled in his broken Spanish. Those were the words I waited for twelve hours a day, everyday, seven days a week, week after week. And the thought of not hearing them again saddened me.

As we drove home Papa did not say a word. With both hands on the wheel, he stared at the dirt road. My older brother, Roberto, was also silent. He leaned his head back and closed his eyes. Once in a while he cleared from his throat the dust that blew in from outside.

Yes, it was that time of year. When I opened the front door to the shack, I stopped. Everything we owned was neatly packed in cardboard boxes. Suddenly I felt even more the weight of hours, days, weeks, and months of work. I sat down on a box. The thought of having to move to Fresno and knowing what was in store for me there brought tears to my eyes.

That night I could not sleep. I lay in bed thinking about how much I hated this move. ◆

A little before five o' clock in the morning, Papa woke everyone up. A few minutes later, the yelling and screaming of my little brothers and sisters, for whom the move was a great adventure, broke the silence of dawn. Shortly, the barking of the dogs accompanied them.

While we packed the breakfast dishes, Papa went outside to start the "Carcanchita." That was the name Papa gave his old black '38 Plymouth. He bought it in a used-car lot in Santa Rosa in the winter of 1949. Papa was very proud of his car. "Mi Carcanchita," my little jalopy, he called it. He had a right to be proud of it. He spent a lot of time looking at other cars before buying this one. When he finally chose the "Carcanchita," he checked it thoroughly before driving it out of the car lot. He examined every inch of the car. He listened to the motor, tilting his head from side to side like a parrot, trying to detect any noises that

spelled car trouble. After being satisfied with the looks and sounds of the car, Papa then insisted on knowing who the original owner was. He never did find out from the car salesman. But he bought the car anyway. Papa figured the original owner must have been an important man because behind the rear seat of the car he found a blue necktie.

Papa parked the car out in front and left the motor running. "Listo" (ready), he yelled. Without saying a word, Roberto and I began to carry the boxes out to the car. Roberto carried the two big boxes and I carried the two smaller ones. Papa then threw the mattress on top of the car roof and tied it with ropes to the front and rear bumpers.

Everything was packed except Mama's pot. It was an old large galvanized pot she had picked up at an army surplus store in Santa Maria the year I was born. The pot was full of dents and nicks, and the more dents and nicks it had, the more Mama liked it. "Mi olla" (my pot), she used to say proudly. ✦

I held the front door open as Mama carefully carried out her pot by both handles, making sure not to spill the cooked beans. When she got to the car, Papa reached out to help her with it. Roberto opened the rear car door and Papa gently placed it on the floor behind the front seat. All of us then climbed in. Papa sighed, wiped the sweat off his forehead with his sleeve, and said wearily, "Es todo" (that's it).

As we drove away, I felt a lump in my throat. I turned around and looked at our little shack for the last time.

At sunset we drove into a labor camp near Fresno. Since Papa did not speak English, Mama asked the camp foreman if he needed any more workers. "We don't need no more," said the foreman, scratching his head. "Check with Sullivan down the road. Can't miss him. He lives in a big white house with a fence around it."

When we got there, Mama walked up to the house. She went through a white gate, past a row of rose bushes, up the stairs to the front door. She rang the doorbell. The porch light went on and a tall husky man came out. They exchanged a few words. After the man went in, Mama clasped her hands and hurried back to the car. "We have work! Mr. Sullivan said we can stay there the whole season," she said, gasping and pointing to an old garage near the stables.

The garage was worn out by the years. It had no windows. The walls, eaten by termites, strained to support the roof full of holes. The loose dirt floor, populated by earth worms, looked like a gray road map.

That night, by the light of a kerosene lamp, we unpacked and cleaned our new home. Roberto swept away the loose dirt, leaving the hard ground. Papa plugged the holes in the walls with old newspapers and tin can tops. Mama fed my little brothers and sisters. Papa and Roberto then brought in the mattress and placed it in the far corner of the garage. "Mama, you and the little ones sleep on the mattress. Roberto, Panchito, and I will sleep outside under the trees," Papa said.

E COMPREHENSION

Write the answers.

1. How long did Panchito work in the fields during the day and during the week?

2. Why did Panchito's family have to move?

3. The sentence "It was that time of year" has two meanings in the story. What are those two meanings?

4. Why did Papa think his carcanchita had been owned by an important man?

5. Use details from the story to describe the garage that Panchito's family moved into.

F WRITING

Write a passage that compares Panchito with the Okie children at Weedpatch Camp.

Use details from "The Dirty Thirties" and "The Circuit" to answer these questions in your passage:

1. What job do Panchito and the Okie children have?

2. Where do Panchito and the Okie children come from?

3. Which state do Panchito and the Okie children live in?

4. Which languages do Panchito and the Okie children speak?

5. How does Panchito's home in the garage compare to the homes of the Okie children at Camp Weedpatch?

Write at least six sentences.

END OF LESSON 69

A | WORD LISTS

1 | Spanish Words

1. corrido
   [koh-REE-doh]
2. quince
   [KEEN-say]
3. tortilla
   [tohr-TEE-yuh]
4. vámonos
   [VAH-moh-nohs]

2 | Spanish Phrases

1. chili con carne
   [CHEE-lay kohn KAR-nay]
2. carne con chile
   [KAR-nay kohn CHEE-lay]
3. tienen que tener cuidado
   [tee-EHN-en KAY teh-NER kwee-DAH-doe]

3 | Spanish Review

1. braceros
2. carcanchita
3. es todo
4. listo
5. mi olla
6. ya es hora

4 | Vocabulary Words

1. savor
2. vineyard

B | VOCABULARY DEFINITIONS

1. **savor**—When you enjoy something as much as you can, you *savor* it.
- Here's another way of saying *Shawn enjoyed every bite of the apple as much as he could: Shawn savored every bite of the apple.*
- What's another way of saying *Lan enjoys freedom as much as she can?*

2. **vineyard**—A field where grapevines grow is called a *vineyard*.
- What's another way of saying *The grape pickers worked in a field where grapevines grow?*

C | VOCABULARY FROM CONTEXT

1. One of the braceros played the guitar and sang **corridos.**

2. After Rosa said, **"Vámonos"** to her friends, she left the playground with them.

The Circuit

Part 2

Early next morning Mr. Sullivan showed us where his crop was, and after breakfast, Papa, Roberto, and I headed for the vineyard to pick.

Around nine o'clock the temperature had risen to almost one hundred degrees. I was completely soaked in sweat and my mouth felt as if I had been chewing on a handkerchief. I walked over to the end of the row, picked up the jug of water we had brought, and began drinking. "Don't drink too much; you'll get sick," Roberto shouted. No sooner had he said that than I felt sick to my stomach. ✿ I dropped to my knees and let the jug roll off my hands. I remained motionless with my eyes glued on the hot sandy ground. All I could hear was the drone of insects. Slowly I began to recover. I poured water over my face and neck and watched the black mud run down my arms and hit the ground.

I still felt a little dizzy when we took a break to eat lunch. It was past two o'clock and we sat underneath a large walnut tree that was on the side of the road. While we ate, Papa jotted down the number of boxes we had picked. Roberto drew designs on the ground with a stick. Suddenly I noticed Papa's face turn pale as he looked down the road. "Here comes the school bus," he whispered loudly in alarm. Instinctively, Roberto and I ran and hid in the vineyards. We did not want to get in trouble for not going to school. The yellow bus stopped in front of Mr. Sullivan's house. Two neatly dressed boys about my age got off. They carried books under their arms. After they crossed the street, the bus drove away. Roberto and I came out from hiding and joined Papa. "*Tienen que tener cuidado*" (you have to be careful), he warned us. ♦

After lunch we went back to work. The sun kept beating down. The buzzing insects, the wet sweat, and the hot dry dust made the afternoon seem to last forever. Finally the mountains around the valley reached out and swallowed the sun. Within an hour it was too dark to continue picking. The vines blanketed the grapes, making it difficult to see the bunches. "*Vámonos,*" said Papa, signaling to us that it was time to quit work. Papa then took out a pencil and began to figure out how much we had earned our first day. He wrote down numbers, crossed some out, wrote down some more. "*Quince*" (fifteen dollars), he murmured.

When we arrived home, we took a cold shower underneath a waterhose. We then sat down to eat dinner around some wooden crates that served as a table. Mama had cooked a special meal for us. We had rice and tortillas with *carne con chile*, my favorite dish.

The next morning I could hardly move. My body ached all over. I felt little control over my arms and legs. This feeling went on every morning for days until my muscles finally got used to the work.

It was Monday, the first week of November. The grape season was over and I could now go to school. I woke up early that morning and lay in bed, looking at the stars and savoring the thought of not going to work and of starting sixth grade for the first time that year. Since I could not sleep, I decided to get up and join Papa and Roberto at breakfast. I sat at the table across from Roberto, but I kept my head down. I did not want to look up and face him. I knew he was sad. He was not going to school today. He was not going tomorrow, or next week, or next month. He would not go until the cotton season was over, and that was sometime in February. I rubbed my hands together and watched the dry, acid stained skin fall to the floor in little rolls.

When Papa and Roberto left for work, I felt relief. I walked to the top of a small grade next to the shack and watched the "Carcanchita" disappear in the distance in a cloud of dust.

Two hours later, around eight o' clock, I stood by the side of the road waiting for school bus number twenty. When it arrived I climbed in. No one noticed me. Everyone was busy either talking or yelling. I sat in an empty seat in the back.

When the bus stopped in front of the school, I felt very nervous. I looked out the bus window and saw boys and girls carrying books under their arms. I felt empty. I put my hands in my pants pockets and walked to the principal's office. When I entered I heard a woman's voice say: "May I help you?" I was startled. I had not heard English for months. For a few seconds I remained speechless. I looked at the lady who waited for an answer. My first instinct was to answer her in Spanish, but I held back. Finally, after struggling for English words, I managed to tell her that I wanted to enroll in the sixth grade. After answering many questions, I was led to the classroom. ✦

Mr. Lema, the sixth grade teacher, greeted me and assigned me a desk. He then introduced me to the class. I was so nervous and scared at that moment when everyone's eyes were on me that I wished I were with Papa and Roberto picking cotton. After taking roll, Mr. Lema gave the class the assignment for the first hour. "The first thing we have to do this morning is finish reading the story we began yesterday," he said enthusiastically. He walked up to me, handed me an English book, and asked me to read. "We are on page 125," he said politely. When I heard this, I felt my blood rush to my head; I felt dizzy. "Would you like to read?" he asked hesitantly. I opened the book to page 125. My mouth was dry. My eyes began to water. I could not begin. "You can read later," Mr. Lema said understandingly.

For the rest of the reading period I kept getting angrier and angrier with myself. I should have read, I thought to myself.

During recess I went into the restroom and opened my English book to page 125. I began to read in a low voice, pretending I was in class. There were many words I did not know. I closed the book and headed back to the classroom.

Mr. Lema was sitting at his desk correcting papers. When I entered he looked up at me and smiled. I felt better. I walked up to him and asked if he could help me with the new words. "Gladly," he said.

The rest of the month I spent my lunch hours working on English with Mr. Lema, my best friend at school.

One Friday during lunch hour Mr. Lema asked me to take a walk with him to the music room. "Do you like music?" he asked me as we entered the building.

"Yes, I like Mexican *corridos*," I answered. He then picked up a trumpet,

blew on it and handed it to me. The sound gave me goose bumps. I knew that sound. I had heard it in many Mexican corridos. "How would you like to learn how to play it?" he asked. He must have read my face because before I could answer, he added: "I'll teach you how to play it during our lunch hours."

That day I could hardly wait to get home to tell Papa and Mama the great news. As I got off the bus, my little brothers and sisters ran up to meet me. They were yelling and screaming. I thought they were happy to see me, but when I opened the door to our shack, I saw that everything we owned was neatly packed in cardboard boxes.

E COMPREHENSION

Write the answers.

1. Why didn't Papa want Roberto and Panchito to go to school when they were working in the vineyard?

2. The story says, "The mountains around the valley reached out and swallowed the sun." What does that mean?

3. Why was Roberto sad on the first day Panchito went to school?

4. Use details from the story to explain how Panchito felt when he saw the cardboard boxes. Why did he feel that way?

5. Why is the story called "The Circuit"?

F WRITING

• Pretend Panchito wants to write a letter to Mr. Lema on the night before his family leaves to find more work.

Write the letter to Mr. Lema.

Be sure your letter answers these questions:

1. Why did you have to leave the school?

2. Why are you grateful to Mr. Lema?

3. How do you feel about your life outside of school?

4. What do you hope to do in the future?

Write at least six sentences.

END OF LESSON 70

A WORD LISTS

1 Hard Words	2 Animal Names	3 Word Endings	4 Vocabulary Words
1. Asian	1. bandicoot	1. admiration	1. endangered
2. Australian	2. chimpanzee	2. competition	2. extinct
3. chemical	3. grizzly bear	3. destruction	3. habitat
4. fuel	4. leopard	4. extinction	4. reserve
5. survival	5. parakeet	5. pollution	5. resources
		6. population	6. species

B VOCABULARY DEFINITIONS

1. **species**—A type of plant or animal is called a *species* of plant or animal. Domesticated dogs are one species of animal. Although there are many different kinds of domesticated dogs, they are all the same species. Domesticated cats are another species of animal. People, cows, and goats are three more species of animals.
- What's another name for a type of plant or animal?

2. **extinct**—When a species of plant or animal no longer exists, that species is *extinct*.
A species of bird that no longer exists is called an extinct species of bird.
- What would we call a species of fish that no longer exists?

3. **endangered**—When a species of plant or animal is in danger of becoming extinct, it is an *endangered* species.
A species of lizard that's in danger of going extinct is an *endangered species* of lizard.

- What would we call a species of monkey that's in danger?

4. **habitat**—The natural home of a plant or animal is called its *habitat*.
Here's another way of saying *The tiger's natural home is the jungle: The tiger's habitat is the jungle.*
- What's another way of saying *The polar bear's natural home is in the far north?*

5. **reserve**—A place set aside for wild animals is called a *reserve*.
A place set aside for lions is called a *lion reserve.*
- What would we call a place set aside for elephants?

6. **resources**—*Resources* is another word for *supplies*.
Supplies found in nature are called *natural resources*. These resources include water, wood, food, and minerals.
- What do we call supplies found in nature?

Endangered Species
Part 1

When a species of animal becomes extinct, every animal of that species dies out all over the earth. Among the species in danger of extinction are the African elephant, the chimpanzee, the rhinoceros, the blue whale, and the grizzly bear. Animal species that are in danger of extinction are called **endangered species.** All of these beautiful animals may soon vanish from the earth forever.

Extinction is nothing new. Throughout the history of the earth, millions of species of plants and animals have died out. What is new today is the rapid rate of extinction. Increasing numbers of people make greater demands on the earth for shelter, food, and fuel. As humans use up more and more of the earth's resources, other species have less and less.

In the past, people used the earth's resources with little thought to the effect on other creatures. Now people all over the world are becoming aware of the ways humans are endangering other animals.

Overhunting

Overhunting is one of the ways animals become endangered. Any species that has fewer babies than the numbers killed by hunters is on the road to extinction.

People kill animals they think are pests. During the 1800s, hunters in the United States shot Carolina parakeets in great numbers to keep them from eating fruits and nuts. This overhunting helped make Carolina parakeets extinct. Wolves have been hunted almost to extinction because they kill livestock and because people fear them.

People often kill animals for their fur or other body parts. African elephants are killed for their tusks, and rhinoceroses for their horns. Cheetahs and leopards are killed for their fur.

People also capture animals from the wild to sell to pet dealers or collectors. Dozens of species of parrots are seriously endangered because of this activity.

Messing with Mother Nature

Wild animals that have lived in a particular area for a long time are called native animals. These native animals can become endangered when people introduce a new species into the area. When people brought rabbits to Australia, the rabbits upset the balance among native animals. Now the bandicoot, a native Australian mammal, is losing out to the rabbit in the competition for survival.

Pollution caused by people also kills many animals. Chemicals released into the world often have far-reaching effects. Acid rain falling into lakes and rivers kills both fish and the animals that depend on the fish for food. Poisons cause similar problems. When people spray poisons over farms and swamps to kill insect pests, sometimes great numbers of fish, birds, and mammals die off as well. ◆

Habitat Destruction

The most serious threat to wildlife is destruction of their natural homes—their habitat. Rain forests, for example, are home to almost half the world's plant and animal species. As people clear rain forests for timber and farming, plants and animals in the rain-forest habitat become endangered.

Habitat destruction goes on everywhere. Bulldozers clear land for houses, shopping malls, factories, and farms. People cut down trees, grasses, and bushes. The plants destroyed may not seem important to humans. But when plants disappear, the animals that depend on those plants for food and shelter suffer. Other species that depend on those animals are affected in turn. All these plants and animals are connected to each other in some way.

In the next lesson, you will read about four animal species that are very different from each other but have one thing in common: they are or were endangered species. Some of these animals are dying out, but others are coming back.

D | COMPREHENSION

Write the answers.

1. What happens when a species of animal becomes extinct?

2. Use details from the article to explain why the rate of extinction is increasing.

3. Use details from the article to explain why people hunt and capture animals.

4. The article makes a claim about what can happen to native animals when people introduce a new species to an area. What is that claim?

5. What evidence does the article give to support that claim?

E | WRITING

Use the following outline to write a passage that explains how animal species can become endangered.

> Animal species can become endangered or extinct for several reasons.
>
> a. Overhunting is one reason.
>
> b. Messing with Mother Nature is another reason.
>
> c. Habitat destruction is another reason.

Use details from the article to answer these questions in your passage:

1. How can overhunting endanger animal species? Give an example.

2. How can messing with Mother Nature endanger animal species? Give an example.

3. Why do people destroy habitats?

4. How can habitat destruction endanger animal species?

Write at least six sentences. Begin with the main-idea sentence.

END OF LESSON 71

A WORD LISTS

1	Hard Words
1.	enforce
2.	foreign
3.	preserve
4.	starvation
5.	successfully
6.	primate

2	Animal Names
1.	orangutan
2.	peregrine falcon
3.	tortoise

3	Place Names
1.	Antarctica
2.	Australia
3.	Borneo
4.	Galápagos
5.	Java
6.	Sumatra

4	Vocabulary Words
1.	century
2.	confine
3.	decline
4.	solitary

B VOCABULARY DEFINITIONS

1. **century**—A period of one hundred years is called a *century*.
   What's another way of saying *The store opened one hundred years ago?*

2. **confine**—When you cannot leave a place, you are *confined* to that place.
   Here's another way of saying *The dog could not leave the yard: The dog was confined to the yard.*
   • What's another way of saying *The survivors could not leave the island?*

3. **decline**—If the number of things gets less and less, the number *declines*.
   • Here's another way of saying *The number of people living in Flatville keeps getting less and less: The number of people living in Flatville keeps declining.*
   • What's another way of saying *The number of wolves got less and less because of hunting?*

4. **solitary**—Animals that live alone are called *solitary* animals.
   • What's another way of saying *Tigers are animals that live alone?*

Endangered Species
Part 2

In the last lesson, you learned that some animal species can become endangered because of overhunting, messing with Mother Nature, and habitat destruction. In today's lesson, you will read about four animal species that are or were endangered: the tiger, the Galápagos tortoise, the orangutan, and the peregrine falcon.

The Tiger

Tigers are among the most impressive animals on earth. People who see tigers in zoos admire them for their beauty and size. But where tigers still exist in the wild, people's admiration is mixed with fear and even hatred. Tigers are beautiful, but they are also dangerous. People and tigers have difficulty living near each other.

Tigers live in the grassy wetlands and forests of India and other Asian countries. The map shows where India is located.

Tigers eat mainly deer and wild hogs. If cattle farmers live nearby, tigers sometimes kill their cattle. Tigers have been known to eat people as well.

Tigers have been a favorite target of hunters for centuries. For hundreds of years, people killed tigers for their beautiful striped skins and to protect livestock. It was not until the 1970s that people realized

Tiger

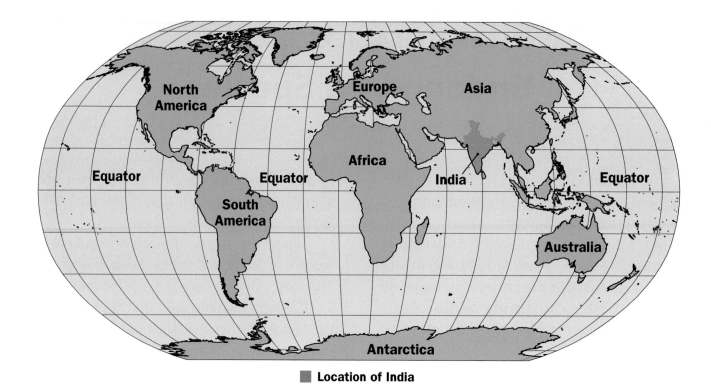

Location of India

tigers were endangered. The government of India banned tiger hunting in 1970 and set up many large tiger reserves.

The reserves were designed to keep people and tigers safe from each other. However, tigers require large reserves to survive, and India is a crowded country. It is hard to keep people who need firewood and land out of the tigers' reserves; and as the tiger population increases, it is hard to keep the tigers inside the reserves.

Almost everybody agrees that tigers should not become extinct. Yet conflicts between the needs of tigers and the needs of people have not been resolved. As long as these conflicts exist, the future of the tiger remains uncertain.

The Galápagos Tortoise

The Galápagos Islands are located in the Pacific Ocean about six hundred miles west of South America. When European sailors first discovered the islands in the sixteenth century, no people lived there, so the islands' creatures had never developed a fear of people. Birds and tortoises didn't even try to escape when sailors came ashore to catch them.

Sailors killed hundreds of thousands of Galápagos tortoises for food in the centuries that followed. Animals that sailors brought to the islands caused further destruction. Many tortoises died of starvation when they had to compete with goats for plant food. Meanwhile pigs, dogs, and cats ate tortoise eggs and young tortoises. The numbers of tortoises and other native species were greatly reduced.

Galápagos tortoise

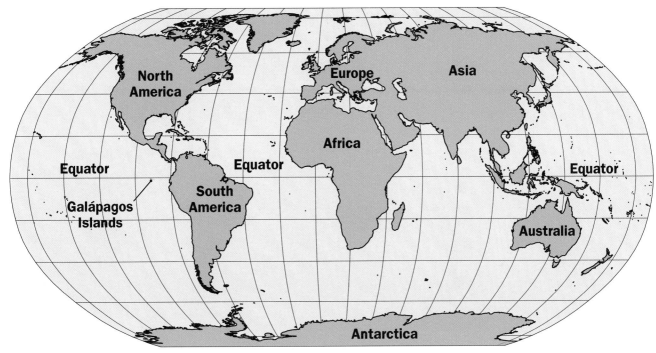

Location of Galápagos Islands

Little was done to help the tortoises until 1959, when the Charles Darwin Foundation was created. To help the tortoises make a comeback, the Foundation set up a breeding station on one of the islands. Tortoise eggs are brought there to hatch, and the young tortoises live in safety until they are too big to be eaten by other animals. Meanwhile, goats have been removed from the islands so that there will be enough plants for the tortoises to eat.

The eggs and the newly hatched young of the Galápagos tortoise continue to be threatened by foreign species. Fortunately, the tortoises that do survive are sturdy beasts. They weigh about one hundred fifty pounds by the age of fifteen and as much as five hundred pounds when fully grown. They can live for a century or more. These peaceful giants may still be saved from extinction.

The Orangutan

The orangutan is a very intelligent animal whose name means "person of the forest." Orangutans are primates, like apes,

Orangutans

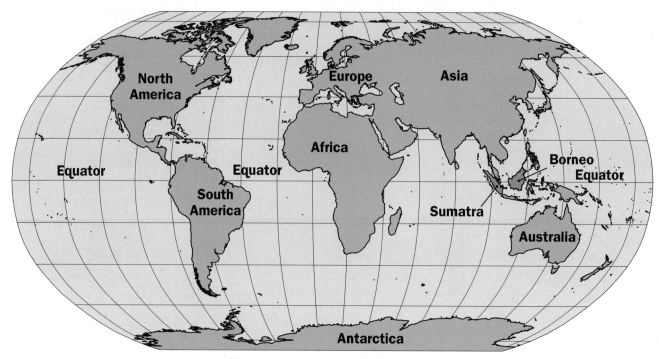

Location of Borneo and Sumatra

monkeys, and people. Female orangutans live with their children, but male orangutans are solitary animals. They live alone because they eat almost nothing but fruit, which is hard to find. If orangutan families stayed together, they could not find enough fruit to support the entire group.

Hunters have reduced orangutan populations. Orangutans are killed for meat or are taken from the forest to be sold as pets. But the greatest threat to their survival is the loss of their rain forest homes. Orangutans once lived in rain forests ranging from southern China to the island of Java. Now they are confined to rain forests on just two islands, Borneo and Sumatra. Unfortunately, the forests on these islands are being cut down for timber or burned for farmland. Shrinking areas of forest support fewer and fewer orangutans.

Efforts are now being made to save the orangutan in the wild. Special areas of rain forests have been set aside, and laws against hunting the creatures are enforced. Breeding in zoos and labs may help to keep the species alive. In the end, though, orangutans will be saved from extinction only if enough of their rain forest habitat is preserved. ♦

The Peregrine Falcon

The peregrine falcon is one of the world's great birds of prey. Its streamlined body is built for speed and strength. It kills its prey

Peregrine falcon

by catching it "on the wing" or by making vertical dives at speeds up to two hundred miles per hour.

Peregrine falcons were once found in nearly all parts of the world. They were described as the world's most successful flying bird. Then suddenly during the 1950s and 1960s there was a worldwide population crash of peregrine falcons.

Scientists noticed that the falcons were no longer successfully raising their young. They discovered that the shells of the falcons' eggs had become so thin that the eggs were breaking when adult falcons sat on them. The problem of shell-thinning was traced to a poison called DDT.

DDT was widely used in the 1950s and 1960s to kill insects. This poison does not break down when it enters the environment. At first, people thought this was a good thing because DDT would continue to kill unwanted insects for a long time. But DDT was killing many animals besides insects.

When small animals ate the insects, they ate the DDT as well. And when larger animals ate the smaller ones, the DDT became more dangerous. Birds of prey, including peregrine falcons, received the most dangerous amounts of DDT. Their populations declined rapidly because many of the birds could no longer lay eggs that would hatch. *

When the United States finally banned the use of DDT in 1972, there were no American peregrines left in the eastern United States except in zoos. The falcon population in western states was also greatly reduced. Breeding programs were begun to save the falcons from extinction.

In the East, baby falcons in zoos were carefully raised so they would be able to survive in the wild. People used falcon-shaped puppets to feed the baby falcons so the birds would learn to expect food from other falcons, not from people. Raising falcons to live outside zoos was a difficult task, but by 1980, the birds were successfully released into the wild.

In the West, thin-shelled eggs were removed from falcon nests and replaced with plaster eggs. After the real eggs hatched, the chicks were returned to the nest to be raised by adult falcons.

Since the 1980s, thousands of peregrine falcons have been released into the wild. The falcon has been brought back from the brink of extinction—but it is not out of danger. It will take the efforts of many people to save the falcon and other rare creatures, all of which are important strands in the web of life.

D COMPREHENSION

Write the answers.

1. Use details from the article to describe three ways that Galápagos tortoises were endangered by foreign species.

2. Use details from the article to explain how the breeding station protects tortoises.

3. What reasons do people have for destroying the orangutans' habitat?

4. Explain how thin eggshells caused falcon populations to decline.

5. Why did people in zoos use falcon-shaped puppets to feed baby falcons?

E WRITING

Use the following outline to write a passage that explains why certain animal species are or were endangered.

Several animal species are or were endangered.

a. The tiger is endangered.

b. The Galápagos tortoise was endangered.

c. The orangutan is endangered.

d. The peregrine falcon was endangered.

Use details from the article to answer these questions in your passage:

1. Why is the tiger endangered?

2. How are people trying to protect tigers?

3. Why was the Galápagos tortoise endangered?

4. How do people protect Galápagos tortoises?

5. Why is the orangutan endangered?

6. How do people protect orangutans?

7. Why was the peregrine falcon endangered?

8. How did people save peregrine falcons from extinction?

Write at least eight sentences. Begin with the main-idea sentence.

A WORD LISTS

1 | Hard Words

1. Brooklyn Dodgers
2. Ebbets Field
3. Jackie Robinson
4. Philadelphia Phillies
5. umpire

2 | Vocabulary Words

1. biography
2. bold
3. daring
4. dugout
5. major league
6. plant

B VOCABULARY DEFINITIONS

1. **biography**—A *biography* is the history of a person's life written by somebody else.
- What do we call the history of a person's life as written by somebody else?

2. **bold**—A person who is confident and brave is a *bold* person.
- What's another way of saying *Doli is confident and brave?*

3. **daring**—A person who takes chances is a *daring* person.
- What's another way of saying *Firefighters are people who take chances?*

4. **dugout**—In a baseball game, the main place where players stay when they're not playing is called the *dugout*. The dugout faces the baseball field.
- In a baseball game, what do we call the main place where baseball players stay when they're not playing?

5. **major league**—A group of sports teams that play each other is called a sports *league*. A *major league* is a league with the best players.
- What's a major league?

6. **plant**—*Plant* is another word for *factory*. Another name for a steel factory is a *steel plant*.
- What's another name for an automobile factory?

Facts about Baseball

You're going to read a biography of a famous baseball player named Jackie Robinson. You need to know some facts about baseball to understand the biography.

The picture shows a game between two baseball teams, the Reds and the Blues. There are nine players on each team. All nine Blues are in the field. One player from the Reds is standing at home plate. That player is called the batter. The other Reds players are in the dugout, waiting for their turn at bat.

The pitcher on the blue team throws the baseball toward the catcher, who plays behind home plate. There are basemen at first base, second base, and third base. First base is to the right of home plate, and third base is to the left. Between second base and third base is another player called the shortstop. In the outfield, there are three more players: the left fielder, the center fielder, and the right fielder.

When the pitcher throws the ball, the batter tries to hit the ball to a spot where nobody on the blue team can catch it. Then the batter runs as far as possible around the bases, starting with first base. If the batter can touch all three bases and then touch home plate, the batter scores a run.

The picture also shows an umpire dressed in black right behind the catcher. The umpire calls out "Strike!" for good pitches and "Ball!" for bad pitches.

This biography of Jackie Robinson is told by a narrator who is fictional. Even though the narrator is fictional, he tells facts about Jackie Robinson.

D READING INFORMATIONAL TEXT: Biography

Jackie Robinson

Chapter 1

The year 1947 was a long time ago, but I can remember some things about that year as if they happened yesterday. At that time, I worked in a meat-packing plant in Brooklyn, which is part of New York City. The work was hard, and I didn't like it very much. But I had one great interest that made the days more exciting: I was a fan of the Brooklyn Dodgers, our local baseball team.

The Dodgers used to play in Ebbets Field. And when the Dodgers played on Saturday or Sunday, I'd be there in the stands. I'd be yelling at the umpire. I'd be booing the players from the other teams. And I'd be cheering like mad for the Dodgers.

For me, the games wouldn't end when they were over on the field. At work the next Monday, we'd talk about the weekend games, and we'd go over every play. I couldn't even begin to count the hours we spent talking about the Dodgers. We'd argue about who was the best hitter, who was the best first baseman, or who was the best pitcher. But we'd always agree on one thing—the Dodgers were the greatest. Even if they didn't win, they were the best team to watch. They were bold and daring. They were tough. And when they played baseball, they played the real thing. ♦

The other day I went to the place where Ebbets Field used to stand. It's not there anymore. There's nothing but city there now. But when I stood on the corner where the entrance used to be, I had a strange feeling. It was almost as if the clock had turned back to 1947. I could almost see Ebbets Field, with a line of fans waiting to get in. I could almost hear the great roar that came from the stands when a Dodger hit a home run.

I must have stood on that corner for ten minutes, thinking back to 1947. A lot of games went through my mind, and I remembered a lot of great players. But as I stood there, the one player that my mind kept going back to was Jackie Robinson.

It's amazing, but I can remember watching a game at Ebbets Field when a man turned toward me and said, "Excuse me, sir, why is that player wearing a Dodger uniform?"

I answered, "Don't you read the papers? That's Jackie Robinson."

I'd read about Jackie Robinson. He was the first African American to play major league baseball, the very first one. And that day in April 1947 was the first time anybody ever saw an African American playing in a major league baseball game. ★

If I'd known then what I know now, I would have stood up and yelled, "Yay for Jackie!" I would have said, "He's the greatest! We should be shouting for joy that he's in a Dodger uniform!" But many Dodger fans were not cheering. They were asking each other why a black man was dressed in a Brooklyn Dodgers uniform.

Robinson was in a tight spot. He knew how some of the white fans and players felt about him. He knew they were looking for the slightest excuse to throw him out of the major leagues. When he walked out there on the first day at Ebbets Field, he looked like the loneliest person in the world. He was the only black player on the field—the only black player in the major leagues.

Some of the other players on the Dodgers wouldn't even talk to Robinson. They wouldn't joke with him or help him out or stick up for him. Can you imagine what that's like—when the men on your team aren't with you? And the team's fans don't cheer for you?

Can you imagine how lonely Robinson must have felt each time he walked up to the plate with his bat? Sometimes, when I think about that day and realize what a fine, gentle person Robinson was, I get kind of choked up. But as I said, I didn't know much about Jackie Robinson back then.

E COMPREHENSION

Write the answers.

1. Pretend a batter from one baseball team is standing at home plate. Use details from the "Facts about Baseball" passage to list the nine baseball players from the other team who are on the field.

2. After a batter hits a ball where nobody can catch it, how does the batter score a run? Use details from the "Facts about Baseball" passage to explain your answer.

3. Why didn't the Dodger games end for the narrator when they were over on the field?

4. Why did many of the fans not cheer for Jackie Robinson during the first game he played for the Dodgers?

5. Use details from the biography to explain why Jackie Robinson looked like the loneliest person in the world during his first game at Ebbets Field.

F WRITING

Write a passage that answers this main question:

- What challenges did Jackie Robinson face during his first game with the Dodgers?

Use details from the biography to answer these other questions in your passage:

1. How many African American players were in the major leagues at that time?

2. How did many of the Dodger fans feel about Robinson?

3. How did many of the Dodger players treat Robinson?

4. How did Robinson probably feel when he came up to bat?

Write at least six sentences.

END OF LESSON 73

A WORD LISTS

1 | Related Words

1. add / additional
2. compete / competitor
3. restrict / restriction

2 | Names

1. Branch Rickey
2. Eddie Stanky
3. Pee Wee Reese
4. New York Yankees

3 | Vocabulary Words

1. inning
2. insult
3. pennant
4. rookie
5. steal a base

B VOCABULARY DEFINITIONS

1. **inning**—A baseball game is divided into *innings*. During each inning, both teams get a turn at bat.
• What do both teams get during an inning?

2. **insult**—A comment or a gesture that is supposed to make you mad is an *insult*.
• What do we call a comment or a gesture that is supposed to make you mad?

3. **pennant**—A sports team that wins its league gets a flag called a *pennant*.

4. **rookie**—A baseball player who is playing his or her first full year on a team is called a *rookie*.
• What do we call a baseball player who is playing his or her first full year on team?

5. **steal a base**—In baseball, when a runner *steals a base*, the runner touches the next base before the batter hits the ball. Runners on first base try to steal second base.
• Which base do runners on second base try to steal?

C STORY BACKGROUND

More Facts about Baseball

In the last lesson, you learned facts about the players on a baseball team. Here are some facts about how baseball is played.

The game lasts nine innings unless there is a tie. The number of innings is easy to remember because it's the same as the number of players on the field, not counting the batter. That number is nine.

During each inning, both teams have a turn at batting. First the visiting team bats in the "top" of the inning until it makes three outs. Then the home team bats in the "bottom" of the inning until it also makes three outs. The inning ends after the last out in the bottom of the inning. Then the players start another inning.

	1	2	3	4	5	6	7	8	9	10	11
Dodgers	1	5	0	0	0	0	0	0	0	0	3
Phillies	0	0	2	2	0	0	2	0	0	0	0

If a game is tied at the end of nine innings, the teams play additional innings. They continue to play until one team is ahead of the other at the end of an inning.

The scoreboard shows the results of a game between the Dodgers and the Phillies. The number at the top of each column is the inning number. The number in each box below the inning number shows how many runs the team scored during that inning. The Dodgers were the visiting team, so their runs appear at the top of each inning. The Phillies were the home team, so their runs appear at the bottom of each inning.

D READING INFORMATIONAL TEXT: Biography

Jackie Robinson

Chapter 2

After Jackie Robinson's first game with the Dodgers, we had a lot of arguments at work. Some of the workers thought Robinson had every right to be in the majors, but others didn't agree. One man kept saying, "If you're a Dodger fan, you've got to be behind the whole team. That means you've got to be behind every player. When you're against one player, you're against the whole team." What he said kept running around in my head, and later on, I admitted to myself that he had a good point. But I still wasn't a big fan of Jackie Robinson.

I began to change my mind after the third game of the season, when Robinson hit his first major league home run. But what really changed my mind was a game between the Dodgers and the Philadelphia Phillies. During that game, the Phillies players yelled at Robinson from the dugout and called him names. Instead of yelling back, Robinson just ignored them.

At first, we thought Robinson had no fight in him, but then we began to learn the true story. Robinson had made a deal with Branch Rickey, the general manager of the Dodgers. Rickey wanted to give black players a chance to compete in major league baseball. He didn't like the idea that talented black athletes couldn't play in the major leagues. So he picked Robinson to be the first black player in the majors. Rickey knew that if Robinson failed, other black players would have a tough time getting into the majors.

Rickey also knew that other major league teams didn't want black players. A couple of teams even said they wouldn't play the Dodgers if a black player was on the team. Rickey knew there would be problems—big problems. So he selected a player who was strong enough to take insults without fighting back. That player was Jackie Robinson.

Before Robinson put on a Dodger uniform, he promised Rickey he wouldn't fight or argue or cause any kind of trouble. Rickey knew that if anything happened, some white people wouldn't even consider who was really at fault. Instead, they would just say, "Jackie Robinson is a troublemaker. Throw him out of the majors."

Can you imagine how much courage it took not to fight back and argue? Can you imagine what it would be like to know that you're as good as any other player on the field and listen to people call you names? ♦

During that game with the Phillies, every player on the Dodgers knew that Robinson had made a bargain with Rickey. They could see he had a lot of courage because he was keeping the bargain. So when the Phillies kept calling Robinson names, the second baseman for the Dodgers, Eddie Stanky, told the Phillies, "Why don't you yell at somebody who can answer back?" Then the Dodger shortstop, Pee Wee Reese, went over and put his arm around Robinson's shoulder. He was showing everybody he was on Robinson's side.

I started to get on Robinson's side, too. There was no way the Phillies could call him names. Robinson was a Dodger, and as far as I was concerned, I was going to stick up for him against the whole Phillies team.

After that game, I became one of Robinson's biggest fans. He was something to watch. He seemed to stir up the whole team and make all the players play better. Sure, he could hit the ball. But when he got on base, that's when the action really started. He could steal a base as fast as you can blink your eye. He'd drive the pitchers on the other teams crazy. One pitcher said that when he pitched to Robinson, he would rather have him hit a home run than get a base hit. He said that with Robinson on the bases, he'd get so nervous he could hardly pitch for the rest of the inning. ✦

Jackie Robinson stealing second base

The Dodgers really started to play great ball in 1947, and the player most responsible for the team's success was Jackie Robinson. It wasn't just his batting and his base stealing that fired up the team. It was the man. He was a fierce competitor, and he played baseball as if his life depended on it. The other Dodger players seemed to pick up this fierce way of playing. They were daring and confident. You never saw anybody loafing on that team.

Robinson played so well and became such a leader that the Dodgers won the National League pennant in 1947. Near the end of the season they had a Jackie Robinson Day at Ebbets Field. Before the game, people made speeches about Robinson and how much they admired him. When it was Robinson's turn to talk, the crowd cheered long and loud.

After winning the National League pennant, the Dodgers played the New York Yankees in the World Series. I don't want to talk about that series, because the Yankees won it. But the Dodgers still had a great year. Best of all, they had a new star— Jackie Robinson.

When the 1947 season was over, the National League gave Robinson the Rookie of the Year award. That winter, I did a lot of reading about Jackie Robinson. I read just about everything I could find. And the more I read, the more I realized how much courage that man had.

E COMPARING ACCOUNTS

Work the items.

Account A

The other day I went to the place where Ebbets Field used to stand. It's not there anymore. There's nothing but city there now. But when I stood on the corner where the entrance used to be, I had a strange feeling. It was almost as if the clock had turned back to 1947. I could almost see Ebbets Field, with a line of fans waiting to get in. I could almost hear the great roar that came from the stands when a Dodger hit a home run.

Account B

The Brooklyn Dodgers played in Ebbets Field from 1913 to 1957. The field was located in the Flatbush area of Brooklyn, New York City. Ebbets Field was the smallest stadium in the National League, and it was very hard to park near the field. For these and other reasons, the Dodgers moved to Los Angeles after the 1957 season. Ebbets Field was torn down in 1960 and replaced by apartment buildings.

1. What does *account A* focus on?

2. What does *account B* focus on?

3. Is Ebbets Field still standing?

4. Is item 3 answered by *account A* only; *account B* only; *both* accounts; or *neither* account?

5. In what year did the Dodgers first play in Ebbets Field?

6. Is item 5 answered by *account A* only; *account B* only; *both* accounts; or *neither* account?

7. How did Ebbets Field compare to other stadiums in the National League?

8. Is item 7 answered by *account A* only; *account B* only; *both* accounts; or *neither* account?

F COMPREHENSION

Write the answers.

1. How did Branch Rickey want to change major league baseball?

2. What agreement did Jackie Robinson make with Rickey before the 1947 season?

3. Use details from the biography to explain how Robinson kept that agreement during the game with the Phillies.

4. Why did pitchers get so nervous when Robinson got on base?

5. Use details from the biography to explain what qualities Robinson had that inspired the Dodgers to play great baseball.

G WRITING

Write a passage that answers this main question:

- Do you think Robinson made the right choice when he promised Rickey that he would take insults without fighting back?

Use details from the biography to answer these other questions in your passage:

1. What would some people think if Robinson did fight back?

2. What else might happen if Robinson did fight back?

3. What happened when Robinson didn't fight back?

Write at least six sentences.

END OF LESSON 74

A | WORD LISTS

1 | Hard Words

1. complain
2. George
3. Georgia
4. orchard

2 | Types of Schools

1. high school
2. junior college
3. college
4. university

3 | Types of Degrees

1. associate degree
2. bachelor's degree
3. advanced degree

4 | Vocabulary Words

1. long jump
2. mechanic
3. Olympics
4. punt
5. quarterback
6. schedule

B | SCHOOLS AND DEGREES

1. When you finish eighth grade or ninth grade, you will go to **high school.** High school ends when you finish twelfth grade. You can go to several types of schools after you finish high school.

2. A **junior college** is a two-year school where you can get an **associate degree.**

3. A **college** is a four-year school where you can get a **bachelor's degree.**

4. A **university** is a school where you can get both a **bachelor's degree** and an **advanced degree.**

C VOCABULARY DEFINITIONS

1. **long jump**—When athletes compete in a *long jump*, they run up to a line and jump as far as they can.
- What are athletes competing in when they run up to a line and jump as far as they can?

2. **mechanic**—A *mechanic* is a person who fixes automobiles and other machines.
- What do we call a person who fixes automobiles and other machines?

3. **Olympics**—The *Olympics* is a festival where athletes from all over the world compete in different types of sports. The Olympics occur in both the summer and the winter.
- What do we call a festival where athletes from all over the world compete in different types of sports?

4. **punt**—In football, a *punt* is a type of kick. A player from one team punts the football toward the other team. A player from the other team tries to catch the football and return the punt.
- In football, what is a punt?

5. **quarterback**
- What does the *quarterback* on a football team do?

6. **schedule**—When you *schedule* an event, you figure out where and when the event will happen.
- Here's another way of saying *Benito figured out where and when the meeting would happen: Benito scheduled the meeting.*
- What's another way of saying *The teacher figured out where and when a field trip would happen?*

D READING INFORMATIONAL TEXT: Biography

Jackie Robinson

Chapter 3

I began to read everything I could find about Jackie Robinson, and I learned a lot. I learned he was born in a small town in Georgia. When Robinson was still a baby, his mother moved the family to California. Robinson had three older brothers and an older sister. There was a lot of love in that family, but there was little money. The Robinsons were so poor that they sometimes did not have enough to eat.

Even though there was a lot of love in the family, you still wonder how Robinson ever made it. If you looked at Robinson a few years later, you'd have even more doubts that he'd ever be able to climb out of the world he lived in. When he was a young teenager, he became a member of a street gang—the Pepper Street Gang. They'd throw things at cars on the street. They'd knock out street lights at night. They'd go into nearby orchards and pick fruit from the trees. And sometimes they'd get caught by the police.

Robinson's mother didn't like what was happening to her son, but he wanted to belong to a group. He wanted to be like some of the other kids in the neighborhood.

An auto mechanic named Carl Anderson helped Robinson look at the world in a different way. Anderson worked near Robinson's house. One day, he heard Robinson complaining to his mother that all the other kids were in the gang, so why shouldn't he be? Anderson told Robinson, "You're behaving just like a sheep." Anderson explained that sheep are stupid animals because they all follow one sheep without even thinking. Then he told Robinson, "You've got a good head, so use it—unless you want to be like a stupid sheep."

Robinson remembered what Anderson had said, so he started playing sports. One of Robinson's older brothers, Mack, was already a talented athlete. When Mack went to junior college, he set a record by jumping 25 feet.

Later, Mack went to the Olympics and won a silver medal in the 200-meter dash. Let me tell you, that young man had talent. ♦

Robinson imitated everything his brothers did. He ran; he jumped; he practiced. In high school, he played football, basketball, and baseball. He was a star in all three sports.

After high school, Robinson went to a junior college. By now, sports were his whole life. He was a quarterback on the football team. In basketball, he was also a star. During one basketball game, he scored a record number of points. In baseball, he was named the most valuable player in his junior college league. As you might guess, he was also a star in track.

One day showed just what a fierce competitor Robinson was. There was a baseball

Jackie Robinson competing in the long jump while at UCLA

game scheduled in one city and a track meet in another city 40 miles away. These events were scheduled at the same time, and Robinson was on both the baseball team and the track team. The track coach asked Robinson which sporting event he wanted to compete in. Robinson said, "Both." And he did compete in both.

The track coach arranged for Robinson to compete in the long jump early, before the other events. The idea was for Robinson to compete in the long jump, get into a waiting car, be driven 40 miles, and play in the baseball game, which would already be under way. So Robinson did his first long jump. It was a good jump, a little over twenty-three feet. That was enough to win the event.

But Robinson wasn't satisfied. He said, "I can do better than that." So he jumped again. The second jump was more than a foot farther than the first.

The driver who was taking Jackie to the baseball game said, "Fantastic. Now let's get out of here."

Robinson shook his head and said, "I can do better than that." So he went for his third try. And what do you think? He jumped twenty-five feet, six and a half inches—more than half a foot farther than the record set by his brother Mack.

Finally, Robinson darted off the field, jumped into the car, and changed into his baseball uniform on the way to the game. There were only five innings left by the time they got there, but Robinson still managed to get two hits and help his team to a victory.

When Robinson finished junior college, he decided to go on to the University of California at Los Angeles (UCLA), which was close to his family's home. Robinson had a lot of reasons for going to UCLA, but the main reason was his brother Frank.

Unlike Jackie and Mack, Frank wasn't a star athlete. But he could coach, and he spent a lot of time working with Jackie, particularly when Jackie was getting started in high school and junior college. So Jackie chose UCLA because it was close to Frank.

This part of Robinson's story has a sad ending. While Robinson was at UCLA, Frank was killed in an accident. That made Robinson feel terrible, but he turned his sadness into strength, and he played football, basketball, and baseball, and he ran track better than ever.

In football, Robinson set a college record for returning punts, and he led the team in scoring. In basketball, he was the top scorer in UCLA's league, even though he didn't get to play in all the games. In track, he was the best long jumper. Strangely enough, the sport he did the worst in was baseball. He was great when he got on base, but he didn't bat well.

Robinson was the first athlete in the history of UCLA to play on four teams— football, basketball, baseball, and track. In 1941, he was considered the best all-round college athlete in the United States. He could do anything. If any person ever deserved a chance to play professional baseball with the best players in the world, it was Jackie Robinson.

But Robinson was black, and in 1941, black athletes weren't allowed to play in the major leagues. Those leagues were only for white players.

E COMPREHENSION

Write the answers.

1. When he was in the Pepper Street Gang, how was Robinson like a sheep?

2. One day, Robinson competed in both a track meet and a baseball game. What did that show about his character?

3. Use details from the biography to explain why Robinson's choice of going to UCLA had a sad ending.

4. The biography says that when Robinson was at UCLA, "Strangely enough, the sport he did the worst in was baseball." Why is that so strange?

5. Why couldn't Robinson play in the major leagues in 1941?

F WRITING

- Today's chapter shows part of a conversation where Carl Anderson tries to convince Jackie Robinson to leave the Pepper Street Gang.

Write an imaginary conversation between Anderson and Robinson.

- Begin when Anderson tells Jackie "You're behaving just like a sheep."

- You can use statements from the chapter in your conversation. Your conversation should also answer these questions:

1. How is Robinson's behavior like a sheep's behavior?

2. Why does Robinson like belonging to the gang?

3. What could Robinson belong to instead?

4. How does the conversation end?

- Use this format:

Anderson: You're behaving just like a sheep.

Robinson: (Show Robinson's reply.)

Anderson: (Show Anderson's reply.)

(Have Anderson and Robinson talk back and forth until the end.)

Write at least six sentences.

A WORD LISTS

1 | Hard Words

1. miner
2. minor
3. Negro leagues
4. regardless

2 | Names

1. Germany
2. Hawaii
3. Japan
4. Montreal
5. Pearl Harbor
6. Rachel Isum

3 | Vocabulary Words

1. career
2. decent
3. officer
4. organization
5. restricted to
6. scout

B VOCABULARY DEFINITIONS

1. **officer**—In an army, an *officer* is a person who commands soldiers. Officers in the United States Army include lieutenants, captains, majors, colonels, and generals.

2. **organization**—Sometimes a business is called an *organization.*
   • What's another name for a business?

3. **scout**—A baseball *scout* is a person who looks for players that a baseball team might hire.

C VOCABULARY FROM CONTEXT

1. Eva was so interested in working as a coach that she decided to make coaching her **career.**

2. Jobs were so hard to find that Gamal couldn't earn a **decent** living.

3. The hotels were **restricted to** white people, so no other people could go into them.

Jackie Robinson
Chapter 4

In 1941, Jackie Robinson was a big college star, but his family was still poor. His brother Mack could only find odd jobs, like cleaning up yards. A couple of years before, Mack had been the pride of the United States, winner of a medal in the Olympics. But now he couldn't even get a decent job. Why? Because he was black, and there weren't many good jobs for black people.

Jackie thought about his family and said to himself, "There is no point in continuing with this sports career." What would he get for the hours he put into practicing? What difference would it make that he had more sports talent than just about anybody in the world? He was black, and black players didn't play major league baseball, major league football, or any other major league sport. They could only play in the Negro leagues. The players in those leagues didn't earn much money, and they led a tough life.

So Jackie quit school and took a job, and then another job. Then, on Sunday, December 7, 1941, something terrible happened. The Japanese attacked Pearl Harbor, which is in Hawaii. On the same day, the United States declared war against Japan and Germany. The United States was now fighting in World War Two.

The day the United States entered World War Two was a sad day. I remember sitting by the radio all day long, listening to the news. At first, we figured that the war would be over in a couple of months, but it lasted until 1945.

In the spring of 1942, Jackie joined the United States Army. He was such a strong leader that he became an officer at an Army camp in Kansas. Black soldiers at the camp weren't allowed to sit next to white soldiers in the snack bar. Instead, the black soldiers had to eat in a small section that didn't have enough seats.

Jackie complained to the Army about the way black soldiers were treated at the camp. Finally, the Army increased the number of seats for black soldiers, but they still had to eat in their own section. ♦

When Jackie got out of the Army in 1944, he wanted to marry a young woman named Rachel Isum. She was studying to be a nurse, and she had known Jackie since he'd been at UCLA.

Rachel lived in California, and Jackie wanted to be near her, but he couldn't get a good sports job in California. So in 1945, he went to Kansas City and took a job with the most famous Negro League team—the Kansas City Monarchs. Jackie earned more money than he had in other jobs, but when the Monarchs went from city to city, it was the same old story. The team could not stay in the same hotels white people stayed in. Often the players had to sleep in the team bus. In some cities, the players couldn't even eat in restaurants because the restaurants were restricted to white people. So the players ate sandwiches on the bus.

After a while, Jackie got tired of traveling with the Monarchs. He didn't get to see

Jackie Robinson in his Kansas City Monarchs uniform

Rachel very often because he was moving around all the time, so he decided to quit the Monarchs, go back to California, and try to get a job there. In the back of his mind, he had a great desire to play major league baseball. But that didn't seem possible. To Jackie, it seemed that as long as he stayed in baseball, he would go from city to city in the Monarchs' bus and feel like somebody who didn't really belong anywhere.

Just when Jackie was about to quit the Monarchs, something happened that changed his whole life. The Monarchs were playing in Chicago. One of the baseball scouts from the Brooklyn Dodgers told Jackie that Branch Rickey, the team president of the Dodgers, was thinking of starting a new league for black players. The scout told Jackie that this league would pay the players more money and offer better living conditions. Jackie was interested, so he agreed to meet with Rickey.

Rickey wasn't really thinking of forming a new league. Instead, he wanted his scouts to find an outstanding black baseball player for the major leagues. This player had to have enough courage to stand up against the trouble he would experience as the first black player. Rickey wanted a player who could thrill the crowd with his skill. He wanted a player who would be a leader and who wouldn't quit.

Rickey had been looking at many black players. But when he met with Jackie Robinson, he knew he had found the right man. He already knew a lot about Jackie from his scouts' reports. He knew Jackie was smart, that he was brave, and that his coaches admired him.

Imagine how Jackie felt on that day in August 1945 when he walked into Rickey's office. Jackie had almost accepted the idea that he would never play in the major leagues. Imagine how he felt when he heard Rickey say, "I'll tell you the real reason you're here. You were brought here to play for the Dodger organization. I want you to start with our top minor league team, the Montreal Royals. If you do well, you'll get to play for the Brooklyn Dodgers."

Jackie sat there shocked, trying to make sense out of what Rickey had told him. The Montreal Royals were the best minor league team in the whole Dodger organization. Every year, the best players from the Royals and other minor league teams would move up to the major leagues.

Then Rickey and Jackie talked about how hard it would be for Jackie to be the first black player in the major leagues. Rickey said, "I need someone who is strong enough to take insults without fighting back." He told Jackie that white people would be watching him. If Jackie got into the slightest trouble, many of them would blame him, regardless of whose fault the trouble really was.

"It's not going to be easy," Rickey said. And it certainly wasn't.

Jackie Robinson signing a contract with Branch Rickey

E COMPREHENSION

Write the answers.

1. Use details from the biography to explain why Jackie decided to quit school when he was at UCLA.

2. When Jackie was in the Army, how did he improve conditions for black soldiers?

3. How were players on the Monarchs treated differently from white people?

4. What did Branch Rickey want his scouts to find?

5. Why did Rickey want Jackie to take insults without fighting back?

F WRITING

- Today's chapter shows only part of the conversation between Branch Rickey and Jackie Robinson.

Write the whole conversation between Rickey and Robinson.

You can use statements from the biography in your conversation. Also use details from the biography to answer these questions in your conversation:

1. What challenges will Jackie face?

2. How does Robinson feel about those challenges?

3. How does Rickey want Robinson to handle those challenges?

4. What plan do they agree to at the end?

Use this format:

- Rickey: (Show the first thing Rickey says.)

- Robinson: (Show Robinson's reply.)

- (Have Rickey and Robinson talk back and forth until the end.)

Write at least six sentences.

A WORD LISTS

1 Hard Words	**2** Vocabulary Review	**3** Vocabulary Words
1. dribble	1. career	1. balk
2. fielding	2. decent	2. contract / contract
3. release	3. officer	3. cousin
	4. organization	4. stadium
	5. restricted	
	6. scout	

B VOCABULARY DEFINITIONS

1. **balk**—When a baseball pitcher pretends to throw a pitch, the play is illegal, and it's called a *balk*.
The penalty for making a balk is that any runners who are on base get to advance one base.

2. **contract**—A written agreement is called a *contract*, which is pronounced *CON-tract*.
• What is a written agreement called?

3. **cousin**—A child of your aunt or your uncle is called your *cousin*.
• If two children have the same grandparents, are the children cousins?

4. **stadium**—A large building that surrounds a sports field is called a *stadium*.
• What's another way of saying *Ebbets Field*?

Jackie Robinson
Chapter 5

During their meeting, Branch Rickey made it very plain that Jackie Robinson would have a tough time playing for the Montreal Royals. He said Jackie would be all alone and the other players would resent him. The last thing he said was that Jackie should marry Rachel. Then he added, "You're going to need her with you from now on." A few months later, in February 1946, Jackie and Rachel were married in Los Angeles.

When word got out that Jackie had signed a contract with Montreal, all the papers carried the story. In March 1946, Jackie joined the Royals for spring training in Florida. For a while, Rachel was just about the only friend Jackie had.

The first time Jackie walked into the locker room with the other Montreal players, he tried to be friendly, but they didn't

Jackie and Rachel Robinson on their wedding day

talk to him. The coaches and trainers talked to him, but not the other players.

Each day Jackie got dressed in his new uniform and walked onto the field. He saw the wives of the players sitting in the stands and watching the practice. Then he saw Rachel sitting all by herself. Jackie was hurt and angry. There she was, the person he loved more than anybody in the world, and the other wives wouldn't even talk to her.

Rachel would smile at Jackie and wave. He would smile and wave back. Jackie knew he wasn't the only one who had to be brave. One day Jackie told Rachel he hated to see her treated that way. But she smiled, shook her head, and said, "Don't worry. Life will soon be better for us. And thanks to you, life will soon be better for all black athletes." ♦

That is what Jackie had to keep reminding himself—that he would make things better for other black athletes. Every time he wanted to fight, and every time he didn't think he could take it anymore, he remembered that he was doing something important. He told himself that even though he had to suffer, he was doing something that could help other black players. So he worked and worked, and he worked even harder.

One day, the Royals played a practice game with the Dodgers. At first, the fans yelled at Jackie. He was scared, but he was also determined.

Jackie was in the field, playing second base. A Dodger batter smashed a fast ground ball that looked like a hit. Jackie raced for the ball, scooped it up, and in one quick motion, fired it to the first baseman. The batter was out, and people in the stands started to say things like, "Did you see that man move?" and "What speed!" Jackie made a lot of dazzling plays in that game, and the fans were impressed.

The first game Montreal played after spring training in Florida was held across the river from New York City. The Royals played a minor league team called the Jersey City Giants. The stadium was crowded with people who had come to see Jackie. The first time Jackie was up to bat, these people didn't have much to cheer about. He tapped a little ground ball that dribbled toward the shortstop. Out!

But the next time Jackie was up, he brought all the fans to their feet. Two Montreal players were on base. The pitcher threw Jackie a sizzling fast ball. Crack! By the sound of the bat, the fans knew the ball was gone. There it went, a shot over the left field fence. It was a home run, with three players scoring. When Jackie crossed home plate, both players who had just scored shook his hand and slapped him on the back. ✦

The next time Jackie was up, he got on first base with a hit. Before the pitcher settled down, Jackie stole second base, and the crowd went wild. On the next pitch, Jackie stole third base. The pitcher got so rattled with Jackie dancing around on third base that he pretended to make a pitch. That's a balk, which meant that Jackie could walk to home plate and score.

The crowd cheered and shouted. That game showed the kind of baseball that Jackie could play. He was daring and always ready to take a chance. He was so good at stealing bases that the other team couldn't throw the ball fast enough to get him out.

When Jackie arrived in Montreal after the Royals had won three games on the road, the fans loved him, and he loved the city.

There were still rough times ahead for Jackie. During one game, a player in the other team's dugout put a black cat onto the field and yelled, "Hey, Jackie, there's your cousin!"

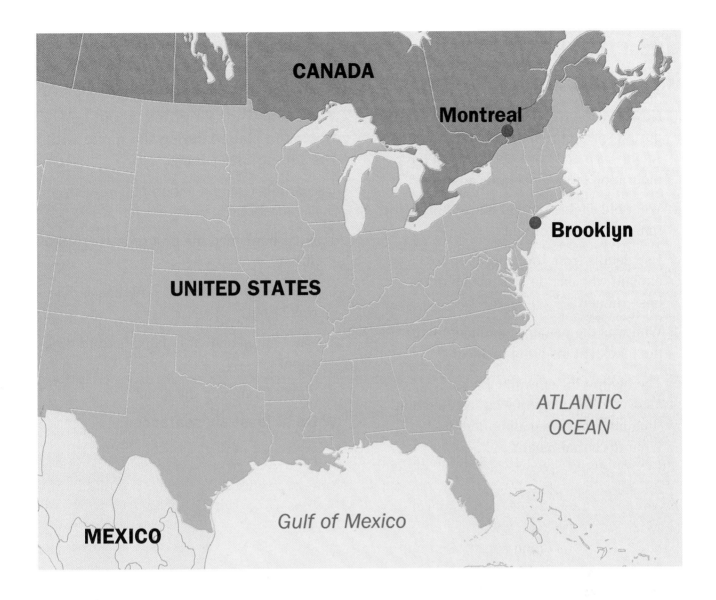

Jackie looked over at the cat and said nothing. But a few moments later he was at bat, and he made his bat do all his talking for him. He smashed the ball and ran like a streak to second base. When one of the Montreal players hit a single, Jackie scored. As he went past the dugout of the other team, he said in a very pleasant tone, "Well, I guess my cousin is pretty happy now."

By the end of the season, Jackie had answered every player on the other teams who insulted him. He answered in a language they all understood. The Montreal Royals won their minor league pennant, and Jackie Robinson was the top batter in the league.

D COMPREHENSION

Write the answers.

1. How was the treatment Rachel received during spring training like the treatment Jackie received? Use details from the biography to support your answer.

2. What did Jackie remind himself of every time he wanted to fight?

3. Use details from the biography to explain why Jackie was such a great base runner.

4. Why was the player's comment about the black cat insulting to Jackie?

5. The biography says that Jackie answered the players who insulted him "in a language they all understood." What does that mean?

E WRITING

• Pretend you are a sports reporter.

Write a newspaper article about how Robinson played during the game with the Jersey City Giants.

Use details from the biography to answer these questions in your article:

1. What happened the first time Jackie was at bat?

2. What happened the second time Jackie was at bat?

3. What happened after Jackie's third time at bat?

4. Which team won the game?

Write at least six sentences.

END OF LESSON 77

A WORD LISTS

1 Hard Words	2 Vocabulary Review	3 Vocabulary Words
1. horizontally	1. balk	1. defeat
2. Kentucky	2. contract	2. deposit
3. Louisville	3. cousin	3. flamingo
4. typically	4. stadium	4. honor
		5. oppose

B VOCABULARY DEFINITIONS

1. **defeat**—When you beat somebody in a game, you *defeat* that person.
- What's another way of saying *She beat him at checkers?*

2. **deposit**—When you put an object in a place, you *deposit* the object in that place.
- What's another way of saying *They put their money in a bank?*

3. **flamingo**—A *flamingo* is a tall wading bird with long legs and a long neck.
- What is a flamingo?

4. **honor**—An award you receive for good work is called an *honor*.
- What is an award you receive for good work called?

5. **oppose**—When you're against something, you *oppose* that thing.
- What's another way of saying *Some people are against taxes?*

Jackie Robinson
Chapter 6

After the Montreal Royals won their minor league pennant, they played a team from Louisville, Kentucky, in the Junior World Series. The first team to win four games would win the series, which began with three games in Louisville. In those three games, Jackie Robinson got only one hit, and the Royals lost twice.

Jackie was worried about how the fans in Montreal would respond to him now that the Royals were behind in the series two games to one. He was in for a pleasant surprise when the Royals came back to Montreal. The Royals won the Junior World Series four games to two after defeating the Louisville team in three straight games.

Jackie had changed the minds of many people in Montreal. The manager of the Royals had been strongly opposed to having a black player on the team. That was before the beginning of the season. At the end of the season, the manager told Jackie, "You're a great baseball player and a fine gentleman. It's been wonderful having you on the team."

The next year was 1947, which was when I began watching Jackie. For me, it was all new. Sure, I had read some of the reports about Jackie before I saw him play. But he was just so many numbers on a piece of paper. The numbers told me that the man could bat, steal bases, play the field, and win. But still, when I saw him for the first time, I had my doubts.

By the end of Jackie's first season, I was singing a different tune, along with the rest of the Brooklyn fans. We were behind Jackie all the way as he led the Dodgers to a National League pennant. And we stayed behind him for ten years. I remember how proud I was of him each time he earned a new honor, particularly in 1949. In that year, the Dodgers won the National League pennant again, and Jackie was the league's batting champion. He was also named the league's most valuable player.

By 1949, other teams were bringing black players into the major leagues, and that made Jackie feel good. Also during that year, Branch Rickey released Jackie from his promise not to fight back. Rickey said, "You've proved that you're a great player. So now you can do what you want." ♦

During the years that followed, Jackie received honor after honor, and he earned every one of them. He was named to the All-Star Team year after year, and during many of those years, the Dodgers won the National League pennant. But after winning the

pennant, they'd play the New York Yankees in the World Series and lose.

By 1955, people were saying that Jackie was getting too old for the game. He didn't play much during that year, but the Dodgers still made it to the World Series with the Yankees.

The Yankees took the first two games. In the third game, Jackie came to bat with the score tied at two. Most fans cheered encouragement to him, but a few said, "What's Old Man Robinson doing out there?"

They found out. He hit a single. Now he was on base, and now the old magic started. Jackie danced around so much that the pitcher hit the next batter with a pitch. That batter went to first base because he had been hit by a pitch, so Jackie moved up to second base.

The next batter got a single and Jackie shot to third. The bases were now loaded. Jackie kept running toward home plate and stopping. The pitcher became so rattled that he walked the next batter.

Jackie walked home, and the crowd went wild.

The next time Jackie got up to bat, he slugged a clean double, but he stretched it into a triple. He scored when the next batter got a hit. The Dodgers won that game and the next two games. Finally, in the seventh and last game of the Series, Brooklyn won. I couldn't believe it. I never thought I'd see Brooklyn win the World Series, but they did, for the first and only time. ★

People celebrated all over Brooklyn. For a week, every time I'd look at one of the guys at work, we'd smile at each other. We didn't have to say anything. Thanks to Jackie, Brooklyn had won the World Series.

After the 1956 season, Jackie retired from baseball. He was 37 years old, and he had slowed down a lot. I wrote him a letter

Jackie Robinson scoring a run during a Dodgers game

after he retired. I told him I thought he was the greatest and that I'd miss him. He wrote back and thanked me for my letter.

I still have Jackie's letter, and I have a lot of pictures of Jackie and a lot of books about him. But, most of all, I have memories. I've got happy memories, like the memory of Jackie being elected to the Baseball Hall of Fame. I've got sad memories, like the memory of Jackie's son being killed in a car accident in 1971.

The saddest memory of all is of Jackie's death in 1972, just a few days after the Dodgers retired the number he wore on his uniform—42. He was only 53 years old when he died. One of the men I worked with came over and said, "A brave man is dead."

That's what Jackie was, a brave man who could teach all of us about the meaning of the word *courage*. You can search the world over for a person who has more strength, courage, and talent than Jackie Robinson. You're not going to find one. One sportswriter did a good job of describing Jackie in two sentences. The sportswriter wrote, "He would not be defeated. Not by the other team and not by life."

D COMPREHENSION

Write the answers.

1. In this chapter, the narrator describes three of Jackie Robinson's seasons with the Dodgers: 1947, 1949, and 1955. Which season do you think was Jackie's best? Use evidence from the chapter to explain your answer.

2. In 1949, Branch Rickey released Jackie Robinson from his promise not to fight back. Why had Jackie made that promise in the first place?

3. Use details from the biography to explain how Jackie Robinson proved he wasn't too old to play in the 1955 World Series.

4. One of the narrator's friends said that Jackie Robinson was a brave man. What are some examples of Jackie's bravery?

5. One sports writer said, "He would not be defeated. Not by the other team and not by life." What do those sentences mean?

E WRITING

• After Jackie Robinson retired, the narrator wrote him a letter.

Write the narrator's letter to Jackie Robinson.

Use details from the biography to answer these questions in your letter:

1. How did your opinion of Jackie change during his career?

2. Which of Jackie's accomplishments were the most impressive?

3. What did you learn from Jackie?

Write at least six sentences.

A WORD LISTS

1 Hard Words	2 Related Words	3 Vocabulary Words	4 Vocabulary Words
1. delicate	1. coast	1. cycle	1. lumbered
2. jellyfish	2. coastal	2. horizontally	2. polluted
3. lily	3. coastline	3. photosynthesis	3. settle
		4. rhizome	4. typically

B VOCABULARY DEFINITIONS

1. **cycle**—A repeating series of events is called a *cycle*. For example, a day is a cycle that begins at sunrise, continues through morning, afternoon, and night, and ends at sunrise the next morning.
- What is the cycle of seasons, beginning with spring?

2. **horizontally**—If something moves *horizontally*, it moves from side to side. It does not move in a vertical line. It moves in a horizontal line.
- What's another way of saying *The water moved from side to side across the table?*

3. **photosynthesis**—*Photosynthesis* is a process where green plants use sunlight to make food for the plant.
- What's the process that green plants use to make food for the plant?

4. **rhizome**—A *rhizome* is a plant stem that grows underground in a horizontal line.
- What do we call a plant stem that grows underground in a horizontal line?

C VOCABULARY FROM CONTEXT

1. The 300-pound turtle **lumbered** along the beach.

2. Some parts of the ocean are **polluted** because people have dumped garbage or oil into the water.

3. The young turtles **settle** close to shore, where they will live for the next ten years or more.

4. People **typically** work from 9 in the morning to 5 at night.

The Life Cycle

The life cycle of plants and animals goes around and around. The life cycle of birds, for example, begins when baby birds hatch out of eggs. The babies stay in their nest until they're old enough to fly away. Then the birds leave the nest and find mates. The birds and their mates build nests, and the female bird lays eggs in the nest. Then new baby birds hatch out of the eggs, and the cycle begins again: around and around from eggs to birds to eggs.

The following passages about animals and plants from coastal Florida present more examples of life cycles.

Sea Turtles

The mother green sea turtle has finally lumbered all the way up the beach to the dry sand. She digs a hole in the sand with her flippers. Then she deposits more than a hundred round, white eggs into the hole. She thrashes her flippers again, covering the eggs with sand. Exhausted from her task, she drags herself back to the ocean.

Two months go by. The eggs under the sand crack open, and baby turtles hatch. They dig their way out of the sand and go as fast as they can to the ocean before gulls and other sea birds can catch them.

The young turtles who make it to the ocean drift there for several years. They are good hunters. With their strong beaks, they watch for mouthfuls of plants or jellyfish. Eventually they settle close to the shore of southern Florida, where they will live for the next ten years or more.

Life Cycle of a Sea Turtle

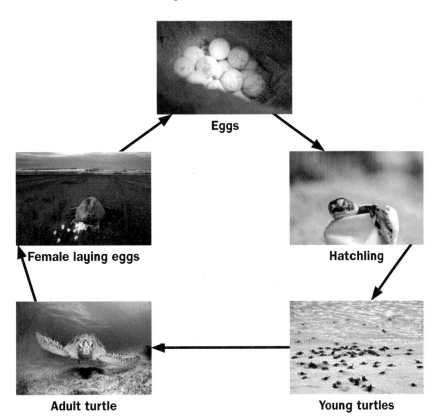

Eggs

Female laying eggs

Hatchling

Adult turtle

Young turtles

Someday the females will swim for hundreds of miles to a nesting beach. They will pull themselves out of the ocean to lay eggs, just as their mothers once did.

Turtle Grass

Sea turtles depend on sea grasses for food and for a place to live. Turtle grass is common in the warm waters near southern Florida, and sea turtles are at home in the underwater meadows of turtle grass.

The turtle grass clings to the ground with its roots and its rhizomes. A rhizome is a special stem that grows underground. The rhizome grows horizontally beneath the sea floor. New shoots come up from place to place along the rhizome. Each shoot grows into grass with roots.

Sea grasses have roots, leaves, and flowers, just like many land plants. Sea grass flowers are small and delicate. The flowers make it possible for sea grass to produce seeds, which grow into plants the same way grass grows from seeds in a garden. So turtle grass can spread by producing seeds and by producing rhizomes.

Turtle grass is like garden grass in another way: turtle grass depends on photosynthesis to make its food. The green leaves take in sunlight that shines through the water and use the light for photosynthesis.

Young sea turtles glide through the clear water around the turtle grass. Turtle grass roots and rhizomes hold the soil in place, so

Turtle grass roots and rhizomes

the water does not often get muddy. Many species of sea animals find food and shelter in this underwater meadow.

Not all of the coastal areas in Florida are this clean and healthy. Some areas are polluted because people have dumped garbage or oil into the water. Neither turtle grass nor turtles grow well in these polluted areas. ◆

Flamingos

Flamingos are tall wading birds that live in large flocks in coastal areas around the world. Hundreds of flamingos typically feed together in the shallow coastal waters of Florida. Many of these flamingos are pink.

Flamingos are like turtles because they both lay eggs. But unlike turtles, flamingos lay only one egg at a time. Flamingo parents take care of their egg until it hatches, and then they take care of their baby.

The mother and father flamingo build a cone-shaped mound of mud for their nest. After the mother lays an egg in the nest, the mother and father take turns sitting on the egg. Unlike a baby turtle, a baby flamingo, or chick, is helpless when it hatches. The chick has feathers that are gray and white, and it calls out in hunger. Both mother and father feed the chick a liquid similar to milk, called crop milk, that they produce inside their throat.

Within just a week, the chick leaves the nest. The chick's parents still feed it, but the chick spends its time with other chicks in a large group. Because flamingos live near shallow water, the chick quickly learns to swim. Soon the growing flamingo learns to eat like an adult. It plunges its head in the water and fills its mouth with plants and small animals. ★

During the dry season, the flock of flamingos must move to a new area where

Adult flamingo feeding crop milk to its chick

they can find food. Hundreds of them take to the air together, their long necks in front, their long legs behind, and their colorful wings flapping. They fly together until they reach a new area with food.

Water Lilies

The ponds where flamingos live are dotted with white and pink flowers with round, green leaves. These are water lilies, which grow in shallow ponds and at the edges of lakes. Like turtle grass, water lilies spread both by rhizomes and by seeds.

The lily's flower and leaves are above water, but its roots dig into the dirt bottom of the pond. A long stem connects the roots to the sweet-smelling flower and the leaves.

The lily's rhizome gradually spreads across the bottom of the pond. On the surface of the pond, a fruit begins to grow inside

Water lilies at the edge of a pond

the flower. The fruit is like a berry, and it has many seeds inside. When the fruit is ripe, the seeds drop into the water. Each seed may start a new water lily plant nearby.

Water lilies provide food and shelter for many kinds of animals. Deer and beaver eat the seeds, leaves, and roots. Fish and frogs hide under the wide, green leaves.

Summary

The life cycles of plants and animals are different in many ways, but they all have the same basic pattern. After a plant or animal is born, it grows up and produces more of its own type of plant or animal. These cycles repeat over and over again, filling our planet with life.

E CHARTS AND GRAPHS

Jackie Robinson's Home Runs

Like many baseball players, Jackie Robinson hit the most home runs per year during the middle part of his career. He hit about a dozen home runs per year when he first started playing with the Brooklyn Dodgers in the late 1940s. In the early 1950s, however, he boosted that total to almost 20 home runs per year. Then he dropped back down to about a dozen per year in the mid-1950s as his baseball career neared its end.

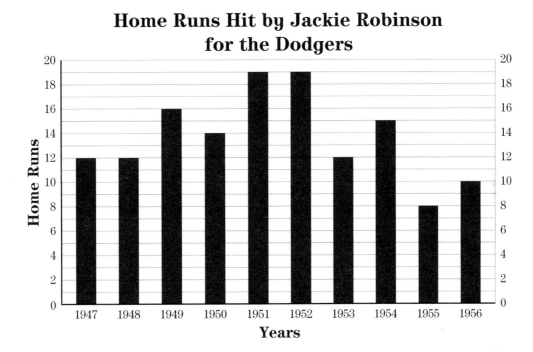

Home Runs Hit by Jackie Robinson for the Dodgers

Work the items.

1. In which year did Robinson hit the fewest home runs?

2. In which years did Robinson hit the most home runs?

3. For the most part, did the number of home runs Robinson hit per year *increase* or *decrease* from 1947 to 1951?

4. For the most part, did the number of home runs Robinson hit per year *increase* or *decrease* from 1952 to 1956?

5. In which part of his career did Robinson hit the most home runs per year: the beginning, the middle, or the end?

6. What information does the graph present that the passage does not present?

7. How does the graph help you understand the passage?

F COMPREHENSION

Write the answers.

1. Use details from the article to describe the life cycle of a female sea turtle, beginning when she is still in an egg.

2. Use details from the text to explain how turtle grass spreads by using rhizomes.

3. How do oceans near the coast get polluted?

4. How does an adult flamingo eat?

5. Name at least three ways that water lilies and turtle grass are the same.

G WRITING

Write a passage that describes the first few months of a flamingo's life.

Use details from the article to answer these questions in your passage:

1. How do the flamingo's parents prepare for its birth?

2. Who takes care of the baby flamingo at first? How?

3. Who does the flamingo spend time with after it leaves the nest?

4. When does the flamingo learn how to swim and eat like an adult?

5. What happens during the dry season?

Write at least six sentences.

END OF LESSON 79

A WORD LISTS

1 Hard Words	**2 Names**	**3 Vocabulary Words**
1. dandelion	1. Nathaniel	1. calculate
2. fragrance	2. Hawthorne	2. gleam
3. fragrant	3. Marygold	3. inhale
4. petal	4. Mediterranean	4. insane
5. perfume	5. Midas	5. sift
6. unreasonable		

B VOCABULARY FROM CONTEXT

1. Jed was always figuring things out. So when he looked at the gifts, he **calculated** what they must have cost.

2. The golden bowl was so bright and polished that it **gleamed** in the sunlight.

3. The swimmer breathed out quickly and then **inhaled** until her lungs were filled with air.

4. People thought that Gad's plan was **insane** because it made no sense.

5. The little girl poured sand into her hand and watched it **sift** through her fingers.

C STORY BACKGROUND

About Myths

Today you will begin reading "The Golden Touch," a myth that takes place thousands of years ago in Turkey, a country on the Mediterranean Sea.

A myth is an old, old story that often includes gods or goddesses. Many myths try to explain how the world began or where people came from. Other myths describe the adventures of ancient heroes or teach us lessons about how to behave.

"The Golden Touch" teaches us a lesson about gold. As you read the myth, think about what it means and if its lesson is still true today.

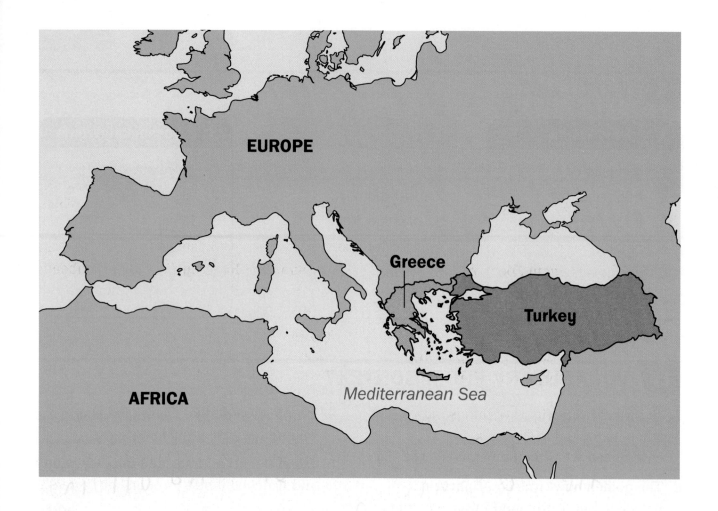

EUROPE

Greece

Turkey

AFRICA

Mediterranean Sea

D READING LITERATURE: Myth

The Golden Touch

Chapter 1

Once upon a time in ancient Turkey there lived a rich king named Midas, who had a daughter named Marygold.

King Midas was very fond of gold, and the only thing he loved more was his daughter. But the more Midas loved his daughter, the more he desired gold. He thought the best thing he could possibly do for his child would be to give her the largest pile of yellow, gleaming coins that had ever been heaped together since the world began. So Midas gave all his thoughts and all his time to collecting gold.

When Midas gazed at the gold-tinted clouds of sunset, he wished they were real gold and that they could be herded into his strong box. ✿ When little Marygold ran to meet him with a bunch of buttercups and dandelions, he used to say, "Pooh, pooh, child. If these flowers were as golden as they look, they would be worth picking."

Retold by Nathaniel Hawthorne.
Adapted for young readers.

And yet, in his earlier days, before he had this insane desire for gold, Midas had shown a great love for flowers. He had planted a garden with the biggest and sweetest roses any person ever saw or smelled. These roses were still growing in the garden, as large, as lovely, and as fragrant as they were when Midas used to pass whole hours looking at them and inhaling their perfume. But now, if he looked at the flowers at all, it was only to calculate how much the garden would be worth if each of the rose petals was a thin plate of gold. ♦

After a while, Midas became so unreasonable that he could scarcely bear to see or touch any object that was not gold. Therefore, he passed a large part of every day in a dark and dreary room in the basement of his palace. His gold was piled in the corners of this room in many different forms. Midas went to this dismal hole whenever he wanted to be particularly happy. After carefully locking the door, he would lift up a bag of gold coins or a golden bowl as big as a hat or a heavy golden bar or a bag of gold dust. He would bring his precious gold objects from the corners of the room into the one bright and narrow sunbeam that came from the window. He only liked the sunbeam because it made his treasure shine.

Midas would then count the coins in the bag or toss up the bar and catch it as it came down or sift the gold dust through his fingers. He would often look at the funny

reflection of his own face in the polished surface of a golden bowl. At those times, he would whisper to himself, "Oh, Midas, rich King Midas, what a happy man you are."

But it was strange to see how the reflection of his face kept grinning at him out of the polished surface of the bowl. It seemed to be aware of his foolish behavior and to make fun of him. ✦

Midas called himself a happy man, but he felt he was not as happy as he might be. His peak of enjoyment would never be reached unless the whole world became his treasure room, filled with his own gold.

One day, Midas was enjoying himself in his treasure room as usual when he noticed a shadow falling over the heaps of gold. He looked up and saw a stranger standing in the bright and narrow sunbeam. The stranger was a young man with a cheerful face. King Midas thought the smile on the stranger's face had a kind of golden glow. And even though the stranger blocked the sunshine, the gleam upon all the piled-up treasures was brighter than before. Even the corners were lit up when the stranger smiled.

Midas knew he had carefully turned the key in the lock and that no human being could possibly break into his treasure room. So Midas concluded that his visitor must be a god. In those days, gods interested themselves in the joys and sorrows of men, women, and children. Midas had met gods before, and he was happy to meet another. The stranger's face was so kind that it seemed as if he had come to do Midas a favor.

E COMPREHENSION

Write the answers.

1. Use details from the text to explain how Midas used to show his love for flowers.

2. When Midas looked at roses now, what would he calculate?

3. Use details from the story to describe the room where Midas went when he wanted to feel happy. Tell where it was located, what it looked like, and what it contained.

4. What was the only reason Midas liked the sunbeam in his treasure room?

5. Why did Midas think the stranger must be a god?

F WRITING

Write a passage that answers this main question:

• How did the love of gold affect Midas?

Use details from the story to answer these other questions in your passage:

1. What did Midas wish when he saw gold-tinted clouds at sunset?

2. Why did Midas think buttercups and dandelions weren't worth picking?

3. What did Midas think about when he looked at roses?

4. Where did Midas spend most of his time? Why?

5. What made Midas happy?

Write at least six sentences.

END OF LESSON 80

A WORD LISTS

1 | Hard Words

1. credit
2. purpose
3. usable
4. wealthy
5. woven

2 | Related Words

1. accompanied / unaccompanied
2. convenient / inconvenient
3. flexible / inflexible

3 | Word Endings

1. anxious
2. delicious
3. precious
4. spacious

4 | Vocabulary Words

1. deserve
2. envy
3. frenzy
4. linen

5 | Vocabulary Words

1. appetite
2. discontented
3. pity
4. secure

B VOCABULARY DEFINITIONS

1. **deserve**—When you *deserve* something, you are worthy of that thing.
- Here's another way of saying *They are worthy of praise: They deserve praise.*
- What's another way of saying *She is worthy of credit for solving the problem?*

2. **envy**—When you *envy* people, you wish you had something they have. If you wish you had a queen's wealth, you envy the queen for her wealth.
- What does it mean when you envy an athlete for his skill?

3. **frenzy**—When you do things in a *frenzy*, you do them in a hurried and excited way.
- Here's another way of saying *She ran around in excitement: She ran around in a frenzy.*
- What's another way of saying *They cooked dinner in a hurry?*

4. **linen**—*Linen* is an expensive cloth that some sheets and clothes are made of.
- What's an expensive cloth that some sheets and clothes are made of?

C VOCABULARY FROM CONTEXT

1. Danilo had a huge **appetite** when he started eating, but when he finished the main part of the meal, he had no room for dessert.

2. Nisha was unhappy about many things, but she was most **discontented** about the mess in the basement.

3. The little boy was so sad and cold that I felt great **pity** for him.

4. King Midas didn't want anybody to steal his treasure, so he looked for a **secure** place to keep it.

D READING LITERATURE: Myth

The Golden Touch

Chapter 2

The stranger gazed about the room, and when his glowing smile had shone on all the golden objects, he turned again to Midas.

"You are a wealthy man, friend Midas," he observed. "I doubt whether any other four walls on earth contain so much gold as this room contains."

"I have done pretty well—pretty well," answered Midas in a discontented tone. "But after all, it is a very small amount when you consider that it has taken me my whole life to gather this much gold. If I could live a thousand years, I might have enough time to grow rich."

"What?" exclaimed the stranger. "Then you are not satisfied?"

Midas shook his head.

"And what would satisfy you?" asked the stranger. "I would like to know."

Midas paused. He felt this stranger had the power to grant any wish. Midas could get whatever he wanted. So he thought and thought and thought. His imagination heaped up one golden mountain after another. But he was unable to imagine mountains that were big enough. At last, a bright idea occurred to King Midas. It seemed really as bright as the glistening metal he loved so much.

Raising his head, he looked the stranger in the face.

The visitor observed, "Well, Midas, I see you have at last hit on something that will satisfy you. Tell me your wish."

"It is only this," replied Midas. "I am weary of collecting my treasures with so much trouble and seeing the heap so small after I have done my best. I wish everything I touch could be changed into gold!"

"The Golden Touch!" exclaimed the stranger. "You certainly deserve credit, friend Midas, for having such a brilliant idea. But are you quite sure this will satisfy you?"

"How could it fail?" said Midas.

"And you will never regret having it?"

"What could make me regret it?" asked Midas. "I need nothing else to make me perfectly happy."

"You shall have your wish," replied the stranger, waving his hand in farewell. "Tomorrow at sunrise, you will find yourself gifted with the Golden Touch." ♦

The stranger then became so terribly bright that Midas closed his eyes. When he opened them again, he saw only one yellow sunbeam in the room. All around him was the glistening precious metal he had spent his life collecting.

Midas did not sleep well that night. His mind was like the mind of a child who has been promised a new plaything in the morning. Day had hardly peeped over the hills when King Midas was wide awake. He stretched his arms out of bed and began to touch objects that were within reach. He was anxious to prove whether the Golden Touch had really come, according to the stranger's promise.

Midas laid his finger on a chair by the bedside, and on other things, but he was disappointed to find they remained exactly the same as before. He was afraid he had only dreamed about the stranger or that the stranger had been making fun of him. And how miserable it would be if Midas had to be content with the little gold he could scrape together by ordinary means, instead of creating gold by a touch.

All this happened while it was only the gray of the morning, with only a streak of brightness along the edge of the sky. Midas was in a very bad mood. He kept growing sadder and sadder until the earliest sunbeam shone through the window and lit up the ceiling over his head. It seemed to Midas that this bright yellow sunbeam reflected in an unusual way on the white covering of the bed. Looking more closely, he was astonished and delighted to find that this linen cloth had been changed into woven gold, the purest and brightest he had ever seen! The Golden Touch had come to him with the first sunbeam!

Midas started up in a joyful frenzy and ran about the room grasping at everything that happened to be in his way. He seized one of the bedposts, and it immediately became a golden pillar. He pulled open a window curtain, and the cord grew heavy in his hand—a mass of gold. Midas took up a book from the table. At his first touch, the cover became solid gold. And when he ran his fingers through the pages, the book became a bundle of thin gold plates, and all the wise words in the book disappeared.

Midas quickly put on his clothes and was overjoyed to see himself in a magnificent suit of gold cloth. The cloth was flexible and soft, but it was heavy. Then Midas drew out his handkerchief, which little Marygold had made for him. That was also gold.

Somehow or other this last change did not quite please King Midas. He would have rather had his little daughter's handkerchief remain just as it was when she climbed upon his knee and put it into his hand.

But it was not worthwhile to worry about a handkerchief. Midas now took his spectacles from his pocket and put them on his nose to see more clearly. But he discovered that he could not possibly see

through them, for the glass had turned into a plate of yellow metal. They were worthless as spectacles, but valuable as gold. It seemed rather inconvenient to Midas that, with all his wealth, he could never again be rich enough to own a pair of usable spectacles.

"It is no great problem," he said to himself. "Every great good is accompanied by some small inconvenience. The Golden Touch is worth the loss of a pair of spectacles. My own eyes will serve for ordinary purposes, and little Marygold will soon be old enough to read to me."

Wise King Midas was so excited by his good fortune that the palace did not seem large enough for him. He therefore went downstairs, and he smiled when the handrail of the staircase became a bar of gold as his hand passed over it. He lifted the door latch. It was brass only a moment ago, but it became golden when his fingers left it. He went into the garden, where he found a great number of beautiful roses in full bloom and others in all the stages of lovely bud and blossom. Their fragrance was delicious in the morning breeze.

But Midas knew a way to make them far more precious, to his way of thinking. So he went from bush to bush and used his magic touch until every flower and bud was changed to gold. By the time this work was completed, King Midas was called to breakfast. The morning air had given him an excellent appetite, and he quickly returned to the palace.

Jackie Robinson's Rookie Year

1947 was a great year for Jackie Robinson. That's the year he started playing for the Brooklyn Dodgers and became a star. He was great in the field, but his most impressive achievements had to do with hitting the ball. He had more than 170 hits and more than 70 walks, which meant he was on base a lot. He also had very few strikeouts—less than 40. Those are great numbers, so great that he got the Rookie of the Year award from the National League.

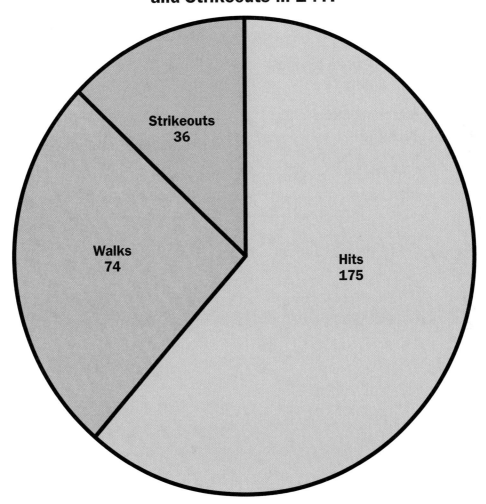

Jackie Robinson's Hits, Walks, and Strikeouts in 1947

Work the items.

1. How many hits did Robinson have in 1947?

2. How many walks did Robinson have in 1947?

3. How many strikeouts did Robinson have in 1947?

4. Is the combined number of Robinson's walks and strikeouts more than the number of hits?

5. How does the pie chart help you understand the passage about Robinson's rookie year?

F | COMPREHENSION

Write the answers.

1. Why did Midas decide to ask for the Golden Touch?

2. Do you think Midas made a good choice or a bad choice when he asked for the Golden Touch? Use details from the story to support your answer.

3. Use details from the story to explain what happened to the book that Midas touched.

4. Why wasn't Midas pleased when his handkerchief turned to gold?

5. What problems do you think Midas will have when he eats breakfast?

G | WRITING

Write a passage that compares what Midas's book and spectacles were like before and after they were turned into gold.

Use details from the story to answer the following questions in your passage:

1. How did Midas use those objects before he turned them into gold?

2. What made those objects valuable to Midas before they were turned into gold?

3. How can Midas use those objects now?

4. How valuable are those objects now?

Write at least six sentences.

END OF LESSON 81

A WORD LISTS

1 | Word Practice

1. appearance
2. breakfast
3. experiment
4. nimble
5. potato
6. woven

2 | Vocabulary Review

1. deserve
2. envy
3. frenzy
4. linen

3 | Vocabulary Words

1. grief
2. imitation
3. occupied
4. ornament
5. wither

B VOCABULARY FROM CONTEXT

1. All the kindergarten students felt **grief** when the class hamster died, and some even cried.

2. The new painting was such a good **imitation** of the old painting that it was hard to tell them apart.

3. Forrest was so **occupied** with the chess game that he didn't hear his phone ring.

4. The plate was covered with curvy lines, squiggles, and other **ornaments,** but it was still just a plate.

5. After the rose bloomed, it began to **wither,** and then it died.

C READING LITERATURE: Myth

The Golden Touch
Chapter 3

On this particular morning, King Midas's breakfast consisted of hotcakes, some nice little fish, roasted potatoes, fresh boiled eggs, and tea. There was also a bowl of bread and milk for his daughter, Marygold. This was a breakfast fit for a king!

Little Marygold had not yet made her appearance, so her father ordered her to be called. Then Midas seated himself at the table and waited for his daughter to arrive before beginning his own breakfast. Midas really loved his daughter, and he loved her even more this morning because of his good fortune. It was not long before he heard her coming along the hallway, crying bitterly.

Marygold's crying surprised Midas because she was almost always cheerful and hardly shed a spoonful of tears in a year. When Midas heard her sobs, he decided to put the girl into better spirits by giving her a surprise. So he leaned across the table and touched her pretty bowl. The bowl was instantly changed to gleaming gold, but because Midas did not touch the bread and milk, they did not change.

Meanwhile, Marygold slowly and sadly opened the door. She held her apron at her eyes and sobbed as if her heart would break.

Midas asked, "What is the matter with you this bright morning?"

Marygold, without taking the apron from her eyes, held out her hand and showed Midas one of the roses that had recently changed to gold.

"Beautiful!" exclaimed her father. "And what is there in that magnificent golden rose to make you cry?"

"Ah, dear Father," answered the child through her sobs. "It is not beautiful, but the ugliest flower that ever grew. As soon as I was dressed, I ran into the garden to gather some roses for you because I know you like them. But all the beautiful roses that smelled so sweet and had so many lovely colors are spoiled! They have become quite yellow, just like this one, and they no longer have any fragrance. What is the matter with them?" ♦

Midas said, "Pooh, my dear little girl. Please don't cry about it." Midas was ashamed to admit that he had brought about the change which saddened her. "Sit down and eat your bread and milk. But don't be sad. You can easily exchange the golden rose for an ordinary one that would wither in a day."

"I don't care for such roses as this!" cried Marygold, tossing it away. "It has no smell, and the hard petals stab my nose!"

The child now sat down at the table, but she was so occupied with her grief that she did not even notice the wonderful change in her bowl. Perhaps this was for the best. Marygold usually took pleasure in looking at the odd figures that were painted on the bowl, yet these ornaments were now entirely lost in the yellow metal.

Midas, meanwhile, had poured out a cup of tea, and the teapot, which had been brass, was gold when he set it down. He thought to himself that it was unusual to eat off golden plates, and he began to worry about keeping his treasures safe. The cupboard and the kitchen would no longer be a secure place to keep articles so valuable as golden bowls and teapots.

As he was thinking these thoughts, he lifted a spoonful of tea to his lips and, sipping it, was astonished to notice that the instant his lips touched the liquid, the tea became liquid gold, and the next moment, it hardened into a lump.

"Ugh!" Midas exclaimed.

"What is the matter, Father?" little Marygold asked, gazing at him with the tears still in her eyes.

"Nothing, child, nothing," said Midas. "Eat your bread and milk before they get cold."

He looked at one of the nice little fish on his plate and touched it with his golden fork and then experimented by touching its tail with his finger. To his horror, it immediately changed from a fried fish into a gold fish. But it was not like a goldfish that people often keep in fish bowls. It was a metal fish that looked as if it had been made by a goldsmith. Its little bones were now golden wires; its fins and tail were thin plates of gold; and there were the marks of the fork in it. It was a very pretty piece of work—except King Midas would rather have had a real fish in his dish instead of this valuable imitation. ★

He thought to himself, "I don't quite see how I am to eat any breakfast."

He took one of the hotcakes and had scarcely broken it when it turned yellow. If it had been an ordinary white hotcake, Midas would have prized it a good deal more than he now did. Almost in despair, he helped himself to a boiled egg, which immediately changed the same way the fish and hotcake had changed.

"Well, this is a problem," he thought, leaning back in his chair and looking with envy at Marygold as she ate her bread and milk with great satisfaction. Midas said to himself, "My breakfast is quite valuable, but I cannot eat it."

Midas thought he might solve his problem by moving faster. He snatched a hot potato and attempted to cram it into his mouth and swallow it in a hurry. But the Golden Touch was too nimble for him. He found his mouth full of solid metal, which so burnt his tongue that he roared aloud. He jumped up from the table and began to dance and stamp about the room, feeling both pain and fright.

"Father, dear Father," cried Marygold. "What is the matter? Have you burnt your mouth?"

"Ah, dear child," groaned Midas sadly. "I don't know what is to become of your poor father."

And truly Midas was a person you should pity. Here was the richest breakfast that could be set before a king, but its richness was worth absolutely nothing to Midas. The poorest farmer, sitting down to his crust of bread and cup of water, was far better off than King Midas, although the fine food that Midas had before him was worth its weight in gold. And what was he to do? Already, Midas was extremely hungry. How would he feel by dinnertime? How many days could he survive on golden food?

Midas's hunger and despair were so great that he groaned aloud and very sadly, too. Marygold could endure it no longer. She gazed at her father a moment to discover what was the matter with him. Then with a sweet and sorrowful desire to comfort him, she started from her chair. She ran to Midas and threw her arms about him. He bent down and kissed her. At that moment, he felt that his little daughter's love was worth a thousand times more than the Golden Touch.

"My precious, precious Marygold!" he cried.

But Marygold made no answer.

D COMPREHENSION

Write the answers.

1. Use details from the story to explain why Marygold disliked the golden roses.

2. The story says that Midas was a person you should pity. Use details from the story to explain why you should pity him.

3. Why was the poorest farmer better off than Midas?

4. At the end of the chapter, Midas feels that Marygold's love is worth a thousand times more than the Golden Touch. Use details from the story to explain why he feels that way.

5. What do you think Midas will do in the next chapter? Why?

E WRITING

Write a passage that explains how Midas's feelings about the Golden Touch changed during Chapter 3.

Use details from the story to answer these questions in your passage:

1. Why was Midas so happy at the beginning of the chapter?

2. Why was Midas looking forward to breakfast?

3. Why was Midas ashamed about Marygold's golden rose?

4. How did Midas's feelings about the Golden Touch change when he tried to eat his food?

5. At the end of the chapter, what did Midas think was more valuable than the Golden Touch?

Write at least six sentences.

END OF LESSON 82

A | WORD LISTS

1 | Hard Words

1. beloved
2. moisten
3. soften
4. wring

2 | Related Words

1. hate / hateful
2. stretched / outstretched

3 | Vocabulary Words

1. deceitful
2. dimple
3. musician
4. perpetual clock
5. sincerely

B | VOCABULARY DEFINITIONS

1. **deceitful**—When you deceive somebody by telling a lie, you are being *deceitful.*
- Here's another way of saying *The man told a lie to the woman: The man was deceitful with the woman.*
- What's another way of saying *The woman told a lie to the man?*

2. **dimple**—A little dent in a person's cheeks or chin is called a *dimple.*
- What do we call a little dent in a person's cheeks or chin?

3. **musician**—A person who plays a musical instrument is called a *musician.*

- What do we call a person who plays a musical instrument?

4. **perpetual clock**—A *perpetual clock* is an expensive type of clock that can run without electricity and doesn't need to be wound up.
- What do we call a clock that can run without electricity and doesn't need to be wound up?

5. **sincerely**—*Sincerely* is another word for *honestly.*
- What's another way of saying *I honestly want to help you?*

C | READING LITERATURE: Myth

The Golden Touch
Chapter 4

What had Midas done? The moment his lips touched Marygold's forehead, a change had taken place. Her sweet, rose-colored face changed to a glittering yellow color, with yellow teardrops on her cheeks. Her beautiful brown hair took the same yellow color. Her soft and tender little form grew hard and rigid as she stood within her father's arms. She was the victim of her father's insane desire for wealth. Marygold was no longer a human child, but a golden statue.

Midas began to wring his hands. He could neither bear to look at Marygold, nor bear to look away from her. He could not believe she had changed to gold. But as he glanced at her, he saw the precious little figure, with a yellow teardrop on its yellow cheek. Her expression was so warm and tender that Midas hoped her expression would soften the gold and make it become flesh again. But she remained gold. So Midas could only wring his hands and wish he was the poorest man in the whole world. He would gladly have exchanged all his wealth to bring back the rose color to his dear child's face.

While Midas was feeling this terrible despair, he suddenly noticed somebody standing near the door. Midas bent down his head without speaking, for he recognized the figure as the stranger who had appeared the day before in the treasure room. The stranger's smile seemed to shed a yellow light all around the room. It gleamed on little Marygold's image and on the other objects that had been changed by the touch of Midas.

"Well, friend Midas," said the stranger, "how do you like the Golden Touch?"

Midas shook his head. "I am very miserable," he said.

"Very miserable? Indeed!" exclaimed the stranger. "And why is that? Have I not faithfully kept my promise to you? Didn't you get everything your heart desired?"

"Gold is not everything," answered Midas. "And I have lost all that my heart really cared for."

"Ah, so you have made a discovery since yesterday," observed the stranger. "Let us see, then. Which of these two things do you think is really worth the most—the gift of the Golden Touch or one cup of clear, cold water?" ♦

"The water!" exclaimed Midas. "I would love to have it moisten my throat."

The stranger continued, "Tell me which is worth more, the Golden Touch or a crust of bread?"

"A piece of bread," answered Midas, "is worth all the gold on Earth."

The stranger then asked, "And is the Golden Touch worth more than your own little Marygold as she was an hour ago?"

"Oh, my child, my dear child is worth a thousand Golden Touches," cried poor Midas, wringing his hands. "I would not have given one small dimple in her chin for the power to change the whole Earth into gold!"

"You are wiser than you were, King Midas," said the stranger, looking seriously at him. "I believe your heart has not been entirely changed from flesh to gold. You appear to understand that common things are more valuable than the riches so many people struggle for. Tell me now, do you sincerely desire to rid yourself of this Golden Touch?"

"Yes, yes!" Midas exclaimed. "The Golden Touch is hateful to me!"

"Go, then," said the stranger, "and plunge into the river that glides past your garden. Then take a vase of the river water and sprinkle it over any object you want to change from gold into its original material. If you do this sincerely, you may possibly repair the mischief your greed has caused."

King Midas bowed low, and when he lifted his head, the stranger had vanished.

Midas lost no time in snatching up a vase (which immediately turned to gold) and running to the riverside. As he scampered along and forced his way through the bushes, the leaves turned yellow behind him, as if autumn had come to one narrow strip of bushes. On reaching the riverbank, Midas plunged into the water without even pulling off his shoes.

"Poof, poof, poof," snorted King Midas as his head came out of the water. He was still holding the vase, and his eyes widened as he watched it change from gold into the good, honest clay it had been before he had touched it. He was also aware of a change within himself. A cold, hard, and heavy weight seemed to have gone out of his chest, and his clothes felt lighter, although they were soaking wet. ✴

King Midas charged back to the palace. The servants did not know what to make of it when they saw their royal master running around with a vase of water. They did not know all the evil that Midas had caused, and that the water was more precious to Midas than an ocean of liquid gold. The first thing he did was to sprinkle handfuls of the water over the golden figure of little Marygold.

As soon as the water fell on Marygold, the color came back to her cheeks, and she began to sneeze and sputter. She was astonished to find herself dripping wet and to see her father throwing still more water over her.

"Please stop, dear Father," she cried. "See how you have soaked my nice outfit."

Marygold did not know she had been a little golden statue; nor could she remember anything that had happened since the moment she ran with outstretched arms to comfort poor King Midas.

Her father did not think it necessary to tell his beloved child how very foolish he had been. Instead, he decided to show how much wiser he was now. He led little Marygold into the garden, where he sprinkled the remainder of the water over the rosebushes.

Two things, however, reminded King Midas of the Golden Touch for the rest of his life. One was that the sands of the riverbank sparkled like gold. The other was that little Marygold's hair now had a golden tint.

When King Midas became an old man and sat with Marygold's children on his knees, he was fond of telling them this marvelous story. When he finished, he would say, "To tell you the truth, my dear grandchildren, ever since that morning I have hated the very sight of gold except for your mother's beautiful golden hair."

D CHARTS AND GRAPHS

Jackie Robinson's Hits per Year

You can understand why Jackie Robinson decided to retire by comparing the number of hits he got each year with the Dodgers. During his first year, he got 175 hits. He had almost as many hits the next year, and then he really took off in his third year, when he had 203 hits. After that year, his numbers decreased during most years until they bottomed out in his next-to-last year, when he had only 81 hits. He retired the next year.

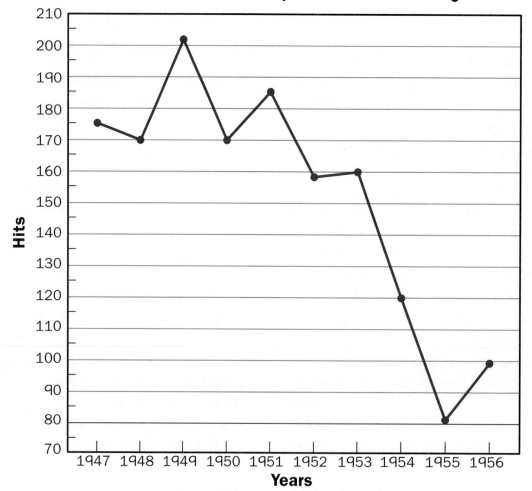

Jackie Robinson's Hits per Year with the Dodgers

1. How many hits did Robinson get in 1947?

2. How many hits did Robinson get in 1948?

3. How many hits did Robinson get in 1949?

4. Did Robinson's hits per year mostly *increase* or *decrease* after 1949?

5. How does the line graph help you understand the passage?

E COMPREHENSION

Write the answers.

1. At the beginning of the chapter, why was Midas ready to give up all his wealth?

2. The story says that Midas "could neither bear to look at Marygold nor bear to look away from her." Use details from the story to explain why Midas felt that way.

3. What did Midas mean when he said, "Gold is not everything"?

4. The stranger claims that "common things are more valuable than the riches so many people struggle for." What evidence does Midas give to support that claim?

5. What is the main theme of "The Golden Touch"?

F WRITING

• Pretend that Midas has to convince the stranger to take away the Golden Touch, so he gives the stranger a speech.

Write Midas's speech to the stranger.

Use details from the story to answer these questions in your speech:

1. What does Midas want the stranger to do?

2. How does Midas feel about having the Golden Touch?

3. What important things has Midas lost?

4. What lesson has Midas learned about gold?

5. Which objects have more value than gold?

6. How sincere is Midas?

Write at least six sentences.

END OF LESSON 83

A WORD LISTS

1 | Hard Words

1. grimy
2. license
3. olive
4. raisin
5. weird

2 | Word Practice

1. album
2. guitar
3. pastry
4. skyward

3 | Spanish Words

1. conjunto
   [kohn-HOON-toh]
2. empanada
   [em-puh-NAH-duh]
3. familia
   [fah-MEEL-yuh]
4. lobos
   [LOH-bohs]

4 | Spanish Names

1. Fausto
   [FOW-stoh]
2. Lupe
   [LOO-peh]
3. Lydia
   [LI-dee-uh]

5 | Vocabulary Words

1. freeway
2. muscular
3. pew
4. stash
5. warehouseman

B VOCABULARY DEFINITIONS

1. **freeway**—A free highway with many lanes of traffic is called a *freeway.*
- What's another way of saying *You don't have to pay tolls on a free highway?*

2. **muscular**—When a body part has strong muscles, it is *muscular.* An arm with strong muscles is a muscular arm.
- What's another way of saying *The tennis player had legs with strong muscles?*

3. **pew**—A bench that people sit on in a church is called a *pew.*
- What is a pew?

4. **stash**—When you *stash* something, you put that thing in a safe and secret place.
- What's another way of saying *Jordan hid the money in a shoebox?*

5. **warehouseman**—A man who lifts and moves items in a warehouse is called a *warehouseman.*
- What does a warehouseman do?

VOCABULARY FROM CONTEXT

1. Fausto liked listening to **conjunto** music, but he also liked country music and rock.

2. The family ate **empanadas** that were stuffed with chicken.

3. There were many brothers and sisters in Lupe's large **familia.**

4. In Spanish, Little Red Riding Hood meets a **lobo** on the way to her grandmother's house.

D STORY BACKGROUND

American Bandstand

Today you will begin reading "The No-Guitar Blues," a realistic short story about a boy named Fausto who lives in Fresno, California. Fausto wants to play the guitar, and the story mentions real musical shows and musicians, such as "American Bandstand" and Los Lobos.

"American Bandstand" was a dance show that ran on TV from 1952 to 1989. Young people in the TV studio danced around while a famous band or singer played on the stage. Millions of kids and teenagers watched "American Bandstand" in their homes, and some danced or played along.

Los Lobos has been playing since the 1970s, and they are one of the most famous bands of all time. They play many kinds of music, from *conjunto* to rock and roll. They appeared on "American Bandstand" in 1985, when "The No-Guitar Blues" takes place.

E READING LITERATURE: Realistic Short Story

The No-Guitar Blues

Gary Soto

Part 1

The moment Fausto saw the group Los Lobos on "American Bandstand," he knew exactly what he wanted to do with his life— play guitar. His eyes grew large with excitement as Los Lobos ground out a song while teenagers bounced off each other on the crowded dance floor.

He had watched "American Bandstand" for years and had heard Ray Camacho and the Teardrops at Romain Playground, but it had never occurred to him that he too might become a musician. That afternoon Fausto knew his mission in life: to play guitar in his own band; to sweat out his songs and prance around the stage; to make money and dress weird.

Fausto turned off the television set and walked outside, wondering how he could get enough money to buy a guitar. He couldn't ask his parents because they would just say, "Money doesn't grow on trees" or "What do you think we are, bankers?" And besides, they hated rock music. They were into the *conjunto* music of Lydia Mendoza, Flaco Jimenez, and Little Joe and La Familia. And, as Fausto recalled, the last album they bought was *The Chipmunks Sing Christmas Favorites.*

But what the heck, he'd give it a try. He returned inside and watched his mother make tortillas. He leaned against the kitchen counter, trying to work up the nerve to ask her for a guitar. Finally, he couldn't hold back any longer.

"Mom," he said, "I want a guitar for Christmas."

She looked up from rolling tortillas. "Honey, a guitar costs a lot of money."

"How 'bout for my birthday next year," he tried again.

"I can't promise," she said, turning back to her tortillas, "but we'll see."

Fausto walked back outside with a buttered tortilla. He knew his mother was right. His father was a warehouseman at Berven Rugs, where he made good money but not enough to buy everything his children wanted. Fausto decided to mow lawns to earn money, and was pushing the mower down the street before he realized it was winter and no one would hire him. He returned the mower and picked up a rake. He hopped onto his sister's bike (his had two flat tires) and rode north to the nicer section of Fresno in search of work. He went door-to-door, but after three hours he managed to get only one job, and not to rake leaves. He was asked to hurry down to

the store to buy a loaf of bread, for which he received a grimy, dirt-caked quarter.

He also got an orange, which he ate sitting at the curb. While he was eating, a dog walked up and sniffed his leg. Fausto pushed him away and threw an orange peel skyward. The dog caught it and ate it in one gulp. The dog looked at Fausto and wagged his tail for more. Fausto tossed him a slice of orange, and the dog snapped it up and licked his lips.

"How come you like oranges, dog?"

The dog blinked a pair of sad eyes and whined.

"What's the matter? Cat got your tongue?" Fausto laughed at his joke and offered the dog another slice. ♦

At that moment a dim light came on inside Fausto's head. He saw that it was sort of a fancy dog, a terrier or something, with dog tags and a shiny collar. And it looked well fed and healthy. In his neighborhood, the dogs were never licensed, and if they got sick they were placed near the water heater until they got well.

This dog looked like he belonged to rich people. Fausto cleaned his juice-sticky hands on his pants and got to his feet. The light in his head grew brighter. It just might work. He called the dog, patted its muscular back, and bent down to check the license.

"Great," he said. "There's an address."

The dog's name was Roger, which struck Fausto as weird because he'd never heard of a dog with a human name. Dogs should have names like Bomber, Freckles, Queenie, Killer, and Zero.

Fausto planned to take the dog to its home and collect a reward. He would say he had found Roger near the freeway. That would scare the daylights out of the owners, who would be so happy that they would probably give him a reward. He felt bad about

lying, but the dog was loose. And it might even really be lost, because the address was six blocks away.

Fausto stashed the rake and his sister's bike behind a bush, and, tossing an orange peel every time Roger became distracted, walked the dog to its house. He hesitated on the porch until Roger began to scratch the door with a muddy paw. Fausto had come this far, so he figured he might as well go through with it. He knocked softly. When no one answered, he rang the doorbell. A man in a silky bathrobe and slippers opened the door and seemed confused by the sight of his dog and the boy.

"Sir," Fausto said, gripping Roger by the collar. "I found your dog by the freeway. His dog license says he lives here." Fausto looked down at the dog, then up to the man. "He does, doesn't he?"

The man stared at Fausto a long time before saying in a pleasant voice, "That's right." He pulled his robe tighter around him because of the cold and asked Fausto to come in. "So he was by the freeway?"

"Uh-huh."

"You bad, snoopy dog," said the man, wagging his finger. "You probably knocked over some trash cans, too, didn't you?"

Fausto didn't say anything. He looked around, amazed by this house with its shiny furniture and a television as large as the front window at home. Warm bread smells filled the air and music full of soft tinkling floated in from another room. ✦

"Helen," the man called to the kitchen. "We have a visitor." His wife came into the living room wiping her hands on a dishtowel and smiling. "And who have we here?" she asked in one of the softest voices Fausto had ever heard.

"This young man said he found Roger near the freeway."

Fausto repeated his story to her while staring at a perpetual clock with a bell-shaped glass, the kind his aunt got when she celebrated her twenty-fifth anniversary. The lady frowned and said, wagging a finger at Roger, "Oh, you're a bad boy."

"It was very nice of you to bring Roger home," the man said. "Where do you live?"

"By that vacant lot on Olive," he said. "You know, by Brownie's Flower Place."

The wife looked at her husband, then Fausto. Her eyes twinkled triangles of light as she said, "Well, young man, you're probably hungry. How about a turnover?"

"What do I have to turn over?" Fausto asked, thinking she was talking about yard work or something like turning trays of dried raisins.

"No, no, dear, it's a pastry." She took him by the elbow and guided him to a kitchen that sparkled with copper pans and bright yellow wallpaper. She guided him to the kitchen table and gave him a tall glass of milk and something that looked like an *empanada*. Steamy waves of heat escaped when he tore it in two. He ate with both eyes on the man and woman who stood arm-in-arm smiling at him. They were strange, he thought. But nice.

"That was good," he said after he finished the turnover. "Did you make it, ma'am?"

"Yes, I did. Would you like another?"

"No, thank you. I have to go home now."

As Fausto walked to the door, the man opened his wallet and took out a bill. "This is for you," he said. "Roger is special to us, almost like a son."

Fausto looked at the bill and knew he was in trouble. Not with these nice folks or with his parents but with himself. How could he have been so deceitful? The dog wasn't lost. It was just having a fun Saturday walking around.

"I can't take that."

"You have to. You deserve it, believe me," the man said.

"No, I don't."

"Now don't be silly," said the lady. She took the bill from her husband and stuffed it into Fausto's shirt pocket. "You're a lovely child. Your parents are lucky to have you. Be good. And come to see us again, please."

F COMPREHENSION

Write the answers.

1. Use details from the story to explain what Fausto wanted to do when he became a musician.

2. Why did Fausto want to earn money?

3. Use details from the story to explain why Fausto thought the dog belonged to rich people.

4. Use details from the story to explain Fausto's plan for Roger.

5. Why did Fausto know he would be in trouble if he took money from the man?

G WRITING

Write a passage that explains what you think Fausto should do with the money the man gave him.

Use details from the story to answer these questions in your passage:

1. Why does Fausto want money?

2. What kind of story did Fausto tell Roger's owners?

3. Why did the man give the money to Fausto?

4. What will happen if Fausto tries to give the money back?

5. What will happen if Fausto keeps the money?

6. What do you think Fausto should do with the money?

Write at least six sentences.

END OF LESSON 84

A WORD LISTS

1 Hard Words	**2** Spanish Words	**3** Vocabulary Words
1. charity	1. chorizo [chor-EET-so]	1. bass / bass
2. chord	2. enchilada [en-chi-LAH-duh]	2. confession
3. eerie	3. guitarrón [ghee-tahr-ROHN]	3. lector
4. privacy	4. hijo [EE-hoh]	4. mimic
5. wrongdoing	5. huevo [WEH-voh]	5. resound
6. zombie	6. papas [PAH-pahs]	6. wicker

B VOCABULARY FROM CONTEXT

1. The **chorizo** looked like a hot dog, but it was much spicier.

2. Pablo made **enchiladas** by filling tortillas with cheese, rolling them up, and baking them in the oven.

3. The guitar made high notes, but the **guitarrón** made notes that were really low.

4. The mother said, "My **hijo** is my only male child."

5. On the Mexican farm, each chicken laid one **huevo** every day.

6. The cook made french fries by slicing the **papas** into thin strips and cooking them in oil.

VOCABULARY DEFINITIONS

1. **bass** [base]—A voice or instrument that makes low sound is called a *bass* voice or instrument.
- What's another way of saying *Pravat played a guitar that made low sounds?*

2. **confession**—When you admit that you did something wrong, you make a *confession.*
- Here's another way of saying *The boy admitted that he had broken the window: The boy made a confession that he had broken the window.*
- What's another way of saying *The girl admitted that she had lied?*

3. **lector**—One of the people who helps with a church service is called a *lector.*
- What is a lector?

4. **mimic**—When you imitate somebody, you *mimic* them.
- What's another way of saying *Selam could imitate a duck quacking?*

5. **resound**—When something *resounds*, it fills a place with sound.
- Here's another way of saying *The singing filled the hall with sound: The singing resounded in the hall.*
- What's another way of saying *The music filled their ears with sound?*

6. **wicker**—Bendable twigs from willows and other trees are called *wicker.*
- What would you call a basket that's made from bendable twigs?

STORY BACKGROUND

Church Services

In part 2 of "The No-Guitar Blues," Fausto wants to make a confession at his church, but he's too late. A confession is what happens when you see a priest in private and admit you have done something wrong.

Instead of making a confession, Fausto attends a mass, which is a type of church service. His church is called Saint Theresa's, and the priest who leads the mass is called Father Jerry. The lector helps with the mass by making announcements. During the mass, people pass around a wicker basket to collect money for the church.

The No-Guitar Blues
Part 2

Fausto went out, and the lady closed the door. Fausto clutched the bill through his shirt pocket. He felt like ringing the door-bell and begging them to please take the money back, but he knew they would refuse. He hurried away, and at the end of the block, pulled the bill from his shirt pocket: it was a crisp twenty-dollar bill.

"Oh, man, I shouldn't have lied," he said under his breath as he started up the street like a zombie. He wanted to run to church for Saturday confession, but it was past four-thirty, when confession stopped.

He returned to the bush where he had hidden the rake and his sister's bike and rode home slowly, not daring to touch the money in his pocket. At home, in the privacy of his room, he examined the twenty-dollar bill. He had never had so much money. It was probably enough to buy a secondhand guitar. But he felt bad, like the time he stole a dollar from the secret fold inside his older brother's wallet.

Fausto went outside and sat on the fence. "Yeah," he said. "I can probably get a guitar for twenty. Maybe at a yard sale— things are cheaper."

His mother called him to dinner.

The next day he dressed for church without anyone telling him. He was going to go to eight o'clock mass.

"I'm going to church, Mom," he said. His mother was in the kitchen cooking *papas* and *chorizo con huevos*. A pile of tortillas lay warm under a dishtowel.

"Oh, I'm so proud of you, Son." She beamed, turning over the crackling *papas*.

His older brother, Lawrence, who was at the table reading the funnies, mimicked, "Oh, I'm so proud of you, my son," under his breath. ♦

At Saint Theresa's he sat near the front. When Father Jerry began by saying we are all sinners, Fausto thought he looked right at him. Could he know? Fausto fidgeted with guilt. No, he thought. I only did it yesterday.

Fausto knelt, prayed, and sang. But he couldn't forget the man and the lady, whose names he didn't even know, and the *empanada* they had given him. It had a strange name but tasted really good. He wondered how they got rich. And how that dome clock worked. He had asked his mother once how his aunt's clock worked. She said it just worked, the way the refrig-erator works. It just did.

Fausto caught his mind wandering and tried to concentrate on his sins. He said a Hail Mary and sang, and when the wicker basket came his way, he stuck a hand reluctantly in his pocket and pulled out the twenty-dollar bill. He ironed it between his palms, and dropped it into the basket. The grown-ups stared. Here was a kid dropping twenty dollars in the basket, while they gave just three or four dollars.

There would be a second collection for Saint Vincent de Paul, the lector announced. The wicker baskets again floated in the

pews, and this time the adults around him, given a second chance to show their charity, dug deep into their wallets and purses and dropped in fives and tens. This time Fausto tossed in the grimy quarter.

Fausto felt better after church. He went home and played football in the front yard with his brother and some neighbor kids. He felt cleared of wrongdoing and was so happy that he played one of his best games of football ever. On one play, he tore his good pants, which he knew he shouldn't have been wearing. For a second, while he examined the hole, he wished he hadn't given the twenty dollars away. ✦

Man, I coulda bought me some Levi's, he thought. He pictured his twenty dollars being spent to buy church candles. He pictured a priest buying an armful of flowers with *his* money.

Fausto had to forget about getting a guitar. He spent the next day playing soccer in his good pants, which were now his old pants. But that night during dinner, his mother said she remembered seeing an old bass guitarrón the last time she cleaned out her father's garage.

"It's a little dusty," his mom said, serving his favorite enchiladas, "But I think it works. Grandpa says it works."

Fausto's ears perked up. That was the same kind the guy in Los Lobos played. Instead of asking for the guitar, he waited for his mother to offer it to him. And she did, while gathering the dishes from the table.

"No, Mom, I'll do it," he said, hugging her. "I'll do the dishes forever if you want."

It was the happiest day of his life. No, it was the second-happiest day of his life. The happiest was when his grandfather Lupe placed the guitarrón, which was nearly as huge as a washtub, in his arms. Fausto ran a thumb down the strings, which vibrated in his throat and chest. It sounded beautiful, deep and eerie. A pumpkin smile widened on his face.

"OK, *hijo*, now you put your fingers like this," said his grandfather, smelling of tobacco and aftershave. He took Fausto's fingers and placed them on the strings. Fausto strummed a chord on the guitarrón, and the bass resounded in their chests.

The guitarrón was more complicated than Fausto imagined. But he was confident that after a few more lessons he could start a band that would someday play on "American Bandstand" for the dancing crowds.

F COMPREHENSION

Write the answers.

1. Why did Fausto want to go to confession?

2. Why did people in the church pass around a wicker basket?

3. Use details from the story to explain why Fausto decided to give the twenty-dollar bill to the church.

4. Why did the adults put more money into the wicker basket when it came around again?

5. The story says that Fausto "felt cleared of wrongdoing." What does that mean?

G WRITING

Write a passage that answers this question:

• Do you think Fausto did the right thing when he gave twenty dollars to the church?

Use details from the story to answer these other questions in your passage:

1. Why did Fausto feel bad about getting twenty dollars from Roger's owners?

2. Why did Fausto decide to give the twenty dollars to the church?

3. What else could Fausto have done with the twenty dollars?

4. Do you think Fausto made the right decision?

Write at least six sentences.

END OF LESSON 85

86

A WORD LISTS

1 | Word Endings

1. Olympus
2. Olympian
3. Olympics

2 | Compound Words

1. earthquake
2. thunderbolt
3. underworld

3 | Greek Goddesses

1. Aphrodite
2. Artemis
3. Athena
4. Demeter
5. Hera
6. Hestia

4 | Greek Gods

1. Apollo
2. Ares
3. Hades
4. Hephaestus
5. Hermes
6. Poseidon
7. Zeus

5 | Vocabulary Words

1. chariot
2. conquer
3. deity
4. disguise
5. miraculous
6. wisdom

B VOCABULARY DEFINITIONS

1. **chariot**—A *chariot* is a two-wheeled cart drawn by horses.
- What's another way of saying *Marcus drove his two-wheeled cart in a race?*

2. **conquer**—When you gain control over something by using force, you *conquer* it.
- What's another way of saying *The army gained control over the city?*

3. **deity**—A god or a goddess is called a *deity.*
- What's another way of saying *Athena was a Greek goddess?*

4. **in disguise**—When you are *in disguise,* you are dressed so that nobody can recognize you.

- What's another way of saying *For Halloween, the children were dressed so that nobody could recognize them?*

5. **miraculous**—Something that is like a miracle is *miraculous.*
- What's another way of saying *The cure was like a miracle?*

6. **wisdom**—When you are wise, you have *wisdom.*
- What's another way of saying *The Scarecrow was wise?*

C READING INFORMATIONAL TEXT: History

Greek Gods and Goddesses

In the next lesson, you will begin reading a myth titled "The Miraculous Pitcher." Like "The Golden Touch," this myth includes gods and teaches us a lesson. The story takes place in Greece, a country that is just a little bit west of Turkey, where "The Golden Touch" took place.

About three thousand years ago, the people who lived in Greece (the Greeks) believed that the world was ruled by gods and goddesses, or deities. They believed that deities lived all over Earth, but the twelve most important deities lived in a magic palace in the clouds on top of Mount Olympus, the tallest mountain in Greece. Because they lived on Mount Olympus, these gods and goddesses were called Olympian deities.

Each Olympian deity had special powers. Some controlled the sun or the ocean, while others had power over love, war, or fire. The list on the next page shows the names and powers of the twelve Olympian deities. It also shows how to pronounce their names.

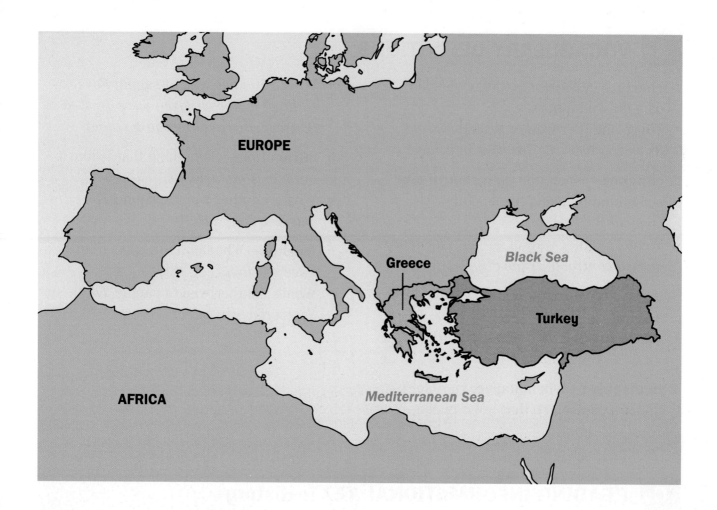

The Olympian Deities

Deity	Power
Aphrodite [af-ruh-DY-tee]	goddess of love
Apollo [uh-PAH-loh]	god of the sun
Ares [AIR-eez]	god of war
Artemis [AHR-tuh-miss]	goddess of hunting
Athena [uh-THEE-nuh]	goddess of wisdom
Demeter [duh-MEE-tur]	goddess of farming
Hephaestus [hih-FACE-tuss]	god of fire
Hera [HAIR-uh]	goddess of marriage
Hermes [HUR-meez]	god of travelers
Hestia [HESS-tee-uh]	goddess of the home
Poseidon [puh-SY-dun]	god of the ocean
Zeus [ZOOss]	god of the sky

Although these twelve deities lived on Mount Olympus, they spent much of their time traveling around Earth trying to help people or to stir up trouble. They also argued with each other and fell in love. In many ways, they were just like people.

The rest of this article gives more details about some of these gods and goddesses. ♦

Zeus

Zeus was king of all the Greek deities. When he was young, he conquered the world with the help of his brothers, Poseidon and Hades [HAY-deez]. Then all three gods agreed to rule over different parts of the world. Zeus ruled the sky, Poseidon ruled the ocean, and Hades ruled the underworld.

As god of the sky, Zeus controlled thunder, lightning, rain, and wind. He sometimes carried a thunderbolt that he would throw in the air to create lightning and thunder. He had a thick beard and a booming voice.

The Greeks believed that Zeus saw and knew everything. He used his knowledge to punish evil people and reward good ones. He could take the form of any animal, and he often traveled in disguise. He was married to the goddess Hera.

Poseidon and Hades

Although Poseidon ruled the ocean, he lived on Mount Olympus and spent a lot of time on dry land. Besides making storms at sea, he could start earthquakes. Poseidon was also the god of horses, and he drove around in a chariot pulled by several of these powerful creatures. He carried a trident—a long spear with three prongs, like a fork. People were afraid of him, and he had many enemies.

Poseidon's brother Hades was the god of the dead. He did not live on Mount Olympus, so he was not an Olympian deity. Instead, he stayed in the underworld, a magic cave below the ground that was surrounded by strange rivers. The Greeks believed that people went to the underworld after they died. Hades sometimes traveled above ground to capture people and bring them to his dark kingdom. ✦

Aphrodite and Ares

Aphrodite and Ares were almost exact opposites, but that didn't stop them from falling in love with each other. Aphrodite was the goddess of love and beauty. Many gods and men were in love with her, and many goddesses and women envied her beauty. She had several love affairs, but the one with Ares is the most famous.

Ares was the god of war. The son of Zeus and Hera, he was quite handsome, with lots of muscles. He wore a helmet and carried a spear, and he was always fighting against other gods and people. Although Ares was more interested in blood than beauty, he fell in love with Aphrodite. In some stories, the two of them get married, but in others she turns him down and marries ugly Hephaestus (the fire god) instead.

Hermes

Hermes was a fast runner who carried messages from Mount Olympus all over Earth. Because he had wings on his sandals, he could fly through the air and cover great distances in just a few seconds. He wore a round hat and carried a winged staff that had two snakes curled around it.

Hermes protected travelers and brought people good luck. He was also full of tricks. He loved playing jokes on the other deities, and sometimes he even stole things from them. He was tall, thin, and handsome, but he never got married. In his spare time, he played music.

D COMPREHENSION

Write the answers.

1. Why were the most important Greek deities called Olympian deities?

2. Use details from the article to explain how the male deities' powers differed from the female deities' powers.

3. In what ways were the Greek deities like people?

4. Why were people afraid of Poseidon?

5. Use details from the article to explain how Aphrodite and Ares were different from each other.

E WRITING

Write a brief report about one of these Olympian deities:

- Apollo
- Athena
- Demeter
- Hephaestus
- Hera
- Hestia

Use at least two reference sources to research your report.

Your report should answer these questions:

1. What does your deity look like?

2. What power or powers does your deity have?

3. How does your deity help or hurt people?

4. What are other interesting stories or details about your deity?

Write at least six sentences.

END OF LESSON 86

A WORD LISTS

1 | Hard Words

1. active
2. disagreeable
3. reflection
4. toil

2 | Compound Words

1. beehive
2. grapevine
3. light-footed
4. mudball
5. nightfall

3 | Word Endings

1. shrilly
2. skillfully
3. wonderfully
4. worthy

4 | Names

1. Baucis
2. Philemon
3. Quicksilver

5 | Vocabulary Words

1. cultivate
2. fertile
3. hospitality
4. staff
5. stately
6. sympathy

B VOCABULARY DEFINITIONS

1. **cultivate**—When you break up the soil in a field, plant seeds, and grow crops, you *cultivate* the field.
- What do you do when you cultivate a field?

2. **fertile**—Land where plants and crops grow well is called *fertile* land.
- What do we call land where plants and crops grow well?

3. **hospitality**—When you are friendly and welcoming to somebody, you show *hospitality* to that person.
- What are you showing when you are friendly and welcoming?

4. **staff**—A *staff* is a wooden or metal stick that comes in different lengths.

People sometimes use long staffs or poles when they hike or ski.
Witches and wizards sometimes use short staffs called *wands*.
- What do we call a wooden or metal stick that comes in different lengths?

5. **stately**—Something that is big and impressive is *stately*.
A stately tree is a big and tall tree that looks impressive.
- What's another way of saying *They lived in a big and impressive house?*

6. **sympathy**—When you feel sorry for somebody, you have *sympathy* for them.
- What's another way of saying *Isra felt sorry for the homeless boy?*

The Miraculous Pitcher

Chapter 1

One evening in Greece, in times long ago, old Philemon and his old wife Baucis sat on a bench next to their cottage door enjoying the calm and beautiful sunset. They had already eaten their supper, and now intended to spend a quiet hour or two before bedtime. So they talked together about their garden, and their cow, and their bees, and their grapevine. But the rude shouts of children and the fierce barking of dogs in the nearby village grew louder and louder, until at last it was hardly possible for Baucis and Philemon to hear each other speak.

"Ah, wife," cried Philemon, "I fear some poor traveler is seeking hospitality in the village. But instead of giving him food and shelter, the villagers have set their dogs on him."

"I do wish the people in the village felt a little more kindness for their fellow human beings," Baucis said. "They bring up their children in this evil way and pat them on the head when they fling stones at strangers."

"Those children will never come to any good," said Philemon, shaking his white head. "To tell you the truth, wife, I would not be surprised if some terrible thing were to happen to all the people in the village, unless they mend their ways. But as for you and me, so long as we have a crust of bread, let us be ready to give half to any poor homeless stranger who may come along and need it."

"That's right, husband," said Baucis. "So we will."

Philemon and Baucis were quite poor, and they had to work hard for a living. Philemon toiled all day long in his garden, while Baucis was always making a little butter and cheese with their cow's milk, or doing something around the cottage. Their food was seldom anything but bread, milk, and vegetables, with sometimes a bit of honey from their beehive. But they were two of the kindest people in the world. They would cheerfully have gone without their dinners any day rather than refuse food to a weary traveler who might come to their door. They felt they should treat guests better and more thoughtfully than they treated themselves.

Their cottage stood on a hill a short distance from the village, which lay in a valley that was about half a mile wide. When the world was new, this valley had probably been the bed of a lake. There, fishes had glided back and forth in the water, and weeds had grown along the shore, and trees and hills had made reflections in the broad and peaceful water. But as the lake had dried up, men had cultivated the soil and built houses on it, so that it was now a fertile spot.

The valley bore no trace of the ancient lake except for a small brook that flowed through the village and supplied the villagers with water. The valley had been dry land so long that oaks had sprung up, and grown great and high, and died with old age, and been followed by other oaks as tall and stately as the first. Never was there a prettier or more fertile valley. The very sight of their rich surroundings should have made the villagers kind and gentle.

But the people of this lovely village were not worthy to dwell in such a beautiful place. They were selfish, hardhearted people and had neither pity for the poor, nor sympathy for the homeless. They would only laugh if anybody told them human beings should love one another.

These people taught their children to be like themselves. They clapped their hands when they saw their boys and girls run after strangers, shout at them, and pelt them with stones. They kept large, fierce dogs. Whenever a traveler came into the village, this pack of disagreeable creatures scampered to meet the traveler, barking, snarling, and showing their teeth.

This unfriendly greeting was hard on poor travelers, especially when they were sick, or feeble, or old. Some would go miles and miles out of their way rather than try to pass through the village. ♦

So now you can understand why Philemon spoke so sorrowfully when he heard the shouts of the children and the barking of the dogs. The noise lasted a long time and seemed to echo all the way through the valley.

"I never heard the dogs so loud," observed the good old man.

"Nor the children so rude," answered the good old wife.

They sat shaking their heads one to another, while the noise came nearer and nearer. At last, they saw two men approaching on foot. Close behind them came the fierce dogs, snarling at their heels. A little farther behind was a crowd of children, who cried shrilly and flung stones at the two strangers with all their might.

From time to time, the younger of the two men turned around and drove back the dogs with a staff he carried in his hand. His companion, who was a very tall person, walked calmly along, as if he didn't notice the fierce children or the pack of dogs. Both travelers were poorly dressed, and they looked as if they didn't have enough money in their pockets to pay for a meal.

"Come, wife," said Philemon to Baucis, "let us go and meet these poor travelers."

"You go and meet them," answered Baucis, "while I see if we can get them anything for supper. A bowl of bread and milk would raise their spirits."

Baucis hurried into the cottage. Meanwhile, Philemon went forward, extended his hand, and said in a hearty tone, "Welcome, strangers, welcome."

"Thank you," replied the younger of the two men. "This is quite a different greeting than we received in the village. Why do you live in such a bad neighborhood?"

"Ah," observed old Philemon with a quiet smile, "I live here so that I may make up for the rudeness of my neighbors."

"Well said, old father!" cried the younger traveler, laughing. "My companion and I need some help. Those children have splattered us with their mudballs, and one of the dogs has torn my cloak."

Philemon was glad to see the younger man in such good spirits. Indeed, the traveler did not seem weary from his long journey, nor upset by the rough treatment he had received.

The younger traveler was dressed in an odd way. The edge of the round cap he wore stuck out over both ears. Although it was a summer evening, he wore a cloak, which he kept wrapped closely around him. Philemon also saw that he had an unusual pair of shoes. But because it was growing dark, the old man could not tell exactly what was strange about the shoes. One thing certainly seemed odd—the traveler was so wonderfully light-footed and active that it appeared as if his feet sometimes rose from the ground.

"I used to be light-footed in my youth," said Philemon to the traveler, "but my feet always became heavier toward nightfall."

"There is nothing like a good staff to help one along," answered the stranger, "and I happen to have an excellent one, as you can see."

The traveler's staff was the oddest looking staff that Philemon had ever seen. It was made of olive-wood, and it had something like a little pair of wings near the top. Two snakes, carved in the wood, curled themselves around the staff. The snakes were so skillfully carved that old Philemon almost thought they were alive, and that he could see them wriggling and twisting.

"A curious piece of work!" said Philemon. "I have never seen a staff with wings!"

D COMPREHENSION

Write the answers.

1. Use details from the story to describe how the villagers treated strangers.

2. How did Baucis and Philemon treat strangers?

3. Why were Baucis and Philemon having so much trouble carrying on a conversation?

4. Why did Philemon speak so sorrowfully when he heard the shouts of the children and the barking of the dogs?

5. The story says the villagers "were not worthy to dwell in such a beautiful place." Use examples from the story to explain what that means.

E WRITING

Write a passage that answers this question:

- Who do you think the younger stranger is?

Use details from the story and the previous lesson to answer these questions in your passage:

1. What kind of hat was the younger stranger wearing?

2. What kind of shoes was he wearing?

3. What did his feet appear to do?

4. What was unusual about his staff?

Write at least six sentences.

END OF LESSON 87

A WORD LISTS

1 Word Endings	**2** Vocabulary Review	**3** Vocabulary Words
1. carelessly	1. cultivate	1. apology
2. continually	2. fertile	2. shrewd
3. humbly	3. hospitality	3. talkative
4. suddenly	4. staff	4. witty
	5. stately	
	6. sympathy	

B VOCABULARY DEFINITIONS

1. **apology**—When you say you are sorry for something you did, you make an *apology*.
- What do you make when you say you are sorry for something you did?

2. **shrewd**—*Shrewd* is another word for *clever*.
- What's another way of saying *The chess player made a clever move.*

3. **talkative**—When you are *talkative*, you talk a lot.
- What's another way of saying *Aunt Bertha talked a lot?*

4. **witty**—Someone who makes remarks in a quick and funny way is *witty*.
- What's another way of saying *Everybody laughed at the clown's quick and funny remarks?*

C READING LITERATURE: Myth

The Miraculous Pitcher
Chapter 2

Philemon and the two travelers continued walking toward the cottage, and they soon reached the bench outside the door.

"Friends," said Philemon, "sit down and rest yourselves here on our bench. My good wife Baucis has gone to see what you can have for supper. We are poor folks, but you are welcome to whatever we have in the cupboard."

The young stranger sat down carelessly on the bench, and his staff fell to the ground. And then something marvelous happened. The staff seemed to get up from the ground by itself. It spread its little pair of wings and flew up to the wall of the cottage. Then it leaned against the wall and stood quite still, except that the snakes continued to wriggle.

Before Philemon could ask any questions, the older stranger drew Philemon's attention from the wonderful staff by speaking to him in a remarkably deep tone of voice. He asked, "In ancient times, wasn't there a lake covering the spot where the village now stands?"

"Not in my day, friend," answered Philemon, "and yet I am an old man, as you see. There were always the fields and meadows, just as they are now, and the old trees, and the little stream murmuring through the valley. My father and his father before him never saw it otherwise, so far as I know. It will probably still be that way when old Philemon is gone and forgotten."

The older stranger observed, "Don't be too sure the valley will always be as it is now." There was something very stern in his deep voice. He shook his head, too, moving his dark and heavy curls. He continued, "Since the people of the village have forgotten affection and sympathy, it would be better if the lake rippled over their dwellings again!"

The older traveler looked so stern that Philemon was frightened. But that was not all, for when the traveler frowned, the twilight seemed suddenly to grow darker; and when he shook his head, there was a roll of thunder in the air.

But suddenly the older stranger's face became so kindly and mild that the old man quite forgot his terror. Still, he could not help feeling that the older traveler must be no ordinary person, even though he was poorly clothed and journeying on foot. Philemon did not think he was a prince in disguise but rather some very wise man, who went around the world in poor clothes, seeking to add to his wisdom.

When Philemon raised his eyes to the stranger's face, he seemed to see a lifetime of thought. ♦

While Baucis was getting supper, the travelers began to talk in a friendly way with Philemon. The younger traveler was extremely talkative, and he made such shrewd and witty remarks that the good old man continually burst out laughing. Philemon thought the younger man was the merriest fellow he had ever seen.

"What is your name?" asked Philemon.

"Why, I am very nimble, as you see," answered the traveler. "So, if you call me Quicksilver, the name will fit well."

"Quicksilver? Quicksilver?" repeated Philemon, looking in the traveler's face to see if he was making fun of him. "It is a very odd name. And your companion there, has he as strange a name?"

"You must ask the thunder to tell you his name," replied Quicksilver, putting on a mysterious look. "No other voice is loud enough."

Philemon turned to look at the older traveler. He was probably the grandest figure that ever sat so humbly beside a cottage door. The older stranger talked in such a grave way that Philemon wanted to tell him everything he knew. This is often how people feel when they meet anyone wise enough to comprehend all their good and evil.

Simple and kindhearted Philemon did not have many secrets to tell. He talked about the events of his past life. He had never been more than ten miles from the very spot where he lived. Baucis and he had dwelt in the cottage since their youth, and they earned their bread by honest labor. They had always been poor but contented.

Philemon told what excellent butter and cheese Baucis made, and how nice the vegetables were that he raised in his garden. He said, too, that because he and his wife loved one another so very much, they both hoped that death might not separate them. They wanted to die together, just as they had lived together.

As the older stranger listened, a smile beamed over his face. "You are a good old man," he said to Philemon, "and you have a good old wife. Your wish will be granted."

And it seemed to Philemon just then as if the sunset clouds flashed brightly from the west and suddenly lit up the sky.

Baucis now had supper ready. She came to the cottage door and began to make apologies for the poor meal that she was forced to set before her guests.

"Had we known you were coming," she said, "my husband and I would have gone without a bite. But I took most of today's milk to make cheese; and our last loaf of bread is already half-eaten. Ah, me! I never feel the sorrow of being poor except when a traveler knocks at our door." ★

"All will be well; do not trouble yourself, my good woman," replied the older stranger kindly. "An honest, hearty welcome to a guest works miracles with any meal."

"A welcome you shall have," cried Baucis, "and likewise a little honey we happen to have left, and also a bunch of purple grapes."

"Why, Mother Baucis, it is a feast!" exclaimed Quicksilver, laughing, "A tremendous feast! And you shall see how eagerly I will feast on it. I think I never felt hungrier in my life."

"Oh dear," whispered Baucis to her husband. "If the young man has such a hearty appetite, I am afraid there will not be half enough supper."

Before Philemon could reply, the travelers stood up from the bench and entered the cottage.

Quicksilver's staff, you will remember, had set itself up against the wall of the cottage. When Quicksilver entered the door,

leaving his wonderful staff behind, it immediately spread its little wings and went hopping and fluttering up the doorstep. It did not rest until it had leaned itself against Quicksilver's chair. Baucis and Philemon, however, were attending so closely to their guests that they did not notice the staff.

As Baucis had said, the supper was quite small. In the middle of the table were the remains of a loaf of brown bread, with a piece of cheese on one side of it and a dish of honey on the other. There was a pretty good bunch of grapes for each of the guests. A medium-sized clay pitcher, nearly full of milk, stood at a corner of the table. But when Baucis had filled two cups and set them before the strangers, only a little milk remained in the bottom of the pitcher. Poor Baucis kept wishing she could provide these hungry folks with a hearty supper.

And, since the supper was so very small, she could not help wishing their appetites were smaller. But, right after they sat down, the travelers both drank all the milk in their cups in one gulp.

"A little more milk, kind Mother Baucis, if you please," said Quicksilver. "The day has been hot, and I am very thirsty."

"Now, my dear people," answered Baucis slowly, "I am so sorry and ashamed. But the truth is, there is hardly a drop more milk in the pitcher."

Quicksilver got up from the table and took the pitcher by the handle. Then he exclaimed, "Why, it appears to me that matters are not quite so bad as you think. There is much more milk in the pitcher."

And he proceeded to fill both cups from the pitcher that was supposed to be almost empty.

D CHARTS AND GRAPHS

Bar Graphs and Line Graphs

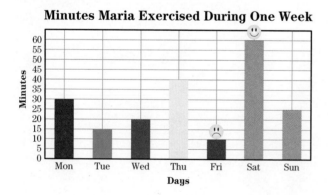

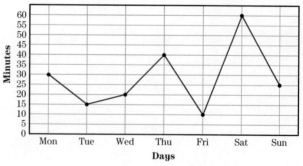

Bar graphs and line graphs can show the same thing, such as how many minutes Maria exercised on each day of the week. The only difference between bar graphs and line graphs is **how** they show the numbers: a bar graph uses separate bars for each day, but a line graph uses a line that goes from one day to the next.

Work the items.

1. What information does each graph show about Maria?

2. How does the bar graph look different from the line graph?

3. Why does the bar graph have a smiling face on Saturday?

4. Why does the bar graph have a frowning face on Friday?

5. How did the number of minutes Maria exercised change from Tuesday to Thursday?

E COMPREHENSION

Write the answers.

1. Why is Quicksilver a good name for the younger traveler?

2. Use details from the story to explain why Quicksilver's staff is magical.

3. Use details from the story to explain why the older traveler might be Zeus.

4. Why was Baucis so worried when the strangers entered her cottage?

5. Why was it strange that Quicksilver was able to refill the glasses with milk from the pitcher?

F WRITING

- Pretend you are Philemon.

Write a speech where you tell the older stranger about your life.

Use details from the story to answer these questions in your speech:

1. How long have you and Baucis lived in the cottage?

2. What's the farthest you've been from the cottage?

3. How do you earn your living?

4. How do you feel about your wife?

5. What is your hope for when you die?

Write at least six sentences.

A | WORD LISTS

1 | Word Endings

1. crusty
2. deliciously
3. unworthy

2 | Vocabulary Review

1. apology
2. shrewd
3. talkative
4. witty

3 | Vocabulary Words

1. abundant
2. astonishment
3. disagreeable
4. inhabitant
5. preparation
6. spacious

B | VOCABULARY DEFINITIONS

1. **abundant**—If something is *abundant*, there is a lot of that thing. Abundant milk is a lot of milk.
- What's a lot of grain?

2. **astonishment**—*Astonishment* is another word for *amazement*.
- What's another way of saying *She felt great amazement?*

3. **disagreeable**—When you are unfriendly and unpleasant, you are *disagreeable*.
- What's another way of saying *Mr. Snedly was unfriendly and unpleasant to everybody?*

4. **inhabitant**—Somebody who lives in a place is an *inhabitant* of that place. A person who lives in the United States is an inhabitant of the United States.
- What do we call someone who lives in South Africa?

5. **preparations**—When you prepare for something, you make *preparations*.
- What's another way of saying *Vani prepared for her vacation?*

6. **spacious**—Something that is *spacious* has a lot of space in it. A house with a lot of space in it is a spacious house.
- What do we call a valley with a lot of space in it?

The Miraculous Pitcher

Chapter 3

Baucis could scarcely believe her eyes. She had certainly poured out nearly all the milk, and she had seen the bottom of the pitcher as she set it on the table.

"But I am old," thought Baucis to herself, "and may be forgetful. I suppose I must have made a mistake. In any case, the pitcher must be empty now."

Quicksilver had turned the pitcher upside down and had poured every drop of milk into the last cup.

"What excellent milk!" observed Quicksilver after finishing his second cup. "Excuse me, my kind hostess, but I must really ask you for a little more."

Of course there could not possibly be any milk left. Baucis lifted the pitcher anyway. To be polite, she went through the motion of pouring milk into Quicksilver's cup but without the slightest idea that any milk would come from the pitcher. She was very surprised, therefore, when so much milk fell bubbling into the cup that it was immediately filled to the brim and overflowed onto the table! She also noticed what a delicious fragrance the milk had. It seemed

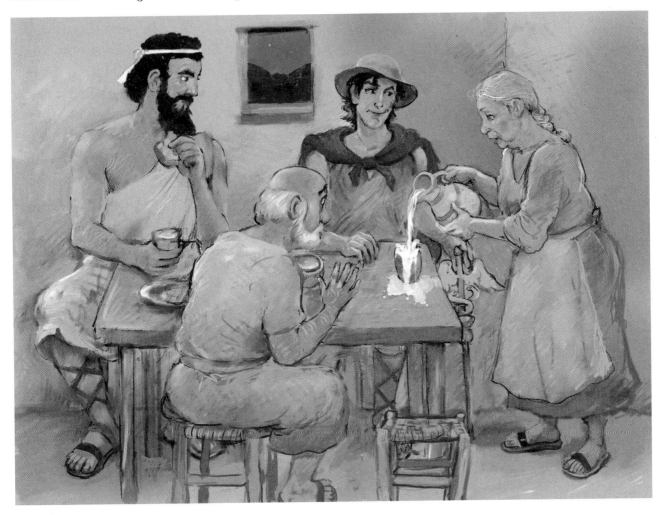

as if Philemon's only cow must have eaten the richest grass in the world.

"And now a slice of your brown bread, Mother Baucis," said Quicksilver, "and a little of that honey."

Baucis cut him a slice. The bread, when she and her husband had eaten it, had been rather dry and crusty. But now it was light and moist. Baucis tasted a crumb that had fallen on the table, and found it more delicious than her bread ever was before. She could hardly believe that it was a loaf of her own. Yet, what other loaf could it possibly be?

Baucis began to think that something very unusual was going on. So, after helping the guests to bread and honey, she sat down by Philemon and whispered what she had seen.

"Did you ever hear of anything like it?" she asked Philemon.

"No, I never did," answered Philemon with a smile. "And I think, my dear old wife, that you have been walking about in a sort of dream. There happened to be a little more milk in the pitcher than you thought, my dear—that is the only possible explanation." ♦

"Ah, husband," said Baucis, "say what you will, but these are very unusual guests."

"Well, well," replied Philemon, still smiling, "perhaps they are. They certainly do look as if they had seen better days; and I am glad to see them having such a good supper."

Each of the guests now took a bunch of grapes. Baucis, who rubbed her eyes to see more clearly, thought the grapes had grown larger and richer. Each grape seemed to be nearly bursting with ripe juice. It was entirely a mystery to her how such grapes could ever have been produced from the old vine that climbed against the cottage wall.

"These are marvelous grapes," observed Quicksilver, as he swallowed one after another. "Where did you gather them?"

"From my own vine," answered Philemon. "You may see one of its branches twisting across the window. But my wife and I never thought the grapes were very fine ones."

"I never tasted better," said Quicksilver. "Another cup of that delicious milk, if you please, and I shall then have eaten better than a prince."

This time old Philemon got up himself and picked up the pitcher, for he was curious to discover whether there was any truth in what Baucis had whispered to him. He knew that his good old wife never lied, and that she was seldom mistaken. But this case was so unusual that he wanted to see into the pitcher with his own eyes.

As Philemon picked up the pitcher, he slyly glanced into it. He saw that it didn't contain a single drop. All at once, however, a little white fountain gushed up from the bottom of the pitcher and rapidly filled it to the brim with deliciously fragrant milk. It was lucky that Philemon, in his surprise, did not drop the miraculous pitcher from his hand.

"Who are you, you wonder-working strangers?" he cried, even more confused than his wife had been.

"We are your guests and your friends," replied the older traveler in his mild, deep voice, which was both sweet and amazing. Then he added, "I would also like another cup of milk."

The older traveler seemed so solemn that Philemon did not ask him any questions. And when Philemon drew Quicksilver aside and asked how a fountain of milk could get into an old clay pitcher, Quicksilver pointed to his staff. ✦

"There is the answer," said Quicksilver. "And if you can figure it out, please tell me. I can't understand my staff. It is always playing such odd tricks as this—sometimes getting me a supper, and quite as often stealing my supper. If I had any faith in such nonsense, I should say the stick was charmed!"

He said no more, but he looked so slyly at Baucis and Philemon that they almost thought he was laughing at them.

The supper was now over, and Baucis begged the travelers to stay the night. They accepted her offer cheerfully. The good woman showed them to the sleeping room. The magic staff went hopping at Quicksilver's heels as he left the room.

Later that night, the good old couple spent some time talking about the events of the evening, and then they lay down on the floor and fell fast asleep. They had given up their sleeping room to the guests and had no other bed for themselves.

Philemon and Baucis arose with the sun, and the strangers made their preparations to depart. Philemon asked them to remain a little longer so that Baucis could milk the cow and bake some bread. The guests, however, seemed to think it better to set out before the day got hot. Therefore, they set out immediately but asked Philemon and Baucis to walk with them a short distance and show them which road to take.

"Ah, me!" exclaimed Philemon, when they had walked a little way from their door. "If our neighbors only knew what great rewards there are for being kind to strangers, they would tie up all their dogs and never allow their children to fling another stone."

Baucis agreed, "It is a sin and a shame for them to behave the way they do! And I'm going to tell some of them what nasty people they are."

With a cunning smile, Quicksilver replied, "I fear you will find none of them at home."

Just then, the older traveler's face took on such a solemn expression that neither Baucis nor Philemon dared to speak another word. They gazed into his face as if it were the sky.

The older traveler spoke. "When a person does not treat the humblest strangers as if they were brothers or sisters, that person is unworthy to exist on Earth." He spoke in tones so deep that they sounded like thunder.

"And anyway, my dear old people," cried Quicksilver, with mischief in his eyes, "where is this village you talk about? On which side of us does it lie? I do not see it."

D COMPREHENSION

Write the answers.

1. The story says the milk had a "delicious fragrance." What does that mean?

2. Use details from the story to describe how the grapes changed.

3. Use details from the story to explain how the pitcher filled up when Philemon looked inside.

4. What was Quicksilver's explanation for the fountain of milk?

5. The older traveler said, "When a person does not treat the humblest strangers as if they were brothers or sisters, that person is unworthy to exist on Earth." What does that mean?

E WRITING

- Do you agree with the following statement?

When a person does not treat the humblest strangers as if they were brothers or sisters, that person is unworthy to exist on Earth.

Write a passage that explains your answer.

Use details from the story to also answer these questions in your passage:

1. What does the statement mean?

2. Which people in the story mistreat strangers?

3. What do you think the older traveler might do to those people?

4. Why would he be able to do that?

5. Do you think it would be right for the older traveler to punish those people? Why or why not?

Write at least six sentences.

END OF LESSON 89

A | WORD LISTS

1 | Related Words

1. sphere / atmosphere
2. thermal / geothermal
3. electric / hydroelectric
4. fertile / fertilizer
5. mischief / mischievous

2 | Planet Names

1. Mercury
2. Venus
3. Earth
4. Mars
5. Jupiter
6. Saturn
7. Uranus
8. Neptune
9. Pluto (dwarf planet)

3 | Vocabulary Review

1. abundant
2. astonishment
3. disagreeable
4. inhabitant
5. preparation
6. spacious

4 | Vocabulary Words

1. decay
2. device
3. predict
4. substance

B | VOCABULARY DEFINITIONS

1. **decay**—When something rots or falls apart, it *decays*.
- What's another way of saying *The old house was rotting and falling apart?*

2. **device**—A piece of equipment that is built for a special purpose is called a *device*.
- What do we call a piece of equipment that is built for a special purpose?

3. **predict**—When you say that something will happen, you *predict* that thing.
- What's another ways of saying *Scientists can say when the sun will rise?*

4. **substance**—*Substance* is another word for *material*.
Water is a substance. Dirt is a substance. Gas is a substance.
- What's another word for *material?*

Roman Deities

By now, you have probably figured out that the two travelers in "The Miraculous Pitcher" are Zeus (the god of the sky) and Hermes (the god of travelers). You can tell that the older traveler is Zeus because he seems to know everything and has a voice like thunder. You can also tell that the younger traveler is Hermes because he's light-footed and carries a magic staff with wings.

The Greeks began telling myths like "The Miraculous Pitcher" about three thousand years ago. Several hundred years later, the people who lived in Rome also began telling myths. Rome was the biggest city in what is now Italy. The map shows where Italy is located. You can see that it's just west of Greece.

Roman myths were similar to Greek myths, but the Roman deities had different names. Some of those names are the same as the names of the planets in our solar system. The table below compares the names of several Greek and Roman deities.

Greek and Roman Deities

Greek Deity	Roman Name	Power
Hermes	Mercury	god of travelers
Aphrodite	Venus	goddess of love
Ares	Mars	god of war
Zeus	Jupiter	god of the sky
Poseidon	Neptune	god of the ocean
Hades	Pluto	god of the underworld

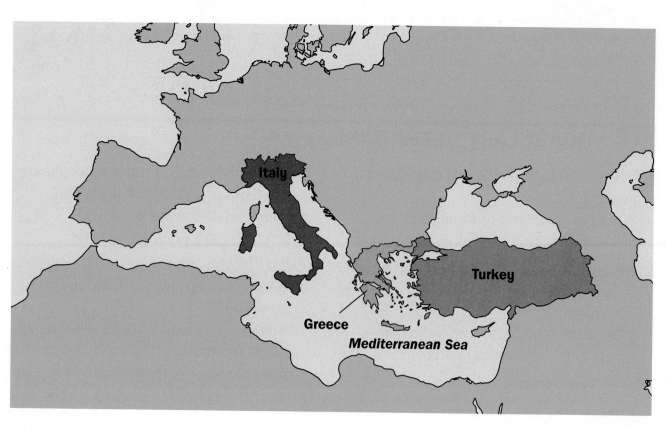

In some ways, the planets are like the Roman deities they are named after. Mercury is the fastest planet, just as Mercury is the fastest Roman god. Venus is the most beautiful planet, and Mars, with its blood-red color, is the most warlike. Jupiter is the biggest planet, and Neptune is blue, like the ocean. Finally, the dwarf planet Pluto is the darkest and farthest from the sun, just like the underworld.

Two more planets are also named after Roman gods. Saturn is Jupiter's father, and Uranus is his grandfather. The only planet that isn't named after a Roman god is Earth.

D READING LITERATURE: Myth

The Miraculous Pitcher
Chapter 4

Philemon and his wife turned toward the valley, where at sunset the day before they had seen the meadows, the houses, the gardens, the clumps of trees, the wide street, and the children. But to their astonishment, there was no longer any village! Even the fertile valley had ceased to exist. In its place they saw the broad, blue surface of a lake, which filled the great valley from brim to brim.

The lake reflected the surrounding hills in its still waters. For an instant, it remained perfectly smooth. Then a little breeze sprang up and caused the water to dance, glitter, and sparkle in the early morning sun.

The lake seemed so strangely familiar that the two old people were greatly puzzled. ✿ They felt as if the village had only been a dream. But then they remembered the dwellings and the faces of the inhabitants. It had not been a dream. The village had been there yesterday, and now it was gone.

"Alas!" cried these kindhearted old people. "What has become of our neighbors?"

"The villagers exist no longer as men and women," said the older traveler in his grand and deep voice, while a roll of thunder seemed to echo in the distance.

Quicksilver said with his mischievous smile, "Those foolish people were all changed into fish. It was only a small change, for they were already the coldest-blooded human beings on earth."

The older traveler continued, "As for you, good Philemon, and you, kind Baucis, you have shown us much hospitality and kindness. You have done well, my dear old friends; therefore, request whatever favor you have most at heart, and it is granted." ♦

Philemon and Baucis looked at one another, and then seemed to answer with one voice. They said, "Let us live together while we live, and leave the world at the same instant when we die, for we have always loved one another!"

"It will be so," replied the older stranger, in a deep, kind voice. "Now look toward your cottage."

They did so. But to their surprise, they saw a tall palace of white marble standing where their humble cottage had been.

"There is your home," said the older stranger, smiling at them. "Show your hospitality in that palace as freely as you did in your humble cottage."

The old folks fell on their knees to thank the stranger, but when they looked up, they were amazed to discover that both he and Quicksilver were gone.

So Philemon and Baucis lived in the marble palace, and they spent much of their time making travelers comfortable.

The milk pitcher was never empty. Whenever friendly guests took a drink from that pitcher, they always found it to be the sweetest milk that ever ran down their throats. But if angry and disagreeable travelers took a sip, they were certain to twist their faces and say that it was a pitcher of sour milk!

Thus, the old couple lived in their palace a long, long time, and they grew older and older. At last, however, there came a summer morning when Baucis and Philemon failed to appear. Their guests searched everywhere, from the top to the bottom of the spacious palace, but they could not find the old couple. ★

Finally, the guests saw two great trees in front of the palace. Nobody remembered ever seeing the two trees before, yet there they stood, with their roots fastened deep into the soil. Their leaves cast a shadow on the palace, and their branches wound together and embraced one another, so that each tree seemed to live in the other.

These trees must have required at least a century to grow, and the guests wondered how they could have become so tall in a single night. Just then, a breeze sprang up and made the branches move. And then there was a deep, broad murmur in the air, as if the two mysterious trees were speaking.

"I am old Philemon," murmured one tree.

"I am old Baucis," murmured the other.

But as the breeze grew stronger, the trees both spoke at once: "Philemon, Baucis, Baucis, Philemon"—as if one were both and both were one, and talking together with a common heart. It was plain enough that the good old couple had been reborn, and were now to spend a quiet and delightful hundred years or so as trees. And oh, what a wonderful shade they gave! Whenever travelers paused beneath the trees, they heard a pleasant whisper of the leaves above their head, and marveled because the sounds seemed to say: "Welcome, welcome, dear traveler, welcome!"

And some kind soul, who knew what would have pleased old Baucis and old Philemon best, built a circular seat around both their trunks, where for many years the weary and the hungry and the thirsty used to sit and drink milk abundantly out of the miraculous pitcher.

E   COMPREHENSION

Write the answers.

1. Which traveler do you think flooded the village? Use evidence from the last chapter to support your answer.

2. How were the villagers like fish before they became real fish?

3. Why did Baucis and Philemon want to die together?

4 Use details from the story to describe how the two trees were like Baucis and Philemon.

5. What is the theme of "The Miraculous Pitcher"?

F   WRITING

Write a story with the same theme as "The Miraculous Pitcher."

Your story should answer these questions:

1. Which person or animal in your story is a stranger?

2. How do most people treat that stranger?

3. Which person treats the stranger differently?

4. What happens in the end?

Write at least six sentences.

END OF LESSON 90

A WORD LISTS

1 | Related Words

1. exhaustible / inexhaustible
2. renewable / nonrenewable
3. scope / microscope

2 | Vocabulary Words

1. carbon dioxide
2. diesel fuel
3. energy resources
4. fossil fuels
5. generator
6. turbine

3 | Vocabulary Review

1. atmosphere
2. fertilizer
3. geothermal
4. hydroelectric
5. mischievous

B VOCABULARY DEFINITIONS

1. **carbon dioxide**—When gasoline, oil, and coal burn, they create a gas called *carbon dioxide*. People and other animals also create carbon dioxide when they breathe.
- What gas do gasoline, oil, and coal create when they burn?

2. **diesel fuel**—*Diesel fuel* is a type of gasoline that is used for large trucks and some cars.
- What do we call a type of gasoline that is used for large trucks and some cars?

3. **energy resources**—Resources that can be used to create energy are called *energy resources*. These resources include the sun, the wind, water, gas, oil, and coal.
- What do we call resources that can be used to create energy?

4. **fossil fuels**—Fuels formed long ago from dead plants and animals are called *fossil fuels*. These fuels include gas, oil, and coal.
- What do we call fuels formed long ago from dead plants and animals?

5. **turbine**—A *turbine* is a machine that spins something around and around. Some turbines are long rods with blades on one end. When water runs through the blades, the rod spins around and around.
- What do we call a machine that spins something around and around?

6. **generator**—A machine that converts spinning forces into electricity is called a *generator*.
- What does a generator do?

Earth's Energy Resources

People use energy every day. They use electric energy to run lights, computers, and televisions. They use energy from natural gas and the sun to heat buildings and power factories. They use energy from batteries and gasoline to drive cars, buses, and trains. All of this energy comes from the Earth's energy resources.

Fossil Fuels

Millions of years ago, before the age of the dinosaurs, Earth's oceans were full of living things, many of them so small that they couldn't be seen without a microscope. For millions of years, the remains of these living things fell to the ocean floor and were covered with layers of mud. Slowly, the remains turned into fossils, and the fossils turned into the oil and gas that we use today, which are called **fossil fuels.**

Fossil fuels are a common energy resource, but they pollute the air when they are used. These fuels produce carbon dioxide and other pollutants. When too much carbon dioxide is released into the atmosphere, the atmosphere gets hotter because carbon dioxide traps heat. In recent years, the Earth has been heating up because of carbon dioxide and other pollutants in the atmosphere. This process is called **global warming.**

From Peat to Coal

Fossil fuels are still forming today, but very slowly. One example is coal, which forms from the remains of trees, ferns, and other plants that fall to the bottom of swamps. Swamps are flat areas that are covered with shallow water.

As millions of years go by, the plant remains slowly build up on the dark, calm bottom of the swamp. The pile grows higher and heavier, putting more pressure on the lower layers. The pressure squeezes the old, decayed plant matter into **peat,** a soft black material that burns. Peat is found in swamps all over the world. Many people use peat for cooking and heating.

When peat stays underground for millions of years, it turns into coal, which burns cleaner and hotter than peat. Because coal is located underground, it must be mined. Coal mines are dangerous places, and they often have tunnels that go far underground. These tunnels sometimes collapse and kill miners. Over the past century, thousands of coal miners in the United States have been hurt or killed in mining accidents.

Coal mines today are safer than in the past, and miners are more careful. Hundreds of miners in the United States used to die each year because of mining accidents, but now only one or two dozen a year die from these accidents.

Mining coal and burning coal also harm the environment. Coal mines leave gaping holes in the land, and smoke from coal fires puts carbon dioxide into the atmosphere, which increases global warming.

Despite all these problems, coal is still an important energy resource. Power plants burn coal to produce electricity, and factories use coal to make steel. Materials that contain coal are used for medicines, paints, and many other products.

Gasoline-burning cars and trucks pollute the air.

Uses for Oil and Gas

Products made from oil and gas are used in many different ways. Most cars and trucks burn gasoline or diesel fuel when they run. Heating oil is used to heat houses and buildings, and natural gas is used for heating and for gas stoves. Oil is also used to make plastic, paint, cloth, fertilizer, and other substances.

When cars and trucks burn gasoline or diesel, they pollute the air with carbon dioxide and other substances. In some cities, the air is so polluted that it makes people sick, and it may even kill people who are old or weak.

Some people try to reduce pollution by riding bicycles, driving electric cars, or using buses, trains, and subways. These types of transportation pollute far less than cars and trucks.

Renewable or Inexhaustible?

Fossil fuels take millions of years to form. If people use up all of Earth's fossil fuels, they won't be able to renew the fuels unless they wait for millions of years. Because fossil fuels can't be easily renewed, they are called **nonrenewable** energy resources.

Some scientists are trying to find **renewable** energy sources, such as plant products. One example is ethanol, a fuel made from corn. Some cars can run on pure ethanol, while others use ethanol mixed with gasoline. People will not run out of ethanol as long as they keep planting corn every year.

Even better than renewable energy sources are **inexhaustible** resources such as sun, wind, and water. These resources can't be used up because there is an unlimited supply. The sun rises every day, rivers keep flowing, and the wind keeps blowing.

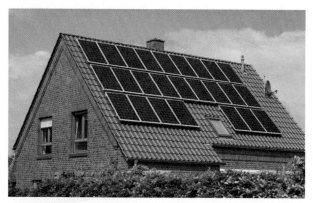
Rooftop solar panels are often used to produce electricity for houses.

Sun Power

Inexhaustible power from the sun is called **solar power.** Many sources of solar power use solar panels that collect sunlight over a large area, such as a roof or a field. Electric power from these panels can be used in homes and buildings. Solar power can also be stored in batteries. Solar batteries are like regular batteries, except they get their power from the sun.

Water Power

Electric power that comes from dams is called **hydroelectric power.** The picture shows that dams are high walls that block rivers. The water behind the dam rises to the top of the dam and forms a lake. Water from the lake rushes down a huge pipe inside the dam. The rushing water spins a turbine. The generator uses the spinning turbine to generate electricity.

Hydroelectric power is clean and inexhaustible, and the lakes behind dams can be used to supply water to nearby farms and towns. But dams are expensive to build, and they create many problems. One problem is that dams can block fish, such as salmon, from swimming up rivers to lay their eggs.

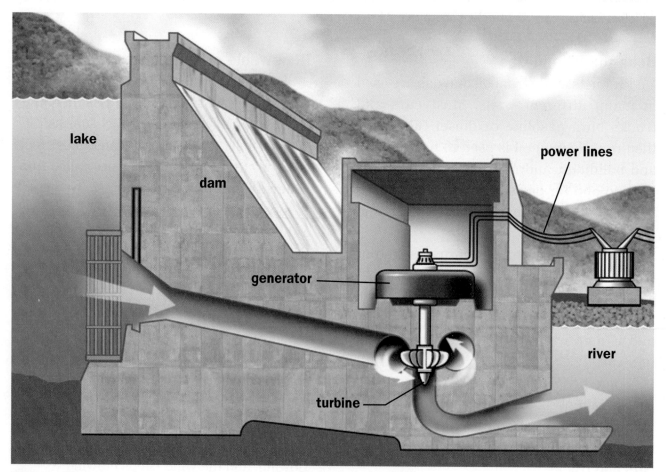
Water rushing through a dam spins a turbine that generates electricity.

Turbines on a wind farm work together to produce electricity.

Another problem is that dams can flood large areas of land where people live and farm.

Wind Power

Before people used electricity, they used spinning power from windmills to grind grain, saw wood, and pump water. Modern windmills, called **wind turbines,** have blades that spin around. A generator inside the wind turbine helps change this spinning energy into electricity. To create more electricity, dozens of turbines can be used together on wind farms. The picture shows a wind farm.

Wind is a clean, inexhaustible resource, but wind turbines have many problems. One problem is that wind turbines can't be used in all places because they need constant, strong winds to work well. Another problem is that wind turbines are very dangerous for birds that fly into the turbine's blades. In

North America, more than 100,000 birds are killed each year by wind turbines. Scientists are trying to solve these problems, but progress is slow.

Geothermal Power

Geothermal power comes from the heat inside the Earth, which is much hotter than the heat on the surface of the Earth. There are several ways to harness geothermal power. One way is to find places where hot water from deep inside the Earth comes to the surface. These places are called **geothermal hot springs.** Water from the hot springs can be used to heat houses. Steam from the water can be used to spin turbines that generate electricity.

In places without hot springs, wells can be drilled to reach hot water far below the surface of the Earth. In other places,

Hot water rises to the surface of the Earth at geothermal hot springs.

water can be injected to hot underground locations. No matter how the hot water is found, it can be used to heat houses and generate electricity. Geothermal power is an inexhaustible resource, and it does little harm to the environment.

Summary

The Earth has many sources of energy. Fossil fuels work well, but they are nonrenewable resources, and burning them pollutes the air. Renewable plant resources, such as corn, can be regrown every year. Inexhaustible resources—such as sun, wind, water, and geothermal—will never run out.

D COMPARING STORIES

Work the items.

1. What is the main theme of "The Golden Touch"?

2. What is the main theme of "The Miraculous Pitcher"?

3. Both stories are a particular kind of story called a ███████ .

4. About how long ago do both stories take place?

5. Both stories have deities who help the main characters.
   What powers do the deities have?

6. Deities play an important role in both stories.
   Would Midas have learned the lesson about gold without a deity's help?

7. Would Baucis and Philemon have been rewarded for their kindness without a deity's help?

8. How is the role of deities in these two stories alike?

E COMPREHENSION

Write the answers.

1. Use details from the article to explain how oil and gas form.

2. Why does the atmosphere get hotter when there's too much carbon dioxide in the air?

3. How is the process of forming oil and gas like the process of forming peat?

4. Use details from the text to explain how mining coal and burning coal harm the environment.

5. What is the difference between **renewable** energy sources and **inexhaustible** energy sources? Give examples to support your answer.

F WRITING

- Pretend you are a mayor who wants to bring solar power, wind power, or water power to your town. Your town gets a lot of sun but only a little wind. You're also close to a river, so you have lots of birds and fish.

Use details from the article to write a passage that answers this question:

- Which type of power should your town choose: solar, wind, or water?

Your passage should also answer these questions:

1. What are the advantages and disadvantages of solar power?

2. What are the advantages and disadvantages of wind power?

3. What are the advantages and disadvantages of water power?

Write at least six sentences.

END OF LESSON 91

A WORD LISTS

1 | Word Practice

1. accuse
2. beauty
3. enormously
4. merchant
5. pirate
6. ridicule

2 | Compound Words

1. anybody
2. folktale
3. halfway
4. horseback
5. shipwreck

3 | French Names

1. Gabrielle
2. Suzanne
3. Barbot
4. Gabrielle-Suzanne Barbot

4 | Vocabulary Words

1. cautious
2. desolate
3. fatigue
4. persuade
5. terrify

B VOCABULARY FROM CONTEXT

1. Ming was very **cautious** with the delicate old vase because it could easily break.

2. There was nothing within a hundred miles of this lonely, **desolate** place.

3. Vanida felt so **fatigued** after working all day that she took a nap when she got home.

4. The lawyer tried to **persuade** the jury that her client was innocent.

5. The movie about ghosts and monsters was so **terrifying** that it was difficult to watch.

Folktales

The next story you will read is a folktale called "Beauty and the Beast." Like myths, folktales are old stories that people told aloud before someone wrote them down. But folktales usually take place more recently than myths. The myths you have just read, for example, take place about three thousand years ago. In comparison, "Beauty and the Beast" takes place just a few hundred years ago, when most countries were ruled by kings and queens.

Another difference is that myths usually include gods and goddesses, but folktales do not. Instead, folktales often have witches, fairy godmothers, genies, or other kinds of magical characters.

"Beauty and the Beast" is one of the most famous folktales of all time. Many movies have been made of the story, and many writers have retold it in their own words. The version you will read was published in 1740 by a French writer named Gabrielle-Suzanne Barbot. She was the first person to write down the story, which is several thousand years old. Barbot probably heard the story as a child and decided to write a modern version.

Beauty and the Beast

Gabrielle-Suzanne Barbot

Chapter 1

Once upon a time there lived a merchant who was enormously rich. His wife had died, but he had six sons and six daughters, and he would give them anything they wanted. They all lived in a magnificent house in a French town.

But one day their house caught fire and burned to the ground, with all the splendid furniture, books, pictures, gold, silver, and precious goods it contained. Yet this was only the beginning of their misfortune. Shortly after the fire, the merchant lost every ship he had upon the sea, either because of pirates, shipwrecks, or fire. Then he heard that the people who worked for him in distant countries had stolen his money. At last, he fell into great poverty.

All the merchant had after those misfortunes was a horse and a little cottage in a desolate place a hundred miles from the town. He moved into the cottage with his children, who were in despair at the idea of leading such a different life. The cottage stood in the middle of a dark forest, and it seemed to be the most dismal place on earth.

The children had to cultivate the fields to earn their living. They were poorly clothed, and they missed the comforts and amusements of their earlier life. Only the youngest daughter tried to be brave and cheerful. She had also been sad at first, but she soon recovered her good nature. She set to work to make the best of things. But when she tried to persuade her sisters to join her in dancing and singing, they ridiculed her and said that this miserable life was all she was fit for. In truth, she was far prettier and more clever than they were. She was so lovely that she was called Beauty.

After two years in the cottage, their father received news that one of his ships, which he had believed to be lost, had come safely into port with a rich cargo. All the sons and daughters at once thought their poverty would be over, and they wanted to set out directly for the town, even though it was winter. But their father was more cautious, so he decided to go by himself with the horse. Only Beauty had any doubt that they would soon be rich again. The other daughters gave their father requests for so many jewels and dresses that it would have taken a fortune to buy them. But Beauty did not ask for anything. Her father noticed her silence and said, "And what shall I bring for you, Beauty?"

"The only thing I wish for is to see you come home safely," she answered.

This reply angered her sisters, who thought she was accusing them of asking for costly things; but her father was pleased. Still, he told her to choose something.

"Well, dear Father," she said, "since you insist upon it, I want you to bring me a rose. I have not seen one since we moved here, and I love them very much." ♦

Early the next morning, the merchant set out on horseback and rode the hundred miles to town as quickly as possible. But when he got there, he found out that his partners had taken the goods the ship had brought. So he found himself poorer than when he had left the cottage. He had only enough money to buy food on his journey

home. To make matters worse, he left town during a terrible snowstorm. The storm was so bad that the merchant was exhausted with cold and fatigue before he was halfway home. Night came on, and the deep snow and bitter frost made it impossible for the horse to carry him any further.

The merchant could not see any houses or lights. The only shelter he could find was the hollow trunk of a great tree, where he crouched all night long. It was the longest night he had ever known because the howling of the wolves kept him awake. And when the day broke, he was not much better off, for the horse had disappeared and falling snow had covered up every path. The merchant did not know which way to turn.

At last, he made out some sort of path, and he started to follow it. It was rough and slippery, so he kept falling down. But the path soon became easier, and it led him to a row of trees that ended at a splendid castle. It seemed very strange to the merchant that no snow had fallen on the row of trees or on the path. Stranger still, the trees were covered with apples and oranges. ✦

"The merchant walked down the row of trees and soon reached the castle. He called out when he arrived, but nobody answered. So he opened the door and called again. Then he climbed up a flight of steps and walked through several splendid rooms. The pleasant warmth of the air refreshed him, and he suddenly felt very hungry; but there seemed to be nobody in this huge palace who could give him anything to eat.

The merchant kept wandering through the deep silence of the splendid rooms. At last, he stopped in a room smaller than the rest, where a bright fire was burning next to a couch. The merchant thought this room must be prepared for someone, so he sat down to wait. But very soon he fell into a heavy sleep.

His extreme hunger wakened him after several hours. He was still alone, but a good dinner had been set on a little table. The merchant had eaten nothing for an entire day, so he lost no time in beginning his meal, which was delicious. He wondered who had brought the food, but no one appeared.

After dinner, the merchant went to sleep again. He woke completely refreshed the next morning. There was still no sign of anybody, although a fresh meal of cakes and fruit was sitting on the little table at his elbow. The silence began to terrify the merchant, and he decided to search once more through the rooms. But it was no use. There was no sign of life in the palace. Not even a mouse could be seen.

E COMPARING THEMES

Work the items.

1. Which story has this theme: "Do unto others as you would have them do unto you"?

2. Which story has this theme: "Love is a powerful force"?

3. Which story has this theme: "You don't have to be born perfect to be outstanding"?

4. Which story has this theme: "Life is more important than gold"?

5. How are all four themes alike?

6. How are the stories with those themes different from each other?

F COMPREHENSION

Write the answers.

1. Use details from the story to show how Beauty was different from her sisters.

2. How was Beauty's request for her father different from her sisters' requests?

3. What was unusual about the row of trees the merchant found?

4. Use details from the text to describe what was unusual about the castle.

5. The story says that "The silence began to terrify the merchant." Why was the silence terrifying to the merchant?

G WRITING

Write a passage that answers this main question:

• Do you think the castle is magic?

Use evidence from the story to answer these other questions in your passage.

1. What was unusual about the row of trees leading up to the castle?

2. What was burning in the room where the merchant stayed?

3. What was on the table when the merchant woke up at night and in the morning?

4. Did the merchant see anybody in the castle?

5. What noises did the merchant hear?

Write at least six sentences.

END OF LESSON 92

A   WORD LISTS

1	Word Practice
1.	curiosity
2.	fault
3.	sensible

2	Related Words
1.	fright / frightful
2.	fury / furious
3.	selfish / selfishness
4.	punished / unpunished

3	Word Endings
1.	condition
2.	mention
3.	permission
4.	possession
5.	solution

4	Vocabulary Words
1.	bidding
2.	distressed
3.	hasty
4.	soothe

B   VOCABULARY FROM CONTEXT

1. Isra climbed into the moving van after **bidding** farewell to her friends.

2. Abe was so **distressed** when his dog died that he started to cry.

3. They were in such a hurry that they ate a **hasty** breakfast.

4. Alexis tried to **soothe** her nerves by breathing deeply and relaxing.

Beauty and the Beast
Chapter 2

After the merchant wandered around the palace, he imagined what it would be like if he owned all the treasures he saw, and he considered how he would divide the riches among his children.

Then he went down into the garden. Although it was winter everywhere else, the sun was shining here. The birds were singing, the flowers were blooming, and the air was soft and sweet. The merchant was so overjoyed with all he saw and heard that he said to himself, "This magic must have been put here for me. I will go and bring my children to share it with me."

The merchant turned down a path that led to the gate. This path had roses on each side of it, and the merchant thought he had never seen or smelled such delightful flowers. They reminded him of his promise to Beauty, so he picked one to take to her.

Suddenly, the merchant heard a strange noise behind him. Turning around, he saw a frightful Beast, who seemed to be very angry. The Beast roared in a terrible voice: "Who told you that you could pick my roses? Wasn't it enough that I allowed you to stay in my palace? Wasn't it enough that I fed you and was kind to you? This is the way you show your thanks—by stealing my flowers! Your selfishness shall not go unpunished!"

The merchant was terrified by these furious words and dropped the rose. He then fell on his knees and cried, "Pardon me, noble sir. I am truly grateful for your hospitality. I did not imagine you would be angered if I took such a little thing as a rose."

But the Beast's anger was not soothed by the merchant's speech. "You are very ready with excuses," he cried, "but that will not save you from the death you deserve."

"Alas," thought the merchant, "if my daughter Beauty could only know what danger her rose has brought upon me." ♦

The merchant feared for his life. In despair, he began to tell the Beast all his misfortunes and the reason for his journey. The merchant also mentioned Beauty's request for the rose. Then he said, "A king's treasure would hardly have bought all that my other daughters asked. But I thought I might at least take Beauty her rose. I beg you to forgive me, for you see I meant no harm."

The Beast thought for a moment, and then he said, in a less furious tone, "I will forgive you on one condition—that you give me one of your daughters."

"Ah!" cried the merchant. "I am not cruel enough to buy my own life at the expense of a child's life. Besides, what excuse could I invent to bring one of my daughters here?"

"No excuse would be necessary," answered the Beast. "She must come willingly. See if any one of them has enough courage and loves you enough to save you. You seem to be an honest man, so I will trust you to go home. I will give you a month to see if any of your daughters will come back with you and stay here, so that you may go free. If none of them is willing, you must come alone after bidding them goodbye forever, for then you will belong to me. And do not imagine that you can hide from me, for if you fail to keep your word, I will come and get you."

The merchant accepted this offer, although he did not really think any of his daughters would come. He promised to return a month later. Then he asked permission to set off at once, but the Beast declared he could not go until the next day.

"Tomorrow you will find a horse ready for you," the Beast said. "Now go and eat your supper, and wait for my orders."

The poor merchant was feeling more dead than alive. He went back to his room, where a delicious supper was already served on the little table. But he was too terrified to eat much, so he only tasted a few of the dishes. After a while, he heard a great noise in the next room.

The Beast appeared and asked roughly if the merchant had eaten well. The merchant answered humbly that he had, thanks to the Beast's kindness. Then the Beast warned him to remember their agreement and to prepare his daughters for what to expect.

The Beast added, "Do not get up tomorrow until you see the sun and hear a bell ring. Then you will find your breakfast waiting for you here, and the horse you are to ride will be ready in the courtyard. It will also bring you back when you come with one of your daughters a month from now. Farewell. Take a rose to Beauty, and remember your promise."

The merchant was glad when the Beast went away, and although he could not sleep, he lay down until the sun rose. When he heard the bell ring, he ate a hasty breakfast and went to pick Beauty's rose. Then he mounted the horse, which carried him off so swiftly that he lost sight of the palace in an instant. Soon, the horse stopped before the door of his cottage.

The merchant's sons and daughters rushed to meet him. When they saw the splendid horse, they thought his journey had gone well. The merchant hid the truth from them at first, but he said to Beauty as he gave her the rose, "Here is what you asked me to bring you. You have no idea what it has cost."

This statement only excited his children's curiosity. At last, he told them his adventures from beginning to end. All his children were unhappy and wept loudly over their lost hopes. They declared that their father should not return to this terrible castle, and they began to make plans for killing the Beast; but the merchant reminded them that he had promised to go back. Then the girls were angry with Beauty. They said it was all her fault and declared that if she had asked for something sensible this would never have happened.

Poor Beauty was distressed. She said, "I have indeed caused this misfortune, but who could have guessed that a rose would cause so much misery? It is only fair that I should suffer. I will go back with Father to keep his promise."

At first, nobody would agree to that solution, and Beauty's father declared that nothing would make him let her go. But Beauty was firm. As the time to depart grew near, she divided all her possessions between her sisters and said goodbye to everything she loved. And on the day of departure, she encouraged and cheered her father as they mounted the horse.

D CHARTS AND GRAPHS

The Trouble with Wool Shirts

Wool shirts are perfect for winter, but they're horrible for summer, unless you live in the far north. In the southern states, wool shirts are just too warm to wear in the hot summer sun, and you quickly start sweating.

Granny Grizzly, the owner of the Clothes Pen store in Alaska, learned about this problem the hard way. Alaska is cold for most of the year, so Granny Grizzly sold wool shirts year-round. The store was so successful that she opened another Clothes Pen store in Florida. Even though Florida is only cold during the winter, Granny Grizzly ordered 1,000 wool shirts for her first year in the Florida store—the same amount she ordered yearly for her Alaska store. The shirts took up a lot of space in the Florida store.

Sales of wool shirts in Florida were good at first. Granny Grizzly sold more than 80 wool shirts in January and more than 90 in February. At that rate, all 1,000 wool shirts would be gone by the end of the year. But then something happened. People stopped buying wool shirts. Sales plummeted to less than 40 in March, less than 30 in April, less than 20 in May, and finally to just a handful in June.

Granny Grizzly realized she had made a mistake by ordering so many wool shirts. She had sold less than 300 shirts, and the other 700 were taking up space in the Florida store. Even worse, she couldn't sell the shirts next year because they would be out of style by then, and nobody would want to buy them. Granny Grizzly felt sheepish about ordering all those shirts, and she told herself, "My Alaska store really pulled the wool over my eyes when I opened a store in Florida." Luckily, the Florida Clothes Pen store survived and now makes most of its money by selling bathing suits.

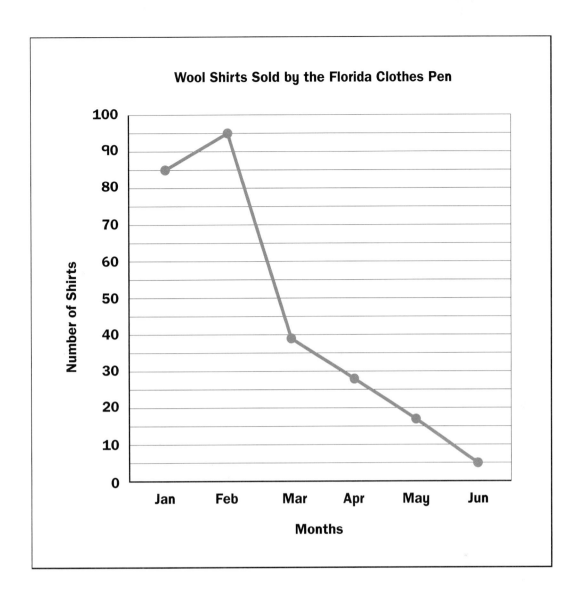

Wool Shirts Sold by the Florida Clothes Pen

Number of Shirts

Months

Work the items.

1. According to the article, how many wool shirts did Granny Grizzly sell in January?

2. According to the graph, exactly how many wool shirts did Granny Grizzly sell in January?

3. In what month were sales of wool shirts at their highest point?

4. In what month were sales of wool shirts at their lowest point?

5. Based on the graph, what do you think will happen to sales of wool shirts in July and August?

6. How does the graph help you understand the story?

E COMPREHENSION

Write the answers.

1. What did the merchant conclude about all the magic he saw in the garden?

2. What did the merchant mean when he said, "I am not cruel enough to buy my own life at the expense of a child's life"?

3. Use details from the story to explain the agreement between the Beast and the merchant.

4. Why did Beauty's sisters blame her for what had happened?

5. Use details from the story to explain why Beauty decided to go to the Beast's palace.

F WRITING

- Pretend you are the merchant telling the story of his adventures to his children.

Tell the last part of your adventures, beginning with when you walked into the Beast's garden.

Use details from the story to answer these questions in your passage:

1. Why did you think the garden was magic?

2. How did you decide to keep your promise to Beauty?

3. What did the Beast threaten to do to you if you didn't obey?

4. On what condition would the Beast forgive you?

5. When did you leave the palace?

6. How did you get home, and what did you bring with you?

Write at least six sentences.

END OF LESSON 93

A WORD LISTS

1 | Related Words

1. arrive / arrival
2. impatient / impatiently
3. mount / dismount
4. obey / disobey
5. paw / pawing
6. respectful / respectfully

2 | Vocabulary Words

1. anxiety
2. dread

B VOCABULARY DEFINITIONS

1. **anxiety**—When you feel worried and nervous, you have *anxiety*.
- What do you feel when you are worried and nervous?

2. **dread**—When you fear something, you *dread* it.
- What's another way of saying *Monsa feared flying in an airplane?*

C READING LITERATURE: Folktale

Beauty and the Beast
Chapter 3

The horse seemed to fly rather than gallop, but it flew so smoothly that neither Beauty nor her father felt frightened. The merchant still tried to persuade Beauty to go back, but she would not listen. While they were talking, night fell, and then, to their great surprise, wonderfully colored lights began to shine in all directions, and splendid fireworks blazed before them. All the forest was lit up, and the air felt pleasantly warm, although it had been bitterly cold before.

The fireworks lasted until Beauty and her father reached the row of orange trees, where statues were holding flaming torches. When they arrived at the palace, they saw that it was lit up from the roof to the ground, and music sounded softly from the courtyard.

"The Beast must be very hungry," said Beauty, trying to laugh, "if he makes all this rejoicing over the arrival of his prey."

But in spite of her anxiety, Beauty could not help admiring all the wonderful things she saw. When the horse stopped in front of the castle, the travelers dismounted, and the merchant led Beauty to the little room he had stayed in before. They found a splendid fire burning and a delicious supper spread on the table.

The merchant knew this supper was meant for them; and Beauty was quite willing to eat, for the long ride had made her very hungry. But they had hardly finished their meal when they heard the Beast approaching. Beauty clung to her father in terror, which became all the greater when she saw how frightened her father was. But when the Beast appeared,

Beauty made a great effort to hide her terror. She bowed to him respectfully and thanked him for his hospitality.

Beauty's behavior seemed to please the Beast. After looking at her, he said, in a tone that might have struck terror in the boldest heart, "Good evening, sir. Good evening, Beauty."

The merchant was too terrified to reply, but Beauty answered sweetly, "Good evening, Beast."

"Have you come willingly?" asked the Beast. "Will you be content to stay here when your father goes away?"

Beauty answered bravely that she was quite prepared to stay.

"I am pleased with you," said the Beast. "You seem to have come of your own choice, so you may stay. As for you, sir," he added, turning to the merchant, "at sunrise tomorrow you will leave. When the bell rings, get up and eat your breakfast. You will find the same horse waiting to take you home. But remember that you must never expect to see my palace again." ♦

The Beast turned to Beauty and said, "Take your father into the next room and help him choose everything you think your brothers and sisters would like. You will find two trunks there; fill them as full as you can. It is only fair that you should send them something precious to remember you by."

Then the Beast went away. Beauty dreaded her father's departure, but she was afraid to disobey the Beast's orders. So they went into the next room, which had shelves and cupboards all around it. They were greatly surprised at the riches the room contained. Beauty and her father went from cupboard to cupboard, selecting precious things, which they heaped into the two trunks. There were splendid dresses fit for a queen, and gorgeous jewels that were heaped on every shelf. After choosing the finest riches and filling the two trunks, Beauty opened the last cupboard. She was amazed to discover that it was completely filled with gold.

She said, "I think, Father, that the gold will be more useful to you. We should remove the other things and fill the trunk with gold."

So they removed the precious things and began heaping gold into the trunks. But the more they put in, the more room there seemed to be. They were able to put back all the jewels and dresses they had taken out, and Beauty even added many more jewels. The trunks were soon so heavy that an elephant could not have carried them.

"The Beast was deceiving us," cried the merchant. "He must have pretended to give us all these things, knowing I could not carry them away."

"Let us wait and see," answered Beauty. "I cannot believe that he meant to deceive us. All we can do is fasten up the trunks and leave them here."

When the merchant and Beauty arose the next morning, they found breakfast ready. The merchant ate his food with a healthy appetite because he secretly believed that he might come back soon and see Beauty. But she felt sure that her father was leaving her forever, so she was very sad when breakfast was over. The time had come for them to part. ★

They went down into the courtyard, where two horses were waiting. One was loaded down with the trunks, and the other was saddled for the merchant to ride. The horses were pawing the ground impatiently waiting to start, so the merchant was forced to bid Beauty a hasty farewell. As soon as he was mounted, he went off at such a pace that Beauty lost sight of him in an instant. Then Beauty wandered sadly back to her room.

Beauty was still sleepy, and she had nothing better to do, so she lay down and fell asleep. She dreamed that she was walking by a brook bordered with trees. In her dream, she was quite sad. Then she saw a prince, more handsome than anyone she had ever seen. His voice went straight to her heart.

"Ah, Beauty," he said, "you are not as unfortunate as you think. In this palace you will be rewarded for all you have suffered. Your every wish shall be granted. I love you dearly, and in making me happy, you will find your own happiness. Be as true-hearted as you are beautiful, and we shall be very happy together."

Beauty asked, "What can I do, prince, to make you happy?"

"Only be grateful," he answered, "and do not trust your eyes too much. Above all, do not desert me until you have saved me from my misery."

Beauty did not know what the prince meant. Suddenly he turned to leave and said, "Dear Beauty, try not to regret all you have left behind you. Just do not be deceived by the way things appear."

Beauty found this dream so interesting that she was in no hurry to wake up. But at last the clock woke her by calling her name softly twelve times. She got up and found dinner waiting in the next room; but eating dinner does not take very long when you are all by yourself, and soon she sat down in the corner on a cozy sofa and began to think about the charming prince she had seen in her dream.

"He said I could make him happy," said Beauty to herself. "I think that the Beast keeps him a prisoner. How can I set the prince free? I wonder why he told me not to be deceived by the way things appear?"

D COMPREHENSION

Write the answers.

1. As Beauty approached the castle, what did she see and hear that made her think the Beast was rejoicing? Use evidence from the story to support your answer.

2. What evidence from the story shows that Beauty was braver than her father?

3. Use details from the story to describe the prince that Beauty saw in her dream.

4. The prince said, "Do not trust your eyes too much." What does that mean?

5. The prince told Beauty that she should not desert him until she had done something. What was that?

E WRITING

Write a passage that answers this main question:

• Do you think the Beast is evil, good, or both good and evil?

Use details from the story to answer these other questions in your passage:

1. What did the Beast threaten to do to the merchant when the merchant picked a rose?

2. What did the Beast want in exchange for sparing the merchant's life?

3. How did the Beast treat the merchant and Beauty when he spoke to them?

4. What did the Beast give to the merchant?

Write at least six sentences.

A WORD LISTS

1 | Hard Words

1. bracelet
2. candlestick
3. lifetime
4. refusal
5. ungrateful

2 | Vocabulary Words

1. chandelier
2. conceal
3. portrait

B VOCABULARY DEFINITIONS

1. **chandelier**—A *chandelier* is a fancy light with branches that hangs from the ceiling. Each branch holds a light bulb or a candle.
• What do we call a fancy hanging light with branches?

2. **conceal**—*Conceal* is another word for *hide*.
• What's another way of saying *She tried to hide her feelings?*

3. **portrait**—A painting, photo, or drawing of a person is called a *portrait*.
• What's another way of saying *The art museum had a room filled with pictures of people?*

C READING LITERATURE: Folktale

Beauty and the Beast
Chapter 4

Beauty began to explore some of the rooms in the palace. The first room she entered was lined with mirrors, and she saw herself reflected on every side. She had never seen such a charming room. Then a bracelet hanging from a chandelier caught her eye. She took it down and was greatly surprised to find that it held a portrait of the prince she had dreamed about. With great delight, she slipped the bracelet on her right wrist and went into a large room filled with pictures. She soon found a portrait of the same handsome prince, as large as life. It was so well painted that he seemed to smile kindly at her.

Beauty tore herself away from the portrait at last and walked into the next room, which contained every musical instrument under the sun. She amused herself for a long time by playing the instruments and singing. The next room was a library. She saw everything she had ever wanted to read, as well as everything she had already read. She thought there were so many books that the rest of her lifetime would not be long enough to read even the titles of them.

By this time it was growing dark, and candles in diamond and ruby candlesticks were beginning to light themselves in every room. Beauty found her supper served at the exact time she preferred to have it, but she did not see anyone or hear a sound. Although her father had warned her she would be alone, she realized her life would not be dull.

After a while, Beauty heard the Beast coming, and she wondered if he meant to harm her. However, the Beast did not seem at all terrifying. He said gruffly, "Good evening, Beauty."

Beauty answered cheerfully, concealing her terror. The Beast asked her how she had been amusing herself, and she told him about all the rooms she had seen.

Then the Beast asked her if she was happy in his palace, and Beauty answered that everything was so wonderful that she was quite happy. After about an hour's talk, Beauty began to think the Beast was not nearly so terrible as she first thought.

At last, the Beast got up to leave and said in a gruff voice, "Beauty, will you marry me?"

Beauty was astonished by his question. She did not know what to say, for she was afraid to make the Beast angry by refusing.

"Say yes or no without fear," the Beast went on.

"No, Beast," said Beauty hastily.

"Since you will not marry me, Beauty" he replied, "I will say good night."

"Good night, Beast," answered Beauty. She was glad her refusal had not made the Beast angry. ♦

After the Beast had gone, Beauty was soon asleep in bed, dreaming of her prince. She dreamed he came to her and said, "Ah, Beauty, why are you so unkind to me?"

Beauty's dreams changed after that, but the charming prince was in all of them. When morning came, her first thought was to look at the portrait and see if it really looked like the prince, and she found that it did.

That morning, Beauty decided to work in the garden. The sun was shining, and all the fountains were spraying trails of sparkling water. She was astonished to find that every place was familiar to her from her dream. She came to the brook where she had first met the prince in her dream. It made her think more than ever that he must be the Beast's prisoner.

After supper that evening, the Beast paid her another visit and asked the same question as before. Then with a gruff "Good night," he left, and Beauty went to bed to dream of her mysterious prince.

The days passed swiftly. Every evening after supper, the Beast came to see her, and always before saying good night, he asked her in his terrible voice, "Beauty, will you marry me?"

Now that Beauty understood him better, it seemed to her that he went away quite sad. But her happy dreams of the handsome young prince soon made her forget the poor Beast.

So the days and nights passed in the same way for a long time, until at last Beauty began to long for her father and brothers and sisters. One night she seemed so sad that the Beast asked her what was the matter.

Beauty was no longer afraid of the Beast. She knew that he was really gentle in spite of his terrifying looks and dreadful voice. So she explained that she wanted to see her home once more. The Beast seemed greatly distressed when he heard this, and he replied, "Ah, Beauty, do you have the heart to desert an unhappy Beast? Is it because you hate me that you want to escape?"

"No, dear Beast," answered Beauty softly, "I do not hate you, and I should be very sorry never to see you anymore. But I long to see my family again. Only let me go for two months, and I promise to come back to you and stay for the rest of my life." ✦

The Beast, who had been sighing while she spoke, now replied. "I cannot refuse anything you ask, even though it might cost me my life. Take the four boxes you find in the room next to yours and fill them with everything you wish to take. But remember your promise to come back when two months are over. If you do not come in good time, you will find your faithful Beast dead."

The Beast stopped for a minute and gave Beauty a ring. "You will not need a horse to bring you back," he said. "Only say good-bye to all your brothers and sisters the night before you leave, and when you have gone to bed, turn this ring around your finger and say, 'I wish to go back to the palace and see the Beast again.' Good night, Beauty. Fear nothing, sleep peacefully, and before long you shall see your family once more."

As soon as Beauty was alone, she hurried to fill the boxes with all the rare and precious things she saw about her, and only when she was tired of heaping things into the boxes did they seem to be full.

Then she went to bed, but she could hardly sleep. When she began to dream of her beloved prince at last, she was sorry to see him stretched upon a grassy bank, sad and weary, and hardly like himself.

"What is the matter?" she cried.

He looked at her sadly and said, "How can you ask me, cruel one? You are leaving me to my death."

"Don't be so sorrowful," said Beauty. "I am only going to show my family that I am safe and happy. I have promised the Beast faithfully that I will come back. He would die of grief if I did not keep my word."

"What would that matter to you?" said the prince. "Do you really care about him?"

"I should be ungrateful if I did not care for such a kind Beast," cried Beauty. "I would die to save him from pain. It is not his fault he is so ugly."

But the prince said nothing, and only turned his face from her.

D COMPREHENSION

Write the answers.

1. Each time the Beast came to see Beauty, what question would he ask her before leaving?

2. Use evidence from the story to explain why Beauty answered no to the Beast's question.

3. After Beauty answers no, the story says that Beauty "was glad her refusal had not made the Beast angry." What does that mean?

4. What did the Beast say would happen if Beauty did not return to the palace in two months?

5. Use details from the story to describe how Beauty's attitude toward the Beast changed in this chapter.

E WRITING

Write a passage that answers this main question:

- Do you think the Beast and the prince are the same person?

Use evidence from the story to answer these other questions in your passage:

1. What did the prince ask Beauty after she refused to marry the Beast?

2. What was strange about the prince's question?

3. How did the Beast feel when Beauty refused to marry him?

4. What did the Beast say might happen to him if Beauty didn't return to the palace in two months?

5. What did the prince say might happen to him if Beauty didn't return to the palace?

Write at least six sentences.

A WORD LISTS

1 Related Words	**2** Word Endings	**3** Vocabulary Words
1. assure / reassure 2. pity / pitiful 3. ugly / ugliness	1. apparently 2. constantly 3. dearly 4. joyfully 5. loudly	1. appearance 2. despite 3. furthermore 4. spell 5. trace

B VOCABULARY DEFINITIONS

1. **appearance**—The way something looks is called its *appearance*.
   When you *trust appearances*, you believe in the way things look instead of understanding what those things really are.
   - What's another way of saying *The young children believed in the way things looked at the magic show?*

2. **despite**—When you do something even though you have a problem, you do that thing *despite* your problem.
   - Here's another way of saying *Olga played soccer even though she had an injury: Olga played soccer despite her injury.*
   - What's another way of saying *Even though it was cold, the postal worker delivered the mail?*

3. **furthermore**—*Furthermore* means *in addition.*
   - What's another way of saying *The witch was evil; in addition, she was powerful?*

4. **spell**—A magic charm is called a *spell*. In some stories, a witch or a wizard might put a spell on somebody and change them into a statue or a frog.

5. **trace**—A clue that something has been somewhere is called a *trace*.
   - A footprint is one kind of trace. What are some other kinds of traces?

Beauty and the Beast

Chapter 5

In Beauty's dream, she was about to speak to the prince, but another person's voice woke her up. When Beauty opened her eyes, she found herself in a room she had never seen before. It was nearly as splendid as the rooms in the Beast's palace. Where could she be, and whose voice had she heard?

Beauty got up and dressed hastily, and then she saw that the boxes she had packed the night before were all in the room. While Beauty was wondering how she got to this strange place, she suddenly heard her father's voice outside the room. She rushed out and greeted him joyfully.

Her brothers and sisters were astonished because they never expected to see her again, and there was no end to the questions they asked her. They told her what had happened to them while she was away.

When Beauty's family heard she had only come for two months, they sobbed loudly. When Beauty was alone with her father, she asked him what her strange dreams could mean, and why the prince begged her not to trust appearances.

Her father thought for a while, and then answered. "You tell me that the Beast, frightful as he is, loves you dearly. You say that the Beast deserves your love for his kindness. I think the prince wants you to marry the Beast despite his ugliness."

Beauty thought her father's answer was right, but still, when she thought of her dear, handsome prince, she did not want to marry the Beast. She wouldn't have to decide about marrying the Beast until her two months were over, so she tried to enjoy herself with her family instead. Although they were rich now and lived in a town again with plenty of friends, Beauty found that nothing amused her very much. She often thought of the palace where she was so happy. Furthermore, she never once dreamed of her dear prince, and she felt quite sad without him.

Her sisters had grown quite used to being without her, and they even found her in the way. But her father begged her to stay and seemed very sad at the thought of her leaving. So Beauty put off her departure. ♦

On the night Beauty was supposed to return to the palace, she had a dismal dream. She dreamed she was wandering on a lonely path in the palace gardens and heard groans coming from a cave. She ran quickly to see what was the matter and found the Beast stretched out upon his side, apparently dying. He said Beauty was the cause of his illness, and he moaned pitifully.

Beauty was so terrified by this dream that the next morning she announced she was going back at once; and that very night she said goodbye to her father and all her brothers and sisters.

As soon as Beauty was in bed, she turned the ring around her finger and said, "I wish to go back to the palace and see the Beast again."

Then she fell asleep instantly, and only woke up to hear the clock saying "Beauty" twelve times. She knew at once that she was in the palace again. Everything was just as before, but Beauty had never known such a long day. She was so anxious to see the Beast again that she felt dinner time would never come.

But when dinner time did come and no Beast appeared, she was frightened. After listening and waiting for a long while, she ran down into the garden to search for him. No one answered her calls, and she could not find a trace of him. At last, she stopped for a minute's rest and saw she was standing near the cave she had seen in her dreams. She entered the cave, and sure enough, there was the Beast, fast asleep. Beauty was glad to have found him. She ran up and stroked his head, but to her horror he did not move or open his eyes.

"Oh, he is dead, and it is all my fault," said Beauty, crying bitterly. But then she looked at him again and saw that he was still breathing. She got some water from the nearest fountain and sprinkled it over his face. To her great delight, he began to wake up. ✦

"Oh, Beast, how you frightened me," she cried. "I never knew how much I loved you until just now, when I feared I was too late to save your life."

"Can you really love such an ugly creature as I?" asked the Beast faintly. "Ah, Beauty, you came just in time. I was dying because I thought you had forgotten your promise. But go back now and rest. I shall see you again soon."

Beauty had expected him to be angry with her, but she was reassured by his gentle voice. She went back to the palace, where dinner was awaiting her. Afterward, the Beast came in as usual, and they talked about the time she had spent with her father. The Beast asked if she had enjoyed herself, and if her family had been glad to see her.

Beauty answered politely and quite enjoyed telling him all that had happened to her. At last, the time came for him to go, and he asked, as he had so often asked before, "Beauty, will you marry me?"

Beauty answered softly, "Yes, dear Beast."

As she spoke, a blaze of light sprang up before the windows of the palace. Beauty turned to ask the Beast what it could all mean but found that he had disappeared. In his place stood her long-loved prince!

"Ah, Beauty," he said. "You have rescued me at last from my terrible spell."

Beauty looked at him in amazement and begged him to explain.

The prince said, "When I was young, a witch put a spell on me and changed me into the Beast. She said that I would keep that form until I met a woman who had enough courage to love me despite my ugliness. You are that woman, and now we will be husband and wife."

The prince came up to Beauty and kissed her. They were married the next day, and they lived happily ever after. And every day, the prince would go into their garden and bring Beauty a rose.

D COMPREHENSION

Write the answers.

1. The story says that the prince begged Beauty "not to trust appearances." What does that mean?

2. The merchant said Beauty should marry the Beast "despite his ugliness." What does that mean?

3. Use details from the story to describe what happened in the dismal dream that Beauty had on the night she was supposed to return to the palace.

4. What was the only way the Beast could change back into the prince?

5. Why are roses so important in this story?

E WRITING

Write a passage that answers this main question:

• Why did Beauty change her mind about marrying the Beast?

Use evidence from the story to answer these other questions in your passage:

1. What did Beauty's father think the prince was telling her?

2. What was happening to the Beast in Beauty's dismal dream?

3. Why did Beauty go back to the palace?

4. What condition was the Beast in when Beauty found him?

5. When did Beauty realize how much she loved the Beast?

6. When did Beauty agree to marry the Beast?

Write at least six sentences

Glossary

A

abandon When you leave a place without planning to come back, you *abandon* that place.

abnormal *Abnormal* is another way of saying *not normal.*

absorb When something *absorbs* water, it soaks up the water.

abundant If something is *abundant,* there is a lot of that thing.

acre An *acre* is a unit of land. The size of an acre is 4,840 square yards.

advantages The *advantages* of a plan are the ways the plan is better than another plan.

agility Someone who moves quickly and easily has *agility.*

anxiety When you feel worried and nervous, you have *anxiety.*

apology When you say you are sorry for something you did, you make an *apology.*

appearance The way something looks is called its *appearance.*

appetite *Appetite* is another way of saying *desire for food.*

astonishment *Astonishment* is another word for *amazement.*

avalanche A landslide of snow, ice, and rock is called an *avalanche.*

B

balk When a baseball pitcher pretends to throw a pitch, the play is illegal, and it's called a *balk.*

bargain When you *bargain* with someone, you try to make a deal with that person.

bass [base] A voice or instrument that makes a low sound is called a *bass* voice or instrument.

beam A ray of light is sometimes called a *beam* of light.

bidding *Bidding farewell* is another phrase for *saying goodbye.*

biography A *biography* is the history of a person's life written by somebody else.

bold A person who is confident and brave is a *bold* person.

bough A main branch of a tree is called a *bough.*

buds Leaves that are forming are called *buds.*

C

calculate When you figure out how much something costs, you *calculate* the cost.

carbon dioxide When gasoline, oil, and coal burn, they create a gas called *carbon dioxide.*

career Your *career* is what you do for a living.

cast When hunting dogs try to find the scent of an animal by sniffing back and forth across the ground, they *cast.*

cautious *Cautious* is another word for *careful.*

century A period of one hundred years is called a *century.*

chandelier A *chandelier* is a fancy light with branches that hangs from the ceiling.

chariot A *chariot* is a two-wheeled cart drawn by horses.

chime When clocks make a ringing sound, they *chime.*

chorizo [chor-EET-so] *Chorizo* is a type of sausage.

circuit When you travel in a circular path, you make a *circuit.*

clutched *Clutched* is another word for *grabbed.*

coil Rope that is wound into a spiral is called a *coil* of rope.

commotion *Commotion* is another way of saying *loud disturbance.*

conceal *Conceal* is another word for *hide.*

confession When you admit that you did something wrong, you make a *confession.*

confine When you cannot leave a place, you are *confined* to that place.

conjunto [kohn-HOON-toh] *Conjunto* is a type of Latin music.

conquer When you gain control over something by using force, you *conquer* it.

contract [CON-tract] A written agreement is called a *contract.*

corridos [koh-REE-dohs] *Corridos* are a type of song sung in Spanish.

cousin A child of your aunt or your uncle is called your *cousin.*

cultivate When you break up the soil in a field, plant seeds, and grow crops, you *cultivate* the field.

cycle A repeating series of events is called a *cycle.*

D

daring A person who takes chances is a *daring* person.

decay When something rots or falls apart, it *decays.*

deceitful When you deceive somebody by telling a lie, you are being *deceitful.*

decent When something is satisfactory, it is *decent.*

decline If the number of things gets less and less, the number *declines.*

defeat When you beat somebody in a game, you *defeat* that person.

deflate When you let air out of something, you *deflate* it.

deity A god or a goddess is called a *deity.*

deposit When you put an object in a place, you *deposit* the object in that place.

deserve When you *deserve* something, you are worthy of that thing.

desolate *Desolate* is another word for *dismal* or *deserted.*

despite When you do something even though you have a problem, you do that thing *despite* your problem.

detect When you notice something, you *detect* it.

determined When you plan to do something no matter what, you are *determined* to do that thing.

device A piece of equipment that is built for a special purpose is called a *device.*

diesel fuel *Diesel fuel* is a type of gasoline that is used for large trucks and some cars.

dimple A little dent in a person's cheeks or chin is called a *dimple.*

disagreeable When you are unfriendly and unpleasant, you are *disagreeable.*

discontented *Discontented* is another word for *dissatisfied.*

distressed *Distressed* is another word for *unhappy.*

down Soft feathers are called *down.*

dread When you fear something, you *dread* it.

drought A *drought* is a period of time without rain.

drowsy *Drowsy* is another word for *sleepy.*

dugout In a baseball game, the main place where players stay when they're not playing is called the *dugout.*

dwarf *Dwarf* is another way of saying *very short.*

E

eliminate *Eliminate* is another way of saying *get rid of.*

embrace *Embrace* is another word for *hug.*

empanada [em-puh-NAH-duh] An *empanada* is a stuffed pastry.

enchilada [en-chi-LAH-duh] An *enchilada* is a rolled tortilla with fillings.

endangered When a species of plant or animal is in danger of becoming extinct, it is an *endangered* species.

energy resources Resources that can be used to create energy are called *energy resources.*

enlarge *Enlarge* is another way of saying *make larger.*

environment Your *environment* is what's around you.

envy When you *envy* people, you wish you had something they have.

exchanged *Exchanged* is another word for *replaced* or *traded.*

extensive Something that is *extensive* covers or affects a large area.

extinct When a species of plant or animal no longer exists, that species is *extinct.*

F

face The steep side of a mountain or cliff is called the *face.*

facilities *Facilities* are places that have a particular purpose.

familia [fah-MEEL-yuh] *Familia* is a Spanish word for *family.*

fatigued *Fatigued* is another word for *exhausted.*

fertile Land where plants and crops grow well is called *fertile* land.

flamingo A *flamingo* is a tall wading bird with long legs and a long neck.

flicker When a fire burns unsteadily, it *flickers.*

flush When your face turns red and hot, it *flushes.*

flyer A piece of paper with an ad on it is called a *flyer.*

fossil fuels Fuels formed long ago from dead plants and animals are called *fossil fuels.*

freeway A free highway with many lanes of traffic is called a *freeway.*

frenzy When you do things in a *frenzy,* you do them in a hurried and excited way.

furthermore *Furthermore* is another way of saying *in addition.*

G

Gee *Gee* is a command that means, "Turn right."

generation A *generation* is a group of people who grow up at the same time.

generator A machine that converts spinning forces into electricity is called a *generator*.

gleamed *Gleamed* is another word for *shined*.

gnaw When you bite or chew something hard, you *gnaw* it.

grapple *Grapple* is another word for *struggle*.

grate When something rubs against a hard surface and makes a harsh sound, it *grates*.

grief *Grief* is another word for *sorrow*.

grit Loose bits of stone and sand are called *grit*.

guilty Somebody who makes a mistake is *guilty* of the mistake.

guitarrón [ghee-tahr-ROHN] A *guitarrón* is a bass guitar.

habitat The natural home of a plant or animal is called its *habitat*.

hasty *Hasty* is another word for *hurried*.

haunted When something disturbs you over and over, it *haunts* you.

have access When you *have access* to something, you are able to get it.

hazard *Hazard* is another word for *danger* or *threat*.

hijo [EE-hoh] *Hijo* is a Spanish word for *son*.

hoarse A voice that sounds rough and harsh is a *hoarse* voice.

honor An award you receive for good work is called an *honor*.

horizontally If something moves *horizontally*, it moves from side to side.

hospitality When you are friendly and welcoming to somebody, you show *hospitality* to that person.

huevo [WEH-voh] *Huevo* is a Spanish word for *egg*.

hurl *Hurl* is another word for *throw*.

ideal When something is perfect, it is *ideal*.

identify When you tell what something is, you *identify* that thing.

imitation An *imitation* is a copy.

in disguise When you are *in disguise*, you are dressed so that nobody can recognize you.

infected A cut that is *infected* becomes swollen and painful.

inhabitant Somebody who lives in a place is an *inhabitant* of that place.

inhale When you *inhale*, you breathe in.

inning A baseball game is divided into *innings*. During each inning, both teams get a turn at bat.

insane *Insane* is another word for *crazy* or *foolish*.

instinct An *instinct* is a behavior that people and other animals are born with.

insult A comment or a gesture that is supposed to make you mad is an *insult*.

intense *Intense* is another way of saying *very strong*.

intently When you do something *intently*, you concentrate on that thing.

jutted out *Jutted out* is another way of saying *stuck out*.

keen If you have *keen* hearing, your hearing is very good.

kennel A *kennel* is a place where dogs or cats are kept.

kerosene *Kerosene* is a type of gasoline that is used in lights and heaters.

laborer A *laborer* does work that doesn't require special skills.

landslide A *landslide* occurs when large amounts of mud and rock slide down from a hill or a mountain.

lean People who are *lean* have very little fat on their bodies.

lector One of the people who helps with a church service is called a *lector*.

ledge A flat shelf on the side of a cliff or a wall is called a *ledge*.

limp When you *limp,* you have trouble walking.

linen *Linen* is an expensive cloth that some sheets and clothes are made of.

lingered on *Lingered on* is another way of saying *kept on going.*

litter A *litter* is a group of animals that are born to the same mother at the same time.

lobo [LOH-boh] *Lobo* is a Spanish word for *wolf.*

long jump When athletes compete in a *long jump,* they run up to a line and jump as far as they can.

lullaby A song that is used to put children to sleep is called a *lullaby.*

lumbered *Lumbered* is another way of saying *moved awkwardly.*

lunge When you charge forward suddenly, you *lunge.*

major league A group of sports teams that play each other is called a sports *league.* A *major league* is a league with the best players.

mechanic A *mechanic* is a person who fixes automobiles and other machines.

migrate When you move from one area to another area, you *migrate* to the other area.

mimic When you imitate somebody, you *mimic* them.

miraculous Something that is like a miracle is *miraculous.*

misery *Misery* is another word for *unhappiness.*

misled When you are *misled,* somebody tricks you.

murmur A *murmur* is a low, soft sound.

muscular When a body part has strong muscles, it is *muscular.*

musician A person who plays a musical instrument is called a *musician.*

mysterious When something is full of mystery, it is *mysterious.*

naked *Naked* is another word for *bare.*

obedient When you obey orders, you are *obedient.*

occupied *Occupied* is another word for *busy.*

officer In an army, an *officer* is a person who commands soldiers.

old-fashioned Something that isn't modern is *old-fashioned.*

Olympics The *Olympics* is a festival where athletes from all over the world compete in different types of sports.

operate When doctors *operate,* they cut into someone's body to make repairs. This process is called an *operation.*

oppose When you're against something, you *oppose* that thing.

organization Sometimes a business is called an *organization.*

ornaments *Ornaments* are decorations or designs.

oval Something that is *oval* is shaped like an egg.

P

papas [PAH-pahs] *Papas* is a Spanish word for *potatoes.*

paradise An ideal place to live in or visit is called a *paradise.*

pennant A sports team that wins its league gets a flag called a *pennant.*

perpetual clock A *perpetual clock* is an expensive type of clock that can run without electricity and doesn't need to be wound up.

persuade *Persuade* is another word for *convince.*

pew A bench that people sit on in a church is called a *pew.*

photosynthesis *Photosynthesis* is a process where green plants use sunlight to make food for the plant.

pity *Pity* is another word for *sorrow.*

plant *Plant* is another word for *factory.*

plentiful When something is *plentiful,* it's in good supply.

pneumonia *Pneumonia* is a type of lung disease.

polluted When the environment is not clean and healthy, it is *polluted.*

portrait A painting, photo, or drawing of a person is called a *portrait.*

pounce When you quickly attack something, you *pounce* on that thing.

poverty When you are very poor, you live in *poverty.*

predict When you say that something will happen, you *predict* that thing.

preparations When you prepare for something, you make *preparations.*

prey An animal that is hunted by another animal is called *prey.*

produce When you make or grow something, you *produce* that thing.

punt In football, a *punt* is a type of kick.

Q

quail A *quail* is a bird that's about the same size as a pigeon.

quarterback A *quarterback* is a type of football player.

quiver *Quiver* is another word for *tremble* or *shake.*

R

rears up When a horse stands up on its back legs, it *rears up.*

recover *Recover* is another way of saying *get better.*

relationship When two things are connected in some way, they have a *relationship.*

relatives Your *relatives* are the people who are part of your family, such as your aunts, uncles, cousins, and grandparents.

reluctant When you are *reluctant* to do something, you really don't want to do it.

resent When you *resent* a person or a thing, you are angry with that person or thing.

reserve A place set aside for wild animals is called a *reserve.*

resound When something *resounds,* it fills a place with sound.

resources *Resources* is another word for *supplies.* Supplies found in nature are called *natural resources.*

restore When you repair something to make it look like new, you *restore* it.

restricted to *Restricted to* is another way of saying *limited to.*

rhizome A *rhizome* is a plant stem that grows underground in a horizontal line.

rhyming couplet A pair of lines that rhyme in a poem is called a *rhyming couplet.*

ridge A long, narrow hilltop is called a *ridge.*

rookie A baseball player who is playing his or her first full year on a team is called a *rookie.*

runners The long, thin strips of metal under a sled are called *runners.*

S

sap The liquid underneath the bark of a tree is called *sap.*

savor When you enjoy something as much as you can, you *savor* it.

schedule When you *schedule* an event, you figure out where and when the event will happen.

scout A baseball *scout* is a person who looks for players that a baseball team might hire.

seawall A *seawall* is a wall that's built in the sea.

secure *Secure* is another word for *safe.*

sedative A *sedative* is a medicine that makes you sleep or feel relaxed.

sediment Small pieces of rock and sand that settle at the bottom of a river, lake, or ocean are called *sediment.*

sensitive Something that can detect things that are very faint is *sensitive.*

settle When you make a home somewhere, you *settle* in that place.

shall *Shall* is another word for *will.*

sharecropper A *sharecropper* is someone who rents land from a farmer.

shrewd *Shrewd* is another word for *clever.*

sift When you pour sand through your fingers, you *sift* the sand.

sincerely *Sincerely* is another word for *honestly.*

slosh When liquid *sloshes,* it splashes around.

sod *Sod* is grass and the dirt underneath.

solitary Animals that live alone are called *solitary* animals.

soothe *Soothe* is another word for *calm* or *comfort.*

spacious Something that is *spacious* has a lot of space in it.

spawn Fish eggs are called *spawn,* so a place where fish lay eggs is called a *spawning ground.*

species A type of plant or animal is called a *species* of plant or animal.

spell A magic charm is called a *spell.*

sprawl When somebody falls down awkwardly, they *sprawl.*

stadium A large building that surrounds a sports field is called a *stadium.*

staff A *staff* is a wooden or metal stick that comes in different lengths.

staggered *Staggered* is another way of saying *walked unsteadily.*

stanza A group of lines in a poem is called a *stanza.*

stash When you *stash* something, you put that thing in a safe and secret place.

stately Something that is big and impressive is *stately.*

steal a base In baseball, when a runner *steals a base,* the runner takes off for the next base before the batter hits the ball.

stocking cap A long and floppy hat is called a *stocking cap.*

stretch A *stretch* is a certain distance along a river, path, or road.

substance *Substance* is another word for *material.*

sympathy When you feel sorry for somebody, you have *sympathy* for them.

talkative When you are *talkative,* you talk a lot.

terrifying *Terrifying* is another word for *frightening* or *scary.*

tolerate When you put up with something, you *tolerate* it.

trace A clue that something has been somewhere is called a *trace.*

treacherous Something that is very dangerous is *treacherous.*

turbine A *turbine* is a machine that spins something around and around.

tussle *Tussle* is another word for *wrestle.*

typically *Typically* is another word for *usually.*

unexpectedly When something happens that you don't expect, it happens *unexpectedly.*

unstable Things that are likely to change are *unstable.*

vámonos [VAH-moh-nohs] *Vámonos* is a Spanish word for "Let's go."

vineyard A field where grapevines grow is called a *vineyard.*

volcanic eruption A *volcanic eruption* is what happens when a volcano erupts.

volunteer When you offer to help, you *volunteer.*

warehouseman A man who lifts and moves items in a warehouse is called a *warehouseman.*

whittled *Whittled* is another word for *carved* or *cut.*

wicker Bendable twigs from willows and other trees are called *wicker.*

wild goose chase When you go on a *wild goose chase,* you are going after something you won't find.

wisdom When you are wise, you have *wisdom.*

wither When something *withers,* it dries up and shrinks.

witness When you see an event happening, you *witness* that event.

witty Someone who makes remarks in a quick and funny way is *witty.*

Fact Game Answer Key

Lesson 78

2.   a.   Lion
     b.   Dorothy

3.   a.   gold
     b.   Yukon River

4.   a.   fact
     b.   fiction

5.   a.   carrying things
     b.   food

6.   a.   scarlet tanager
     b.   salmon

7.   a.   Buck
     b.   Toto

8.   a.   steeplechase
     b.   Liverpool

9.   a.   wild
     b.   domestic

10. a.   tiger
     b.   Galápagos tortoise

11. a.   Land of the North
     b.   Land of the South

12. a.   Jackie Robinson
     b.   Brooklyn Dodgers